The German Working Class 1888-1933

THE POLITICS OF EVERYDAY LIFE

EDITED BY RICHARD J. EVANS

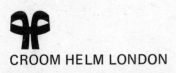

CROOM HELM LONDON

BARNES & NOBLE BOOKS
TOTOWA, NEW JERSEY

© 1982 Richard J. Evans
Croom Helm Ltd, 2-10 St John's Road, London SW11

British Library Cataloguing in Publication Data

The German working class 1888-1933
  1. Labour and labouring classes—Germany—History
  I. Evans, Richard J.
  305.5'6   HD8446

ISBN 0-7099-0431-2

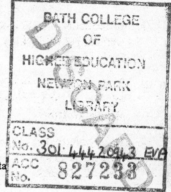
First published in the USA 1982 by
Barnes & Noble Books
81 Adams Drive
Totowa, New Jersey, 07512

Library of Congress Cataloging in Publication Data
Main entry under title:

The German working class, 1888-1933.

    Includes index.
    1. Labor and laboring classes — Germany — History —
Addresses, essays, lectures. 2. Deviant behavior —
Political aspects — Addresses, essays, lectures.
3. Germany — Social conditions — Addresses, essays,
lectures. I. Evans, Richard J.
HD6957.G3G36   1982   305.5'6   81-12724
ISBN 0-389-20118-9 (Barnes & Noble)   AACR2

Printed and bound in Great Britain
by Billing and Sons Limited
Guildford, London, Oxford, Worcester

CONTENTS

TABLES

FIGURE

PREFACE

Recent work on the history of the German labour movement before 1933 has concentrated on the development of a specifically Social Democratic subculture, in which working-class people could spend their entire lives. It has been argued that this comprehensive social subculture, by transmitting down the social scale values and beliefs that were essentially bourgeois in character, and by diverting revolutionary energies into harmless pursuits such as choral singing, gymnastics or bicycling, helped reconcile the German working class to the existing political and social order and so prepared its surrender to German imperialism in 1914 and to the Nazi seizure of power in 1933. This book, by a group of younger German, American and British historians, challenges these views. It argues that historians have concentrated too much on the respectable side of working-class life and have confused Social Democratic values with working-class values. After an introduction analysing the nature and development of the historiography of the German labour movement, separate essays deal with pilferage, drink, industrial sabotage, concubinage, youth gangs and other neglected aspects of working-class culture in the Wilhelmine era and the Weimar Republic. The authors discuss the attitude of the labour movement to this 'rough' side of the everyday life of the German working class. The book documents the growing gulf between proletarian culture and Social Democratic culture and explores its consequences for the struggle against German Fascism and imperialism.

This book is the second publication to emerge from the SSRC Research Seminar Group in Modern German Social History, *The German Family*, edited by Richard J. Evans and W.R. Lee,[1] being the first. Four of the chapters were presented in earlier versions to the second or the fourth meeting of the group, held in January 1979 and July 1980 respectively, and five of the authors took part in one or other, or both, of these meetings. I wish first of all, therefore, to thank the Social Science Research Council for its generous support of the Research Seminar Group through Grant No. HG 113/6/7, and the participants in the group's discussions for the many stimulating and penetrating observations which they made on the papers presented. The SSRC Research Seminar Group in Modern German Social History, which meets regularly at the University of East Anglia, Norwich, provides a forum where British historians of Germany can discuss current research in major areas of German social history with colleagues from Germany, and it is hoped that the meetings of the group will result in further publications in due course. This volume is not, however, a collection of conference proceedings. Not all the papers presented to these two meetings of the group have been included; and three of the contributions to the book originate elsewhere. Rather, it reflects in its general scope and orientation a number of the concerns that emerged from the discussions which took place, above all, at the January 1979 meeting of the group.[2] Following on from this, it represents to a greater degree than is customary in a collection of essays a genuinely collective venture. First drafts of all the essays were circulated among all the contributors and the drafts were then revised in the light of comments and criticisms received. It is to be hoped, therefore, that the resulting collection will have a greater degree of cohesion than is usually the case with publications of this kind.

I am grateful to Verlag Vandenhoek & Ruprecht, Göttingen, and the editors of *Geschichte und Gesellschaft*, for permission to print as Chapter 5 a revised version of an article which first appeared in volume 7, number 2 of that journal. I would also like to thank Cathleen Catt (University of East Anglia) for undertaking the task of translating Chapters 2 and 5, and also for assisting with the preparation of Chapter 3. I am also grateful to Eric Rustad (Columbia University, New York) for his assistance, and to Marjan Bhavsar (University of East Anglia) for undertaking much of the typing. Finally I wish to thank the Alexander von Humboldt-Stiftung Foundation for electing me to a Research Fellowship at the Free University of Berlin and thereby considerably easing the final stages of the book's preparation.

Richard J. Evans
Norwich and Berlin

Notes

1. Croom Helm, 1981.
2. See the detailed report and critique of this meeting in Geoff Eley and Keith Nield, 'Why does Social History Ignore Politics?', *Social History*, vol. 5, no. 2 (1980), pp. 249-71.

ABBREVIATIONS

AfS	*Archiv für Sozialgeschichte*
AfSHD	*Archiv für Soziale Hygiene und Demographie*
AZD	*Arbeiter Zeitung* (Dortmund)
BGB	Bürgerliches Gesetzbuch
BT	*Berliner Tageblatt*
DAAB	Deutscher Arbeiter Abstinenten-Bund
DAZ	*Deutsche Allgemeine Zeitung*
DHSG	Deputation für Handel, Schiffahrt und Gewerbe
Diss.	Dissertation
DMV	Deutscher Metallarbeiter-Verband
DZt	*Dortmunder Zeitung*
E	Evening edition
ev.-luth.	evangelisch-lutherisch
GAD	*General-Anzeiger für Dortmund und die Provinz Westfalen*
GehStA	Geheimes Staatsarchiv Berlin-Dahlem
GG	*Geschichte und Gesellschaft*
HBV	*Jahresbericht des Hafenbetriebsvereins in Hamburg*
HdStW	*Handwörterbuch des Staatswissenschaften*
H.Pol.Dir.	Herzogliche Polizeidirektion
H.St.M.	Herzogliches Staatsministerium
KPD	Kommunistische Partei Deutschlands
LABln	Landesarchiv Berlin
M	Morning edition
MAZ	*Metallarbeiter-Zeitung*
MEW	*Marx-Engels-Werke*
NF	Neue Folge
P	Postal edition
PP	Politische Polizei
Pol.Dir.	Polizeidirektion
RABl	*Reichsarbeitsblatt*
RF	*Die Rote Fahne*
RFB	Roter Frontkämpferbund
RGBl	*Reichsgesetzblatt*
RJ	Roter Jungfront
RWR	Roter Wanderring
SA	Sturmabteilung

SAJ	Sozialistische Arbeiterjugend
SKJV	Senatskommission für die Justizverwaltung
SPD	Sozialdemokratische Partei Deutschlands
StA Br	Staatsarchiv Bremen
StA BS	Staatsarchiv Braunschweig
StJB	Statistisches Jahrbuch für die Stadt Berlin
StA Wf	Niedersächsisches Staatsarchiv Wolfenbüttel
Tab.	Tabelle
VW	*Vorwärts*
VZ	*Vossische Zeitung*
ZfBS	*Zeitschrift für Bevölkerungspolitik und Säuglingsfürsorge*
ZfS	*Zeitschrift für Socialwissenschaft*
ZGStW	*Zeitschrift für die gesamten Strafrechtswissenschaften*

1 INTRODUCTION: THE SOCIOLOGICAL INTERPRETATION OF GERMAN LABOUR HISTORY

Richard J. Evans

I

The historiography of the labour movement in Germany has been dominated not by historians, but by sociologists.[1] The formative interpretations, the major theoretical initiatives, the seminal works, all owe more to the sociological profession than to its historical counterpart. Moreover, German labour history has not merely been strongly influenced by sociology *per se* – in itself no bad thing – but in particular a decisive role has been played by one specific theoretical tradition within the field of sociology – the functionalist or neo-Weberian approach. There are three main reasons for this unusual state of affairs. In the first place, academic historiography in Germany has been more reluctant to admit the legitimacy of labour history than it has elsewhere. Not only has it until recently been politically very conservative, it has also been able to use the highly organised character of the German historical profession – often compared by its critics to a medieval guild (*Zunft*) – to exclude unwelcome outsiders and political radicals. This political conservatism and relative ideological homogeneity has been compounded by an overwhelming concentration on problems of foreign policy, a feature of traditional German historiography which began with the identification of historians with the nationalist movement of the nineteenth century, was strengthened by the widespread opposition in Germany, on largely historical grounds, to the Treaty of Versailles after 1918, and only ended with the final abandonment of the nationalist legacy in the mid-1960s.[2] In Britain, by contrast, even if labour history began within the labour movement itself, it was able to gain a place in the historical profession because universities were less ideologically homogeneous, and because historians were more prepared to admit the legitimacy of other subjects of historical inquiry apart from the central policies of the state.

Second, labour history in Germany tended at first, naturally enough, to be written by intellectuals within the labour movement itself, by members of the Social Democratic Party of Germany (Sozialdemokratische Partei Deutschlands, or SPD). It formed part of the Social

Democratic subculture, isolated from institutions of the dominant culture such as universities, historical societies and learned journals, in a way that had few parallels in other countries. Here the dominant intellectual tone was strongly Marxist; and the major historical accounts to emerge from the labour movement were repudiated or ignored by the historical profession, and suppressed, along with the labour movement itself, in the Third Reich.[3] After 1945, in the Cold War, in which the front line ran through the middle of Germany, this tradition was taken up by the German Communist Party and its successors in East Germany, who produced a large body of work from the early 1950s onwards, all designed more or less consciously to provide a historical legitimation for the East German regime.[4] This made labour history even more suspect in the West, where the Federal Republic was regarded as the heir not of German Social Democracy, but of the regimes established by Bismarck and his successors.

Third, these two features of the German historical tradition combined to create a vacuum which was largely filled by sociologists. The reason for this lay initially in the fact that sociology enjoyed a strong tradition in Germany before 1933, beginning in the late nineteenth and twentieth centuries with such powerful figures as Weber, Michels, Tönnies, Sombart and Schmoller. All of these figures interested themselves at one time or another in the nature of German Social Democracy and its place in the German political system; indeed, with some of them, it formed a basic and central intellectual concern.[5] The German sociologists never established themselves securely in the German academic world, and this tradition too, like that of labour history, was submerged after 1933 and did not fully resurface until the end of the Adenauer era. But instead of migrating to the East, the German sociological tradition found a new home in the United States, where many of its leading exponents lived during the Third Reich. Here indeed it gained new strength, partly through the personal influence of its representatives in American universities, partly through its more general affinities with American liberalism and its consequent intellectual influence on American sociology. From here it was re-imported into West Germany during the 1960s and early 1970s, as part of the Americanisation of West German intellectual life during this period. The influence of sociology increased as the West German historiographical tradition became discredited because of its associations with Germany's nationalist past,[6] and it moved in to fill the intellectual vacuum left by Germany's lack of a non-dogmatic Marxism of the kind which contributed so significantly to the re-invigoration of historical studies in England, France and the United States.[7] The prestige of American sociology in West Germany was completed by its scientific credentials, increasingly necessary in a society where science was coming to provide the major source of intellectual legitimacy.[8]

For all these reasons, the influence of the German-American sociological tradition, already considerable in most areas of historical scholarship in West Germany, has been overwhelming in the field of labour history.[9] The great founders of German sociology were concerned with the problem of the German labour movement because they were, as far as their political beliefs were concerned, middle-class liberals trying to seek an explanation for, and a way out of, their own political impotence. The political system in which the great German sociologists of the pre-1914 era lived was not one in which Liberalism was able to enjoy as much direct political power as it did in contemporary England, America, France or Italy. Government was conducted by the Emperor and his Ministers, who lacked all formal accountability to the Parliament, the Reichstag. Direct parliamentary pressure for reforms was extremely difficult; the most the Reichstag could hope to do was to exert a negative influence by blocking the government's measures. A great deal of legislative responsibility lay with the parliaments of the federated member states of the Empire, the *Länder*. This was especially true of areas of central concern to social reformers (e.g. education). These assemblies were mainly elected on property franchises and were often conservative in complexion. Most important of all, however, was the fact that a vast area of the control of social and political life lay in the hands not of legislatures but of administrative authorities who were not in any way accountable to parliaments. The police were a particularly striking example, for their powers and competence, far wider than in, say, England, included many areas subject across the North Sea to Acts of Parliament. In a very real sense, Germany before 1914 was administered rather than governed.[10]

If liberals like Weber, Tönnies and Michels, therefore, found themselves blocked from this side, they were unable to turn to any mass support to help them change the situation. For unlike their counterparts in Britain or Italy, they had no large or united liberal political party on which they could rely. German liberalism in the late nineteenth and early twentieth centuries was represented by no less than four different political parties, all of them relatively small and ineffectual to an increasing degree on a provincial as well as a national level. Even more serious, German liberalism had been unable to strike any kind of alliance with the labour movement. Almost from the very beginning, the German labour movement had rejected all ideas of an alliance with middle-class liberalism; least of all was it prepared, on the British model, to allow itself to be absorbed by it.[11] In the 1880s the influence of Marxist ideology on the labour movement became paramount. The Social Democratic Party adopted an attitude of uncompromising hostility not only to the state itself but also to all 'bourgeois' political parties, including the liberals. It demonstrated its unwillingness to co-operate by consistently voting against state budgets, and by refusing to join in ceremonies of the Reichstag which implied a recognition of the legitimacy of the Empire (such as the traditional 'cheer for the Kaiser'. It made no secret of the fact that it shortly expected a revolution which would sweep away the entire administrative and political structure of the German Empire. And the SPD was no mere left-wing sect: by the turn of the century it was well on the way to becoming a mass party; by 1914 its membership had topped the million mark; by 1912 it had gained more seats in the Reichstag than any other party despite a gerrymandered electoral system which left urban areas seriously under-represented.[12] With the Social Democrats, there was no compromise, no room for 'fellow travellers'; either one belonged, and submitted oneself to party discipline, including its explicit rejection of co-operation with liberals, or one was condemned out of hand as a 'class enemy'.

Thoughtful liberal reformists were naturally deeply worried by this situation. Some, like Michels, tried to move the Social Democratic Party towards a more flexible position from within;[13] others, like Weber, attempted to persuade liberals, and perhaps themselves, that the SPD was by no means as radical as it seemed. While Michels eventually gave up in disgust, and sought an explanation for the party's continued adherence to a rigidly radical ideology in its gradual bureaucratisation, Weber came to see bureaucratisation as a source of what was for him a positive development — the growth of reformism.[14] Both these views, of course, could be reconciled by arguing — as has since become conventional — that the SPD remained radical in theory, but became increasingly reformist in practice; for the bureaucratic leadership of the party was unwilling openly to challenge the party's radical ideology, enshrined in the Erfurt Programme of 1891, for fear of promoting a divisive internal debate, and it adopted the solution of continuing to pay it lip-service while increasingly ignoring it in day-to-day political affairs.

This interpretation was taken up in the 1950s by the sociologist Günther Roth, who had been brought up in Germany but had been teaching in the United States for some years by the time his book *The*

Social Democrats in Imperial Germany came to be published.[15] Indebted particularly to the neo-Weberian sociologists Reinhard Bendix and Seymour Martin Lipset,[16] Roth advanced the existing sociological interpretation in a number of ways.[17] First, he pointed out that the SPD's isolationism went much further than a mere refusal to co-operate with bourgeois parties. It involved, he said, the creation of a Social Democratic subculture, by which he meant both 'a normative system of sub-societies' and the norms which governed the system.[18]

> The labour movement came to offer to masses of workers a way of life which was significantly different from that of other groups, especially those explicitly supporting the prevailing political and social system. The vehicle for this way of life was a proliferating network of political, economic and cultural organizations.[19]

As the Social Democratic Party became a mass movement, so these organisations came to include almost the whole of social life. A member of the party could read Social Democratic newspapers and borrow from a Social Democratic library books which covered every aspect of life from a Social Democratic point of view; he could spend his leisure in Social Democratic pubs or gymnastic clubs, choirs or cycling societies, he could enrich his life through Social Democratic cultural and artistic associations; his wife could enlist in the Social Democratic Women's Movement and his son in the Social Democratic Youth Movement; if he was injured or ill, he could call upon the Working Men's Samaritan Federation to help him; if he died, there were Social Democratic burial clubs to see he received a decent funeral.[20]

Roth pointed out that the values which governed this subculture were strongly influenced by Marxism, though it was a Marxism attenuated by Social Darwinist evolutionary determinism , for the Social Democrats argued that since the course of history was bound to bring about a proletarian revolution in Germany, it was not necessary for them to do anything to help bring it about: all they had to do was sit tight and wait.[21] Nevertheless, it was clear that the Social Democrats regarded the subculture as a nucleus of the future socialist society; and they constantly emphasised the detachment of its organisations from parallel institutions in the dominant culture. A second point made by Roth about the Social Democratic subculture, however, was that it was by no means as isolated from the dominant culture as it appeared to be. To start with, many if not most party members either failed to understand Marxism or failed to take it seriously. At best, they believed in a series of vulgar Marxist dogmas — class struggle, the progressive immiseration of the proletariat, the labour theory of value, the increasing concentration of the means of production, the inevitability of the social revolution, and so on — without understanding the connections between them.[22] At worst, they echoed the views of one active Social Democrat who told the social investigator Paul Göhre that although he supported the SPD because it was the only party to champion the cause of the workers, he scarcely ever read a Social Democratic newspaper or book and added that he did not 'want to be equal to the rich and distinguished people. There must always be rich and poor.'[23] Analyses of books borrowed from Social Democratic libraries or read by individual Social Democrats, Roth argued, showed that the preferred reading of Social Democrats was 'bourgeois' in character, varying from penny-dreadfuls to the classics of German literature, and taking in popular works on Darwinism, history and religion on the way.[24] Even the party press, which included many daily papers, was, according to Roth, 'an organ for the declaration of faith and for intra-party communications . . . The party press remained unable to attract those readers who fell under the influence of the *Generalanzeiger* press,[25] or to interest intellectuals who were looking for good news coverage.'[26] And in its debates and policy on art and literature, the party demonstrated with particular clarity its inability to escape from bourgeois values, a feature of party attitudes which became stronger with the progressive *embourgeoisement* of the growing corps of paid party functionaries.[27] In a highly influential analysis of social divisions within the party, Roth asserted that

> there seems to be no significant evidence that the embourgeoisement of the leaders created any mass conflict between leaders and led. In contrast, there was sometimes conflict between proletarian functionaries and Social Democratic intellectuals. The intellectuals were often as doctrinaire as they were unsuitable for the routine tasks of lower-ranking positions . . .[28]

In other words, the fundamental division within the party was not between an *embourgeoisé* bureaucracy and a proletarian membership, but between the 'doctrinaire' (i.e. Marxist) intellectuals and the rest of the party, bureaucracy and membership together.

The point was, Roth argued, that while intellectuals may have been able to escape the influence of the dominant culture, ordinary workers, even if (or especially if) they ended up as full-time party functionaries, were not. Religion, education, popular literature and commercial newspapers, the official cult of the monarchy and the pervasive influence of militarism, all combined in his view to dilute the commitment of ordinary Social Democrats to a socialist revolution with a strong dose of allegiance to the existing structure of state and society. Citing the radical liberal historian of Imperial Germany Eckhart Kehr, Roth suggested that the authorities, led by Bismarck's reactionary Minister von Puttkamer and later by Wilhelm II, consciously used church, religion and education to cement the people's loyalty to the German state. This was not without its results on the labour movement: many Social Democratic workers had a 'dual loyalty';[29] some of the SPD's cultural activities 'reinforced the workers' adherence to significant components of the dominant culture';[30] others failed to replace the existing culture in the lives of Social Democratic members, so that bourgeois literature was read side by side with socialist, Bismarck and Wilhelm II were venerated as much as Bebel and Liebknecht, and petty-bourgeois morality dominated personal relations and home life.[31] Beyond this limitation, the Social Democratic subculture, by sealing itself off from the rest of society, effectively prevented the SPD from expanding its constituency into the middle classes. Finally, argued Roth,

> The subculture was 'negatively' integrated into the dominant system because by its very existence it provided an important means for the controlled expression and dissipation of conflict and thus contributed, for decades of peacetime, to the stability of the Empire. Specifically, the Social Democratic subculture furthered political moderation and industrial discipline in the following way: (a) It gave the workers the political and social recognition which the dominant system denied them (b) Radicalism was greatly weakened because both the individual Social Democrat in his industrial job and the party as a whole had to be careful not to provoke retaliatory measures or an intensification of repressive policies. Because of the permissive aspects of the dominant system, party and unions had an overriding interest in legality and therefore strove to protect themselves against complete suppression by fighting Blanquist and anarchist tendencies (c) With the expansion of the labour movement, more and more workers were taught by their own representatives to accept the necessity of authority, discipline, skill and good work performance. Social Democratic workers endeavoured to prove to themselves and to others that radical political aims and personal respectability were not mutually exclusive (d) Indirectly the Social Democratic labour movement enforced better living and working conditions by its mere

presence and thus promoted reformist moderation and industrial peace, even though the unions could not negotiate with big business and even though the Social Democrats did not cooperate on welfare legislation.[32]

In these ways, then, the Social Democratic subculture not only failed to create a viable alternative to the dominant culture, but even contributed to the stability of the dominant culture rather than hastening its downfall.

Recent historiography has, in one respect, gone even further than Roth in exposing the limitations of the Social Democratic subculture, by arguing that it reproduced within itself many of the features of the dominant culture, even where it was apparently successful in constructing an alternative. In this view, the construction of an elaborate and increasingly independent and unpolitical party bureaucracy was a reflection of the nature and the place of the state bureaucracy in German society; the dominance, frequently expressed in the rough, authoritarian behaviour towards subordinates, of the party leader Bebel, was a Social Democratic expression of Bismarck or Wilhelm II's role in Germany itself; the growing impotence of the Party Congress, where more and more issues were decided not in debate but outside, in committee-room intrigues, was a reproduction of the impotence of the Reichstag and the dominance of personal intrigue in national politics; the tendency of the same leading figures, not only Bebel and Liebknecht, but other lesser-known leaders both on a national and on a provincial or local level, to remain in power for decades, showed that the SPD shared the dominant culture's emphasis on respect for authority, age and hierarchy; the party's constant insistence on discipline, its perfectly organised street marches and demonstrations, the orderly structure of promotion within its ranks – usually on the basis of seniority – even the militaristic language which the party commonly used in describing its activities – all these made the SPD into a caricature of the Prussian Army.[33]

With this exception, however, subsequent studies have mostly contented themselves with filling out the details of the picture painted with such ingenuity and persuasiveness by Roth. Thus Hans-Ulrich Wehler has traced the SPD's attitudes to German nationalism and found it by no means so hostile as its formal commitment to internationalism might lead one to suppose;[34] Peter Domann has done the same with the party's view of the monarchy, which, he argues, it was formally committed to abolishing but gradually came to accept in practice;[35] Hans-Josef Steinberg, Klaus Schönhoven and Dieter Langwiesche have shown the weakness of the membership's commitment to Marxism, above all by closely examining the borrowing records of a large number of workers' libraries;[36] Dieter Groh has taken the concept of 'negative integration' and studied its use by, and impact on, the Imperial government and administration;[37] Dieter Dowe has shown that the workers' choral movement sang bourgeois songs as well as proletarian ones;[38] Horst Ueberhorst and others have examined workers' sports and gymnastic clubs and argued that they helped lessen class antagonisms and integrated workers into society;[39] studies of workers' festivals and theatres have argued that these mainly served the function of transmitting traditional or bourgeois culture;[40] and recent work on SPD attitudes to marriage, sex, women, children and the family has consistently argued in the same direction.[41] Major monographic studies arguing against these views have been almost entirely absent in West Germany. The few general surveys of labour history that have appeared, on the other hand, have endorsed them almost without comment.[42]

Clearly this remarkable unanimity is not coincidental; nor can it be ascribed to mere unoriginality or mediocrity on the part of recent scholarship on German labour history, for many of the works which I have mentioned are remarkable for the high quality of their research. Nor do the scholars concerned all come from the same university background or training. The main reason for the wide acceptance of the interpretation developed by Roth and his sociological predecessors lies in the evident sympathy of most established labour historians in West Germany with the ruling Social Democratic coalition in Bonn. Here there is a tendency consciously or unconsciously to facilitate the historical legitimation of the present-day SPD by playing down its radicalism and its commitment to Marxism in the past, and by arguing that its adherence to the Erfurt Programme and its use of Marxist language — highly embarrassing to present-day Social Democrats — was forced on it from outside, by the negative attitude of the state. The SPD is portrayed in this interpretation as having been a predominantly non-revolutionary party from the beginning. This in itself indeed is a reasonable enough line to take; what is more open to question is the way in which this has been interpreted. What prevented the SPD from realising its potential as a broadly based movement of social reform, it is often argued, was above all the hostility of the authorities. By subjecting the party to constant police harassment and by preventing Social Democrats from occupying socially prestigious positions such as those of army officer or university professor, the authorities manoeuvred the SPD into a ghetto. It was thus impossible for the party to make the politically crucial transition

from a labour movement (*Arbeiterbewegung*) to a broadly based democratic party (*Volkspartei*). The verbal radicalism of the party, taken
seriously only by its intellectuals, served as a rhetorical fig-leaf for its
political impotence. Had the state offered the SPD full participation,
the pseudo-Marxism of the party's programme would soon have been
dispensed with. In this way, therefore, the Social Democrats' tradition
is linked to the present-day SPD, and the blame for what is portrayed
as its radical alienation under the Empire is placed on the 'pre-industrial'
authoritarian Prussian state.[43]

It is for these political reasons, then, that Roth's hypotheses have
been accepted in the West German historical profession with such
striking unanimity, a process made easier by the fact that Roth's approach
carries with it the scientific legitimation of the German-American sociological tradition. In the 1960s and early 1970s it undoubtedly exercised
an intellectually liberating influence on German labour history, first by
making the serious study of the subject academically respectable and by
integrating it fully into the German historical profession for the first
time,[44] secondly, in conjunction with the increasingly negative view of
the Empire which followed in the wake of the celebrated Fischer controversy of the 1960s, by inspiring a great deal of important work on the
repressive policies of state and employers towards the labour movement
and thus illuminating the context in which the SPD had to operate,[45]
and finally, by drawing the attention of historians away from ideologies
and institutions and towards the cultural and moral values of the party
and its working-class constituency.[46] However, as monograph after
monograph appears in which the author is forced to confess that he is
doing little more than filling out the details of an already well established
interpretation,[47] it is becoming clear that the functionalist sociological
approach is offering rapidly diminishing returns.

II

At the most general level, then, many of the most widely accepted hypotheses in current West German writing on labour history are consciously
derived from functionalist sociology, and they share the limitations of
this brand of sociological theory. The idea that society is a functioning
system whose interlocking parts all contribute to its 'stabilisation' (in a
favourite phrase of German historians, are *systemstabilisierend*) allows
any social institution or process to be portrayed as contributing to the
social and political *status quo*. By explaining everything, it explains

nothing. And it completely fails to account for or (characteristically, in the *general* context of West German historiography) drastically under-estimates the extent and significance of the social and political changes that a moment's consideration indicates were taking place in Imperial Germany.[48] Using the functionalist model, for example, it is possible, as Roth demonstrates, to argue that the Social Democrats were on the whole a stabilising factor in the Imperial 'system' because they diverted the workers' revolutionary potential into cultural activities which in themselves were a reflection of the dominant culture; or, as Groh and others have suggested, because the more they grew in number, the more reason they gave the ruling elites of industrialists and landowners to bury or paper over their differences and join together in an ever-fiercer defence of the *status quo*.[49] Using these models, there is no reason why we should not explain strikes, street demonstrations and revolutionary speeches as *systemstabiliserend* as well. When it comes to events which it is impossible even in this interpretation to portray as contributing to the maintenance of the *status quo* — notably the Revolution of 1918 — its exponents are reduced to using the metaphor of a temporary break-down in the social order, occasioned by psychological factors (e.g. war-weariness), and give the impression that the 'system' was soon 'stabilised' once more, above all by the actions of the SPD leadership itself.[50] Not only does this view ignore the increasingly deep and violent social antagonisms of the Weimar Republic itself, culminating in a virtual state of civil war during the Depression and ending, of course, with the collapse of the Republic and the Nazi seizure of power, it also neglects, or fails to explain, the continuing periodic outbreaks of mass protest that occurred before 1914 as well, not to mention the progressive radi-calisation of the political right and the growth of anti-Semitism;[51] for there is nothing in the functionalist view which offers an explanation for conflict and change, except in terms of individual psychology; its whole attention is directed towards stability, which, not surprisingly in view of its theoretical premises, it drastically overestimates.

The functionalist or neo-Weberian sociological interpretation of German labour history also adopts a highly simplistic view of the process of the formation of consciousness. The working classes are portrayed as passive receptacles waiting to be filled with ideas poured down from above; by ideologies formulated by intellectuals, attitudes propagated by church and school, or social values and practices developed by the bourgeoisie. This is particularly true of the view which sees the SPD as a caricature of the Wilhelmine state, Bebel as a radical but equally authori-tarian version of Bismarck, the SPD's emphasis on discipline as a derivative of Prussian militarism and so on; but it is equally true of the thesis, almost universally accepted by present-day labour historians in West Germany, that the SPD's verbal radicalism, its isolationism, indeed the very existence of its self-enclosed subculture, were all basically consequences of the hostility of the state towards the labour movement and of the state's refusal to allow the SPD and its members to participate in the dominant institutions of the political and social system. Not only are the mass of SPD members (and the mass of the people in general) seen as mere cyphers without any specific historical tradition of their own, but — in a way highly characteristic of the dominant intellectual culture in Germany — the state is seen as active, society as passive. Little attempt is made to relate the ideas and actions of the labour movement to the specific situation of workers, where, more often than not, the most obvious explanation of the movement's behaviour is to be found. All that has been done is to incorporate the study of labour movement *institutions* into the study of German political history; their relation to *society* has been left largely untouched.

Moreover, while recent labour historians in Germany have paid close attention to tracing bourgeois or reformist elements in the SPD's theory and practice on a wide range of issues, from the monarchy and the nation-state at one extreme to gymnastics and poetry at the other, few have paused to ask precisely the significance of the issues they examine, either for the formation of working-class consciousness or for determining whether the labour movement was radical or reformist. Much, if not most, work on the Social Democratic subculture has concentrated on leisure activities. This is most obvious in the case of the recent proliferation of studies of workers' singing clubs, football teams, bicycling associations, cultural societies and so on, but it is equally true of many studies of more directly political subjects. Thus a recent (generally excellent) examination of anti-Semitism in the pre-1914 SPD has used the party's satirical weekly magazine as one of its main sources,[52] and, more generally, studies of ideology (and particularly Marxist ideology) rely heavily on figures culled from workers' libraries demonstrating the popularity of romantic novels.[53] It is arguable, however, whether leisure activities are the right thing to look at when trying to gauge the extent of the Social Democrats' commitment to socialism and revolution.

Many of the studies carried out in the sociological tradition seem to take as their starting-point an image (perhaps 'ideal type' would be a more appropriate expression) of a revolutionary worker who has never existed outside the fantasies of Lukács,[54] dedicated wholly and exclusively to the cause of revolutionary socialism every waking hour, and presumably dreaming about it as well, since his or her consciousness has been entirely purged of all 'bourgeois' elements. Such an individual has never existed in reality of course; to start at the top, for example, Marx's own wide knowledge of 'bourgeois' literature is well attested, while Lenin's fondness for the ideologically ambiguous adventure stories of Jack London is also well known.[55] No one has ever suggested, however, that any of this impeded their revolutionary thinking or activity, nor is there any reason to suppose anything similar in the case of their followers. More seriously, any individual's consciousness is surely made up of a number of different elements, and it does not really amount to much to show that not all of these were socialist or Marxist.

The categorisation of attitudes and activities into 'bourgeois' on the one hand and 'socialist' on the other is in any case a considerable over-simplification. The quality of being 'bourgeois' is not necessarily inherent in books, recreations, institutions or even ideas and beliefs; they also acquire this quality, or lose it, from the context in which they are placed. The same thing can have a different meaning for different individuals, groups or social classes. The SPD's insistence on the value and impor-tance of the family as an institution, for example, has been seen by some historians as an example of its 'embourgeoisement', of conformity to the bourgeois cult of the family prevalent in Wilhelmine Germany.[56] Equally, however, it is clear that the Social Democrats saw the working-class family, united in its support of the party's beliefs, as an important focus of resistance to the dominant culture purveyed through school, church and army; and that the party also argued for, and in some ways gave practical support to, equality within the family as an alternative to the exclusive domination of the *Paterfamilias* propagated by official ideology.[57] Similarly, though workers' libraries, choirs and so on have often been seen as little more than a means of transmitting bourgeois culture to the proletariat, they can also be seen in a quite different light: as Dieter Dowe has remarked, 'working people's embrace of the best cultural achievements of the past, whether feudal or bourgeois in origin, can. . .be interpreted more meaningfully as a desire to appropriate to themselves the "national culture." '[58] The fact that this was done through *workers'* libraries, *workers'* choral societies and *workers'* clubs was surely a crucial element in defining the meaning of the cultural products involved.

There is a similar one-sidedness in the way in which recent German historiography has approached the dominant cultural institutions of Imperial Germany. School, church and army are generally portrayed as 'socialising agents' whose main function was to imprint the dominant social values on those who passed through them, a view which has been backed up in research mainly through evidence of political conservatism in textbooks and curricula.[59] Here again, quite apart from the failure to perceive that those who entered the primary school, the church congregation or the army barracks already brought values with them in the light of which they would interpret what was offered to them, there is an insufficient awareness of the fact that education, religion and military training were profoundly ambiguous in their potential effects; education enabled workers to read Marx and Bebel as well as Treitschke and Riehl, religion helped them to express moral repugnance at the hypocrisy of the ruling class, and military training taught them how to use weapons and proved an invaluable experience in insurrections such as that of the 'Red Army' in the Ruhr at the beginning of the 1920s.[60] Moreover, it is still by no means clear precisely in what degree these institutions affected the beliefs of those who passed through them; at the most basic level, for example, we do not yet know how often children were absent from school, working illegally or simply playing truant, nor do there appear to be any serious studies of attendance at church or of the social composition of army conscripts.

Finally, recent research, above all on a local level, has begun to reveal – often almost despite itself – that the functionalist sociological interpretation of German labour history is open to question on more detailed empirical grounds. Returning to the theses advanced by Roth, there are in particular two specific points on which some doubt can now be thrown. First, the role of the labour movement in stabilising the social system. This claim rests on three assertions,[61] which I shall deal with in turn:

(1)   *The movement gave the workers political and social recognition and instilled in them a belief in the need for discipline, skill and good work performance.* It must be remembered, however, that this recognition was based specifically on a denial of the legitimacy of the existing political and social system; that discipline was essential for the organisation of revolutionary outbreaks, or even of successful strikes; and that the skilled workers were among the most militant in the work-force, particularly during the First World War.[62]

(2)   *The movement's growth frightened the ruling classes into ever-greater efforts to stabilise the political system.* Here, however, it has long been well known that these efforts met with little success; indeed, if we accept the view that they culminated in the launching of the First World War, then it is clear that they ended in total disaster.

(3) *The labour movement promoted moderation by helping to enforce better living and working conditions.* Here again one can refer to the militancy of skilled workers; but there are also more specific examples which can be offered. In Hamburg[63] the minimum qualification for voting in state elections was an annual income of 1,200 marks sustained over a period of five years. Rising real wages, whether or not they were to some degree a result of pressure from the SPD and the unions, brought an increasing number of working men above this boundary, a process which gave the SPD its first seat on the city council in 1901, and 12 more in 1904. As a result, the city government felt obliged to forestall a further growth in the party's electoral strength by revising the franchise qualifications sharply upwards in 1906, thereby provoking the local SPD into mounting Germany's first-ever political general strike, which was followed by violent riots which the Hamburg police likened to the events of the 1905 Revolution in Russia. All this throws some doubt on any simple equation between the growth of working-class prosperity and the spread of political moderation and reconciliation to the *status quo*.

Second, Roth asserts the identity of party functionaries with ordinary party members, in opposition to the intellectuals in the labour movement. Although it has become conventional, following Roth, to minimise the effects of the bureaucratisation of the labour movement, and to assert that reformist functionaries were only expressing the moderate views of ordinary party or union members against the intransigent and purely theoretical revolutionism of a small and increasingly isolated body of party intellectuals, local studies suggest that it is time that the political importance of the bureaucratisation of the labour movement, first brought to the attention of students by Weber and Michels, was reasserted. Lützenkirchen's study of Dortmund, for example, has shown quite clearly how in the disputes within the local SPD over the budget question in 1908-9, all the speakers who took the reformist line (save two) were middle-ranking or high party or union functionaries, while most of the speakers who opposed them held party posts at the lowest level, the level, in other words, that was nearest to the ordinary member. A struggle followed in which local branches of the Dortmund party attempted — without success — to curtail the freedom of action of the functionaries by forcing Party Congress resolutions to be put to a ballot of all party members and by depriving the party executive and Reichstag deputies of the right to vote at party congresses.[64]

The functionalist sociological interpretation of German labour history, then, is open to criticism on a number of counts. It tends to portray society as a self-regulating system in which every element plays a functional part and in which the possibilities of real change are minimal; it assumes that values are transmitted downwards from active state institutions on to a passive proletariat; it takes its evidence from cultural and leisure activities whose role in the formation of political consciousness is exaggerated; it overplays the significance of 'bourgeois' elements in workers' culture, which it presents as politically important deviations from a purely imaginary construct of permanent and total revolutionary socialist activism; it ignores the fact that 'bourgeois' cultural artifacts, education activities or social institutions can be given quite different meanings and uses according to the situation of the recipient; it fails to note the contradictory effects of improvements in working-class living standards and of the labour movement's imposition of discipline on its members; and it overestimates the success of ruling-class strategies of containment. This catalogue by no means deals with all the many facets of what is beyond doubt a very rich and highly stimulating interpretative tradition, or with the many ways in which its insights have become embedded in the literature; I have reserved one or two of the most important aspects for later in the discussion. Before they can be brought into focus, however, it is necessary to turn to the question of how one might begin to construct an alternative framework of interpretation.

III

The first stop necessary in order to transcend the functionalist sociological interpretation of German labour history is to make a distinction between *Social Democratic* (or *labour movement*) culture and *working-class* culture. Roth, for example, claimed that 'the labour movement came to offer to masses of workers a way of life which was significantly different from that of other groups'.[65] Yet it seems unlikely that the labour movement and its subculture played such a central role in working-class life. It is an obvious point that though it contained over a million members by 1914, the SPD only contained a minority of the working class as a whole. The same is true of the successor parties (Communists, Independent Social Democrats) in the Weimar Republic. Similarly with the trade unions. Even among miners, often thought of as an exceptionally militant group, only a minority belonged to trade unions of any description, and in general only a minority of trade unionists actually belonged to the SPD.[66] The numbers involved in the labour movement's cultural associations, however large, by no means encompassed a majority of the working class. The relationship of many of these associations with the political parties of the labour movement may have been loose or informal, but it is clear that there was a very substantial overlap in membership, and even without this the basic distinction, between labour movement and working class, still holds good. Recognition of this point is spreading among German labour historians: a good deal of work is being carried out on non-socialist labour organisations, and historians are beginning to explore regions of working-class life and experience not encompassed within the labour movement.[67] Yet these beginnings are very slow, as a recent book of essays on 'Workers' Culture' edited by Gerhard A. Ritter indicates;[68] despite the editor's plea for more study of working-class as distinct from socialist culture, the great majority of the studies in the volume deal with socialist cultural organisations. Even major socialist festivals such as May Day did not play a particularly significant role in the life of the working class as a whole, though this seems to be assumed by the essay on it in the book.[69] Certainly, a number of primarily quantitative studies of the labour force in various nineteenth-century factories and towns in Germany have recently been undertaken, and these are rapidly transforming our knowledge of the German proletariat during the Industrial Revolution. Yet these studies are proceeding in a manner that is largely empirical in character, and in most respects are divorced from the existing historiographical debate about the nature of the German labour movement.[70]

The same is the case for another very interesting development in German labour history since the end of the 1970s: the turn to the 'history of everyday life' (*Alltagsgeschichte*) of the working class. A recent collection of essays on 'the social history of everyday life in the Industrial Age', edited by Jürgen Reulecke and Wolfhard Weber, gives some indication of the direction which historical inquiry is taking: there are contributions on miners and metalworkers, on housing and food, on primary schools, religion and sports.[71] The editors see their enterprise as an attempt to recapture 'the various hopes, fears and desires of "ordinary people" ("*Leute*")', which, they argue, run the risk of being neglected in 'technocratically congealed pluralistic societies, when an arrogant bureaucracy, contemptuous of ordinary human beings, seeks to determine everyday life'.[72] The influence of the French *Annales* school is acknowledged; and so too is that of contemporary social science. It follows from this that one of the major weaknesses of the collection lies in the way in which everyday experience is frequently dissolved into categories such as 'norm structures', 'conditions of socialisation', 'need satisfaction', 'behavioural patterns', 'communication networks', etc., etc., thus reproducing static categories of sociology in a context (history) for which many of them are inappropriate. Moreover, although one of the impulses behind *Alltagsgeschichte* is evidently the belief that the development of the labour movement cannot be properly understood without knowledge of the conditions of life and the everyday thought and action of its members and supporters, the development of *Alltagsgeschichte* as a specific area of historical investigation none the less runs the risk of separating social history from political history and of presenting itself as a mere *addition* to labour history, rather than a different way of looking at it.[73] In addition to this, there is a continuing tendency to present the working class as passive rather than active even in its daily experience of life: to write *Alltagsgeschichte*, in the words of Reulecke and Weber, as the history of 'how individual human beings *lived under the conditions* of the spectacular political events and social change processes of modern times, and how *these made themselves felt* in the daily life of the many individual and small groups [of people]'[74] (my italics). Finally, 'the history of everyday life', at least as it has been developed so far, seems to fragment working-class experience, to divorce not only political from social life, but to separate work from leisure, family from factory, and one occupation from another. The sense of what links these things, or what in the way of working-class culture or consciousness, might transcend them, is lost.[75] The problem remains, therefore, of constituting the *working class* and its culture and values as objects of historical study, and of investigating the relationship between these and the institutions, culture and values of the *labour movement*.

A second step by which we might go beyond the functionalist sociological interpretation of German labour history is to move the focus away from leisure. As I have suggested, the sociological interpretation relies heavily for its evidence on investigations of socialist leisure organisations. More recently, historians have begun to move beyond this to examine patterns of working-class leisure in a more general way, including activities and institutions unconnected with the socialist movement, such as football clubs.[76] Implicit in this new approach is still the view that working-class culture means what workers do or think when they are not working. But this was only a small part of the working-class experience. In an era when the working day was far longer than it is now, work stood at the centre of life for most people; through it, the employee was brought into daily contact with the dominant culture (again using the word in its broadest sense, meaning the attitudes and

practices of the ruling classes). The centrality and intensity of this experience far outweighed any influence exerted by bicycling clubs and male
voice choirs on the one hand or by school and military service on the
other. It is to work, therefore, that we should be directing our attention;
to the structure and conditions of employment and unemployment, to
their economic meaning and social or personal significance.[77] Our
starting-point should be the relations of employer and employed, the
nature of work, and the conditions under which people laboured to
secure their existence. It is from this perspective that we should then
look to the social structure and function of leisure activities; from a
study of work and leisure, and from their relations with one another,
and with the labour movement, its ideology and its institutions, that we
can begin to construct a picture of working-class attitudes to state and
society more satisfying than that provided by the functionalist sociological interpretation. What is necessary is not only the penetration of
historical investigation beneath the level of socialist organisation and
labour movement culture to the reality of working-class life and attitudes underneath; it is, rather, the investigation of the relationship
between these two levels that most urgently needs to be studied. For
working-class experience is no more real or authentic than the experience of activists in socialist political or cultural organisations; it
possesses, certainly, its own autonomy and its own creative drive, but it
does not, and cannot, remain unaffected by the ideology and politics
of the labour movement itself. These premises form the starting-point
for the collection of essays presented in this book.[78]

It is necessary at this point, therefore, to return to the specifics of
the 'functionalist sociological interpretation' of German labour history
in order to spell out in more concrete form what the present collection
of studies hopes to achieve. According to Günther Roth, the German
labour movement insisted on legal tactics and fought revolutionary
activism within its own ranks. More generally,

> with the expansion of the labour movement, more and more workers
> were taught by their own representatives to accept the necessity of
> authority . . . Social Democratic workers endeavoured to prove to
> themselves and to others that radical political aims and personal
> respectability were not mutually exclusive.[79]

The recent trends in historical scholarship discussed above have tended
to reinforce this view. The investigation of the labour movement and
the working class in Germany has produced a picture of proletarian

culture that has highlighted its integrative aspects and the extent to which it (allegedly) diverted political energies into harmless, even 'bourgeois', leisure pursuits. Football teams, singing clubs, gymnastic associations, libraries, or even political festivals such as May Day were relatively respectable, generally innocuous activities, and if this is what the working class of Wilhelmine and Weimar Germany spent its time doing, it is scarcely surprising that it lost the taste for revolution, if indeed it had ever possessed it. The Social Democrats, it is argued, taught the proletariat to be law-abiding; but even more than this, the 'traditional' components of working-class culture (miners' festivals, guild practices and the like), which exerted a strong influence on the formation of the Social Democratic subculture, were themselves, it is suggested, profoundly addicted to the observation of rules and conformity to authority.[80] Much of the work that has been carried out on working-class culture has been motivated not least by a desire to establish its authenticity as part of the national culture, and the value of its contribution to cultural life in general, by an urge to counteract the elitist view of the working class as a collection of ignorant, untutored savages with no authentic cultural life of their own.[81] It is this approach, with its narrow definition of 'culture'[82] as the artistic and creative life of a society or group within it, which helps explain why so much attention has been paid by historians to singing clubs, popular festivals, organised sports and the like; though there remains in this a refusal to look at more widespread but perhaps less elevating manifestations of popular culture (in this narrow sense of the word) such as the German equivalent of the music hall (*Variétés* and *Tingeltangels*).[83] Finally, of course, work on German labour history has been indubitably structured by hindsight; by the capitulations of 1914 and 1933, by the need to explain why the seemingly radical socialist left first supported the German government at the outbreak of the First World War, then failed to mount any effective opposition to the Nazi seizure of power.[84] All these various influences, together with the elements of the functionalist sociological interpretation discussed in the earlier parts of this essay, have come together to produce a picture of working-class culture and working-class life in Wilhelmine and Weimar Germany that suppresses almost completely its rough, law-breaking and undisciplined aspects. The result is a drastically distorted view of working-class habits, manners and values which in turn leads to serious misunderstandings about the nature of working-class culture and politics.

Many of the contributions to the present volume counteract this popular image of working-class culture as something worthy, law-abiding and harmless.[85] A necessary premiss is of course a redefinition of the concept of culture — such has already been proposed, though as yet scarcely carried out, by West German students of the subject — to include 'the social history of day-to-day experiences',[86] the whole package of values and practices which informed everyday proletarian life. In the particular case with which we are concerned — working-class culture in Germany — the question at the top of the historical agenda is (as it has always been) the extent to which it rested on either an acceptance or a denial of the legitimacy of the capitalist social order. The first theme running through all the contributions to this volume, therefore, is that of working-class deviance from bourgeois social values and norms. The everyday life of the working class, at work and at leisure, involved constant deviations from the attitudes and patterns of conduct which the bourgeoisie laid down for the attainment of 'respectability'. Working-class culture contained many elements of which the ruling classes disapproved: heavy drinking, for instance, as James Roberts shows in his contribution[87] or even, as James Wickham has suggested, dancing, cinema-going and adolescent sexuality.[88] These deviations were also frequently necessitated by the economic and social situation of the working class; Michael Grüttner's contribution to this volume[89] indicates, for example, how pilferage and small-time crime were built into the structure of work in the Hamburg dockland in the late nineteenth and early twentieth centuries. Dockers considered in effect that they had a right to appropriate part of the wares which they were required to load and unload from ships; and the casual, precarious nature of their employment encouraged them to maximise earnings in any way possible at the times then they were actually working. At moments of tension and conflict too, some workers could again feel few qualms about breaking the law and engaging in what were regarded as crimes of some seriousness and magnitude, as David Crew's contribution on the workers' report to sabotage during the Dortmund steel strike of 1912 seems to indicate.[90]

The question of 'deviance' leads on naturally to the problem of working-class attitudes towards the law. Many historians have pointed out that the law in Wilhelmine Germany (and to a lesser extent in the Weimar Republic as well) discriminated massively against the labour movement. Even though the Social Democratic Party was no longer formally illegal after 1890, its activities were still constantly supervised by the political police, who arrested its members on the slightest pretexts. Few indeed by 1914 were the Social Democratic newspapers and magazine editors who had not spent some time in gaol on a charge of *lèse-majesté* or libel on the police, or as the result of some piece of legal chicanery engineered by the authorities. And countless were the SPD meetings that were broken up and dissolved by the police on one pretext or another, such as constituting a danger to public order. Strikes and union activities were similarly circumscribed by a whole set of legal restrictions and limitations.[91] This system of judicial bias and persecution, conventionally dubbed both by socialists at the time and by subsequent historians as a system of 'class justice' (*Klassenjustiz*), would not, it is generally argued, have existed in a society more liberal or politically 'modern' in its nature.

Yet this argument obscures the real nature of 'class justice' in late-nineteenth- and early-twentieth-century Germany. For the law was structured so as to constitute a massive interference not simply in labour movement activities but also in the daily life of the working class. This is an area which has hardly been touched upon by German historians, although a good deal of work on the growth of police forces and the 'policing of everyday life' has been carried out in the context of Victorian and Edwardian England. As the American observer Raymond Fosdick wrote in 1914:

On every side and at every turn, the German citizen is confronted by newly adopted police regulations. Thus in Berlin, the Police President has recently issued ordinances regulating the color of automobiles, the length of hatpins and the methods of purchasing fish and fowl . . . In Stuttgart, a driver may not snap his whip as he guides his horses in the street; a customer may not fall asleep in a restaurant or a weary man on a park bench; a barber may not keep his official trade card in an inconspicuous place; a cab-driver may not leave his position in front of the railway station during the hours in which the police decree he shall be on duty; a driver may not hold his reins improperly or go through the public streets without having the owner's name in a conspicuous place on his cart or carriage; a delivery boy may not coast on a hand-cart or carriage; a passenger may not alight from a train on the side away from the platform or while the train is in motion; children may not slide on a slippery sidewalk; a citizen may not be impertinent to a public official on duty nor offer any affront to his dignity. These regulations are not only negative, they are often positive; not only general, but particular and directed against specific parties. Thus a house owner *must* sprinkle his street in hot weather when ordered by the police or a certain striker *must* refrain from picketing when so directed or a given contractor *must* remove building encumbrances on demand.[92]

The policing of everyday life in Wilhelmine Germany is another theme which runs through the essays in this book which deal with that particular period. As Stefan Bajohr points out,[93] this extended even into the most intimate spheres of personal life; his contribution on unmarried mothers in Brunswick presents a fascinating account of police attempts to prevent men and women living together and having sexual relations without being married, or even to prevent such people from getting married if they were adjudged to be 'immoral' characters. Similarly, police control of prostitution in Imperial Germany involved a degree of interference with the lives of those concerned that was unknown in England even under the (short-lived) regime of the Contagious Diseases Acts. A special branch of the police existed in every German state to deal with prostitution — the 'Morals Police' (Sittenpolizei). These were enpowered to arrest and subject to a medical examination any women suspected of being a prostitute; those convicted were liable to be inscribed on the official list and subject to the Morals Police Regulations. These were formidable in their scope and extent. Apart from the obligatory medical examinations, there were also provisions confining prostitutes to certain buildings or streets, regulating the hours at which they could go out, and prohibiting them from frequenting at any time a whole range of different, named streets, parks, cafés and other places in the various towns for which these regulations obtained. As has recently been written:

> they present such a close net of possibilities of contravention and prosecution that if she [i.e. the prostitute] is for a moment inattentive, she will then fall foul of them; on the other hand, if she lives according to these rules, she exists within an invisible but ever-present prison.[94]

It is important, however, to bear in mind that such attempts to control everyday life met with only limited success. As Stefan Bajohr points out, most couples living in *wilden Ehen* ('wild marriages') were able to circumvent police restrictions; if they really wanted to marry, they commonly went to London to do so. Similarly, in the case of prostitution, the strength of the Morals Police was altogether inadequate to deal with the scale of the problem which they (of their own choice) confronted or to enforce even a tithe of the regulations which they had drawn up. The Morals Police were complaining by the end of the nineteenth century that prostitution was being increasingly carried on by women 'who for part of the time do a regular job, but who also from time to time sell themselves to men for money, in order to improve their financial situation'.[95] In such circumstances the police themselves became increasingly unwilling to enforce the regulation too vigorously, because the more unpleasant they made the situation of controlled prostitutes, the more prostitutes would be inclined to evade control altogether. None the less, by the early 1900s only a tiny proportion of German prostitutes were inscribed at all. In 1909, in Munich, for instance, less than 9 per cent of the prostitutes actually known to the police were inscribed and regulated; and even these were only part of the whole. The truth was, as one prostitute told the American investigator Abraham Flexner on the eve of the First World War, 'only the stupid are inscribed'.[96]

But working-class resistance to, or evasion of, the policing of everyday life extended well beyond the domestic sphere; it took place even at the workplace itself, and confronted police measures that, unlike the prevention of concubinage or the regulation of prostitution, would not have been considered unfamiliar or excessive in other countries. Erhard Lucas, in his study of the mining town of Hamborn, in the Ruhr, has painted a graphic picture of the ineffectiveness of policing in this community. There were only a few score policemen to deal with a town of 110,000 in 1910; and when one calls to mind the fact that coal-miners in Hamborn returned from work, or even simply went for walks, in groups of 40 to 50, carrying coal-picks in their hands, it is hardly surprising that cases of the 'forcible release of prisoners' figured frequently in the criminal statistics for the town. Drunkenness was extremely common, and crimes of violence made up 22.5 per cent of the overall crime figures for Hamborn in 1900-8. Parts of the town were described as resembling the Wild West. Crime rates for the town as a whole were high.[97] In such new industrial communities, working-class resistance to, or evasion of, police attempts to enforce the law were considerable. Similarly, in the present volume, Michael Grüttner's study of pilfering in the Hamburg docks shows clearly how workers defied the law at the workplace as well as on the streets or in their leisure hours.

Being working-class in Wilhelmine and Weimar Germany meant, therefore, not only constant contraventions of bourgeois moral and social norms; it also meant continual evasion, defiance and disregard of the law and of those whose job it was to enforce it. Law-breaking was woven into the fabric of the everyday life of the working class.[98] Of course it is necessary to distinguish between different elements of the proletariat in this, as in other, contexts. Work in the docks provided more opportunities for pilferage than did some other kinds of employment, and the structure of employment in the docks was also of a kind to encourage illicit ways of supplementing income. Among working-class youth in Berlin during the 1920s, as Eve Rosenhaft shows in her contribution to this volume, only a minority engaged in gang violence, though a great many more must, if they were like working-class adolescent gangs elsewhere, have constantly engaged in petty violations of the law.[99] And the steelworkers of David Crew's contribution only resorted to sabotage, if they did at all, at a moment of extreme tension between workers and employers.

So it would be wrong to conclude that a hard-and-fast line should be drawn between those elements of the working class who broke the law and defied bourgeois morality, and those who did not. Marxist theory has conventionally drawn a distinction between the working class, to whom are ascribed a set of functioning moral, social and political values, and the *Lumpenproletariat*, the 'proletariat of rags', 'a residuum drawn from all social classes, of society's outcasts, whose conduct no political or moral principles can be said to govern'.[100] Certainly Marx tended to use this term as a means of abuse in his writing; Louis Napoleon, for example, appears in the *Eighteenth Brumaire* as a member of the French *Lumpenproletariat*.[101] But more commonly, the term corresponded to what French writers in the nineteenth century called the 'dangerous class', in contrast to the honest 'labouring class'; the one lived off its wits, the other from its work.[102] Such a distinction may in certain circumstances be a useful one. But it has its dangers too, particularly if it is used in the polemical way in which it came to be employed by the labour movement in the late nineteenth century. It must not be taken to imply, as it was by Social Democrats in Imperial Germany, that the working class 'proper' never had any occasion to break the law or defy accepted moral standards. One feature of this book may indeed be a questioning of the conventional use of the term *Lumpenproletariat*, not least by revealing the implications of the ways in which it was used by Marxists in the late nineteenth and early twentieth centuries.[103] More useful may be a distinction between proletariat and sub-proletariat (the residuum of casually employed or structurally unemployed and underemployed, the poorest and most precarious sectors of the working class). In the conditions of employment which obtained in the industrialising economy of Wilhelmine Germany, or the crisis-ridden economy of the Weimar era, the boundary lines between proletariat and sub-proletariat, between stable and unstable, solvent and insolvent, employed and unemployed, permanently engaged and casually hired, were fluid, shifting and hard to discern. Workers changed jobs frequently; sudden lay-offs, dismissals and lock-outs were common. The extent of casual employment was far greater than in more mature capitalist societies.[104] Welfare provisions were inadequate to save a family from destitution when illness, accident or death incapacitated the main breadwinner. In such circumstances recourse to additional, illegal sources of income was common. But even in the higher-earning sectors of the working class, as with lightermen in the Hamburg docks, such recourse was equally common. Nor, as Stefan Bajohr and James Roberts show, do concubinage or heavy drinking seem solely to have been pursuits of the destitute. And sabotage in the Dortmund steel strike of 1912, as David Crew indicates, was probably carried out by workers who were among the most highly and regularly paid in Germany. Certainly it would be exaggerated to suggest that all of the working class were breaking the law and contravening bourgeois morality all of the time, at least in so dramatic a way. But it would be equally erroneous to attempt to maintain any sharp dividing line between those who conformed and those who did not.

In addition to working-class contravention of bourgeois norms, and of the law, a third theme of this book is that such contraventions did not necessarily constitute a repudiation of morality and law *per se*.[105] The most striking illustration of this point is to be found in Michael Grüttner's contribution, where he notes that although dock workers constantly stole from their employers, they did not steal from each other; those who did rob their workmates were ostracised, while the dockers felt no qualms about entrusting the funds of their organisations to fellow workers with previous convictions for stealing from cargoes. Similarly, Eve Rosenhaft notes that although the Berlin *Cliquen* (a sort of cross between street gangs and hiking clubs) in the 1920s constantly engaged in violence, vandalism and theft, a member who made off with the funds of a *Clique* was an exception, and instantly stigmatised as a 'bad character'. And Stefan Bajohr demonstrates that one of the ironies of police attempts to control 'concubinage' was the fact that many of the couples concerned actually wanted to live together in stable marriages and were only prevented from doing so by the law. Working-class culture involved its own sets of values and norms, its own codes of conduct, even though frightened conservatives frequently thought of the working class as a part of society that still existed in a state of nature, without morality, honour or law. Working-class culture, then, did possess its own authenticity, as earlier studies of working-class leisure pursuits have suggested; but this involved a widespread deviance from bourgeois values which a concentration on *organised* leisure, and a concomitant neglect by historians both of informal spare-time activities, and of the culture of work and employment, has largely served to obscure.

IV

The contributions to this book, therefore, present a variety of analyses of which might loosely be termed the 'rough' side of working-class culture in Wilhelmine and Weimar Germany. But it is hoped that they go beyond this and address the major questions about the history of the German labour movement which this introductory essay began by discussing. All the essays attempt to examine not only aspects of working-class culture, but also the relationship in which working-class culture stood to the formal institutions and consciously articulated ideology of the socialist labour movement; in other words, at the relationship between politics and society in the context of the German working class. The earlier drafts of some of the chapters in this book, when they were presented to a conference of the SSRC Research Seminar Group in Modern German Social History, were criticised for allegedly ignoring the political dimension, in an article entitled 'Why does Social History Ignore Politics?', by Geoff Eley and Keith Nield. This criticism, I believe, is misplaced; part of the purpose of the present book indeed is to restore the links between social and political history in this context. Nor does it seem much of an advance to return to the anlaysis of the SPD and its organisations, as Eley and Nield suggest, simply substituting a Gramscian analysis for a more explicitly functionalist one. This seems to be yet another example of how currently fashionable Marxist modes of analysis can lead to a resurrection of conventional political history. In the present book, we hope to look at working-class politics not merely in the context of a theoretical analysis, but also in their relation to working-class culture and modes of life. At its most elementary, this involves looking at what the SPD and the trade unions thought of the 'rough' or 'deviant' side of working-class culture. Predictably enough, in view of what is known about the SPD's own cultural activities, there was a good deal of disapproval, as the contributions to this volume clearly indicate. To this extent, therefore, Günther Roth's picture of the SPD as a disciplining influence on the working class, discussed earlier in this essay, does contain a good deal of plausibility.

Yet this picture is in reality far more complicated than this. In the first place, as I have already suggested, the extent to which the SPD and the unions actually succeeded in their attempts to impose respectability on the proletariat has been seriously exaggerated by the functionalist sociological interpretation of German labour history. The labour movement, indeed, was unable even to do this with its own members, let alone the millions of working-class Germans who remained outside it.[106] The *Schnaps* boycott of 1909, as James Roberts shows, was a failure; so, too, in Michael Grüttner's account, were the efforts made by the trade unions in the First World War and the early Weimar Republic to stop their members among the Hamburg dockers from pilfering cargoes. The party and the unions commonly asserted that those who engaged in 'rough' or deviant behaviour were not organised workers but members of the *Lumpenproletariat*.[107] Yet this was patently untrue, as they themselves were well aware. To some extent such denials were a defensive mechanism against attempts by the authorities, employers and the right-wing press to assert that the labour movement encouraged such activities; that it was the creation of a demoralised, violent, drunken, lazy, thieving and fornicating working class, and that its main aim was to create more room for its members to indulge their base lusts and appetites instead of doing an honest day's work. The conservative press in particular portrayed the labour movement as subversive of all social and moral order.[108] It was necessary to refute such accusations if the movement was to remain credible as a political force or achieve some recognition at the bargaining table. Refuted, therefore, they were, even when — as in the case of dock pilferage, or drink, or participation in suffrage disturbances — the labour movement knew that on a superficial level at least, they were true.

Implicit in such refutations was surely the knowledge that — as I argued earlier in this essay — the working class had its own system of values, that because dockers habitually stole from ship's cargoes, this did not mean that they were congenitally dishonest, that because workers drank large quantities of beer and *Schnaps* in their leisure hours, this did not mean that they were depraved, that because proletarian women had illegitimate children, this did not mean that they were sexually promiscuous. Indeed at times, as Eve Rosenhaft shows in her discussion of the relations between the Communist Party and the violent, juvenile *Cliquen* in Berlin in the Weimar Republic, the labour movement could put this insight to positive use in the struggle against its opponents. Yet such an insight, such tactics, depended on the labour movement's retention of a radical socialist ideology which had as one of its premises a sharp distinction between proletarian and bourgeois morality and behaviour, and a recognition of the social relativity of the latter. As time went on, the Social Democrats, and the 'Free' trade unions with which they were associated, gradually seem to have lost this way of looking at working-class culture, as they retreated from the socialist radicalism of the Wilhelmine era. By 1918-19, as Michael Grüttner shows, the trade unions no longer denied that there was a pilferage problem in the Hamburg docks, but actively urged the most extreme measures to combat it. James Wickham has suggested elsewhere that the failure of the labour movement to adapt to new working-class cultural forms during the Weimar Republic was a major reason for its failure to attract the young.[109]

Certainly, the gradual alienation of labour movement culture from working-class culture was no simple, unilinear development. Some aspects of working-class life had, it seems, always met with SPD and union disapproval. Chief among these was the prevalence of violence; the SPD was ascribing riotous disturbances to the *Lumpenproletariat* as early as 1892. Clearly this was felt to be more politically sensitive than, say, theft, drunkenness or 'concubinage'.[110] Violence had directly political overtones; in 1878 two attempts on the life of the Emperor Wilhelm I — neither of them by socialists — had been the occasion for Bismarck's introduction of the Anti-Socialist Law. Even after the law was allowed to lapse in 1890, any apparent encouragement of violence uttered by a speaker at a Social Democratic assembly could call forth the meeting's dissolution by the attendant policemen and perhaps even provoke the speaker's arrest. Yet this was not the only reason for Social Democratic legalism; nor were its social and political consequences necessarily all of a kind. Social Democrats could observe the letter of the law while constantly attempting to evade it in practice. Countless examples of such evasion could be presented: typical was, for instance, the statement of the SPD speaker and recruiting agent Luise Zietz in 1903: 'when I am forbidden, for example, to deliver a speech in Thuringia, a comrade gives a ten-minute speech then I speak in the discussion period for one and a half hours'.[111] Even when they did counsel observance of the law, for instance on strikes or picketing, Social Democrats did not cease to denounce it as 'class justice' in the most vehement terms. It would be wrong, therefore, to treat Social Democratic 'legalism' in isolation: the important question is how and why the labour movement came to accept the values that lay behind the law, not how it came to observe the letter of the law itself, though of course decades of formal obedience to detested laws and ordinances could not help but blunt the edge of the movement's general critique of 'class justice' in the long run. Labour movement attitudes to political violence must therefore be seen in the wider context of labour movement attitudes towards the dominant culture and the culture of the working class. Such indeed is the approach which the present collection of essays adopts.

The conclusion that seems to emerge from the studies presented here is that while the Social Democratic Party and the 'Free' trade unions remained in touch with some aspects of working-class culture before 1914, there were some areas where an alienation had already taken place long before the outbreak of the First World War. This was above all true of violence, which had an immediate and obvious political significance. Under the Weimar Republic this alienation of labour movement culture from working-class culture became deeper and spread to other areas of working-class life.[112] Thus James Roberts shows how the *Schnaps* boycott was something of an aberration in the party's handling of the alcohol question. Its failure probably reinforced the SPD's willingness to adapt to the realities of working-class culture in this respect before 1914. When we turn to the Weimar Republic, on the other hand, we see a much-reduced tolerance for working-class attitudes being displayed by the party. Only the Communists could be said to have tried to overcome it, and even in their case there were still ambivalences, problems and failures, while the attempt itself cut them off still further from the SPD and so divided labour movement culture ever more deeply within itself. The political significance of these developments is not easy to judge. By discussing the 'rough' side of working-class life, it is far from the intention of this book to resurrect a Bakuninist vision of the criminal, the vagabond and the thief as the vanguard of the socialist revolution;[113] one of the most important lessons of David Crew's contribution is that radical methods could quite easily be used for eminently moderate purposes. Nor is it our intention to romanticise squalor, violence and drunkenness. Yet the problem of assessing the political meaning of working-class culture remains. Were drink, sex, violence and thieving simply ways of making life bearable? Certainly; but this did not mean that they necessarily diverted working-class energies from the political struggle. Michael Grüttner's contribution to this volume shows, indeed, how the Hamburg dockers stole more when their trade union was not doing well, and less when it was; but this does not mean that pilfering acted as a brake on labour militancy. Other factors were responsible for the union's difficulties, as Michael Grüttner shows; and because the union made no real effort to curb pilfering before the First World War, its actual political significance in itself does not seem to have been very great. Similarly, as James Roberts indicates, the 'Beer War' indicates the willingness of workers to take collective action against, and presumably to draw political conclusions from, efforts by the government to tax one of their most cherished habits. On the other hand, it would be too facile to equate deviance from bourgeois social norms with opposition to the capitalist order and conformity to them with acceptance. Radical politics could perfectly go well together with personal respectability, and often did. Nor should respectability be simply equated with acceptance of bourgeois values. Sobriety and punctuality could just as well develop out of working-class experience as out of bourgeois persuasion; their significance also depended on the social and political context. So the problem of the overall political importance of the patterns of behaviour and belief revealed in this book remains; and to try and bring it out, in all its complexity and ambiguity, we have asked Dick Geary to provide a final, general chapter on the problem of assessing working-class attitudes to state and society, written in the light of the previous contributions in the volume.

The studies presented here, then, hope to contribute to the current debate on the history of the German labour movement and working class in a number of ways apart from presenting new research on unfamiliar aspects of working-class life and culture. In the first place, they seek to re-integrate social and political history, the history of the working class and the labour movement, which the rapid development of social-historical research in German labour history is threatening to tear asunder.[114] Second, they hope to demonstrate some of the many ways in which the historian can try to get at the reality of working-class experience in the past, whether, as in Stefan Bajohr's contribution, through oral history allied to a use of quantitative material that carefully avoids the positivist trap into which most quantifying historians seem to fall; or through reading police and official documents 'against the grain', as it were, for what they often reveal, unconsciously and despite the intentions of those who produced them, about socialism and the working class, as in the contribution by Eve Rosenhaft. Third, they aim to free the study of working-class culture from its confusion with labour movement culture, a confusion that is the legacy above all of the 'sociological interpretation' discussed at the beginning of this introductory essay. For, ironically, as Geoff Eley and Keith Nield have pointed out, by emphasising the primacy of the repressive agencies of the German state in producing the 'negative integration' of the labour movement and the containment of the working class, it has ended up by delivering an approach which is almost wholly 'political'.[115] In this book, therefore, we hope to move towards a more genuinely sociological approach, which investigates the relationship of formal political organisations to their social constituencies rather than conflating the two. That this interpretation involves the critical and selective use of sociological concepts is self-evident; and indeed, in general most of the contributions owe something to the 'radical criminology' or new sociology of deviance developed in the 1960s, though the contributors to this book do not see the deviant as necessarily a revolutionary force. So sociological concepts and approaches do, then, permeate this book. In this way, perhaps, we might be contributing, not just to the criticism of the existing 'sociological interpretation', but also to the emergence of a new one.

Notes

1.   This contribution originated as an attempt to develop and present in a more systematic form some of the ideas put forward in my book *Sozialdemokratie und Frauenemanzipation im deutschen Kaiserreich* (Verlag J.H.W. Dietz Nachfolger, Berlin/Bonn, 1979). Different versions were read to the Social History Society Conference on 'Peasants and Proletarians' held in Bristol in January 1979, and to the second meeting of the SSRC Research Seminar Group on Modern German Social History, held at the University of East Anglia later in the same month. I am grateful to the participants in both meetings for their critical comments and suggestions, and particularly to Dieter Dowe for sending me a written résumé of the comments he made at the SSRC meeting. I have also benefited from reading an unpublished paper by David Crew ('The Constitution of "Working-Class Culture" as a Historical Object', read to the fourth meeting of the SSRC Research Seminar Group on Modern German Social History, held at the University of East Anglia in July 1980). I have expanded the paper to include some introductory remarks on the contributions to the present work, but in the earlier sections I have retained the sometimes intentionally provocative formulations which betray the essay's original incarnation in the form of a conference paper. I am grateful to James Roberts, Dick Geary, Michael Grüttner and James Wickham for their comments on the expanded draft. The title is not intended to imply that all sociological influences on historical interpretation should be rejected out of hand; simply that we should adopt a critical stance towards them and give careful consideration to their historical and ideological provenance. It is concerned with one sociological tradition in particular, not with sociology in general. The comments which follow refer mainly to the Wilhelmine period, on which work has concentrated; until very recently, surprisingly little research has been carried out on the labour movement in the Weimar Republic (after 1918-19), and though the very early history of the labour movement was already being intensively studied by the end of the nineteenth century, this was mainly by Marxist writers outside the historical profession.

2.   For fuller accounts and examples of the development of German historiography outlined here, see the introduction to Richard J. Evans (ed.), *Society and Politics in Wilhelmine Germany* (London, 1978), pp. 11-39, and Geoff Eley, 'Memories of Underdevelopment: Social History in Germany', *Social History*, vol. 2, no. 3 (Sept. 1977), pp. 785-91. For a striking example of how this tradition affects even a historian who has previously devoted a whole monograph to the history of the SPD when it comes to writing a *general* account of Wilhelmine

Germany, see Hans-Ulrich Wehler, *Das deutsche Kaiserreich 1871-1918* (Göttingen, 1973), in which 29 pages are devoted to foreign policy, over 70 to government and only 3 to the labour movement.

3. These include both general histories by authors such as Mehring and local studies (of particular importance in Germany) by writers such as Bernstein, Laufenberg and others.

4. See especially *Geschichte der deutschen Arbeiterbewegung* (8 vols., East Berlin, 1966).

5. Among innumerable studies, see for example Arthur Mitzman, *Sociology and Estrangement: Three Sociologists of Imperial Germany* (New York, 1973), on Tönnies, Sombart and Michels; and Wolfgang J. Mommsen, *Max Weber und die deutsche Politik 1890-1920*, 2nd edn (Tübingen, 1974) on Weber.

6. A crucial role here was played by the 'Fischer controversy' of the 1960s: cf. the account in John A. Moses, *The Politics of Illusion* (London, 1975).

7. The reasons for (and some consequences of) this crucial absence are outlined briefly in the introduction to *Society and Politics in Wilhelmine Germany*, pp. 14-15.

8. Cf. my review of R. Rürup (ed.), *Historische Sozialwissenschaft* (Göttingen, 1977) in *Social History*, vol. IV (1979), pp. 367-9.

9. Indeed, the functionalist sociological interpretation has become something of an orthodoxy. A parallel situation exists in the wider field of German political history as a whole: see the discussion in Geoff Eley, 'Defining Social Imperialism: Use and Abuse of an Idea', *Social History*, vol. 3 (1976), pp. 265-90.

10. The standard account of the constitution is E.R. Huber, *Deutsche Verfassungsgeschichte seit 1789, Vol. IV: Struktur und Krisen des Kaiserreichs* (Stuttgart, 1969).

11. Wolfgang Schieder, 'Das Scheitern des bürgerlichen Radikalismus und die sozialistische Parteibildung in Deutschland' in Hans Mommsen (ed.), *Sozialdemokratie zwischen Klassenbewegung und Volkspartei* (Frankfurt am Main, 1974), pp. 17-34.

12. The standard account in English is still Carl E. Schorske, *German Social Democracy 1905-1917: the Development of the Great Schism* (Cambridge, Mass., 1955).

13. For Michels' association with the revisionists see Mitzman, *Sociology and Estrangement*, p. 285. Michels' political evolution after his disillusion with the SPD eventually took him close to Italian Fascism.

14. For Weber, see Mommsen, *Max Weber*, pp. 109-23. In this paragraph I am of course necessarily giving a selective and simplified account of the interpretations advanced by Weber and Michels.

15. Günther Roth, *The Social Democrats in Imperial Germany. A Study in Working-class Isolation and National Integration* (Totowa, 1963).

16. Ibid., p. vii and Preface (by Reinhard Bendix), pp. xii-xiv.

17. It is worth noting that Roth declared himself, with commendable frankness, to be personally 'more sympathetic to the right and center of the Social Democratic movement than to the left' (ibid., p. 324).

18. Ibid., p. 159, note 2.

19. Ibid., p. 159.

20. Roth took only some of the multifarious aspects of the subculture as examples; the picture has been filled out by subsequent research (discussed later in this chapter).

21. Roth, *Social Democrats*, pp. 159-92.

22. Ibid., p. 201.

23. Ibid., p. 196.

24. Ibid., p. 242, note 63.

25. Local (bourgeois) dailies which grew in popularity from *c*.1900.

26. Roth, *Social Democrats*, p. 246. It should be added that this is an extremely unfair remark; in fact the news coverage of the SPD daily press (in newspapers such as *Vorwärts*, the *Hamburger Echo* or the *Leipziger Volkszeitung*) was broad and comprehensive, though of course the news stories covered were presented and interpreted from a Social Democratic point of view.

27. Ibid., pp. 259-60.

28. Ibid., p. 261.

29. Ibid., pp. 214-17.

30. Ibid., pp. 309-10.

31. Ibid., pp. 212-48.

32. Ibid., pp. 315-16.

33. See in particular J.P. Nettl, 'The German Social Democrats 1890-1914 as a Political Model', *Past and Present*, vol. 3 (Apr. 1965), pp. 65-95, and Peter Lösche, 'Arbeiterbewegung und Wilhelminismus: Sozialdemokratie zwischen Anpassung und Spaltung', *Geschichte in Wissenschaft und Unterricht*, vol. 20 (1969), pp. 519-33.

34. Hans-Ulrich Wehler, *Sozialdemokratie und Nationalstaat*, 2nd edn (Göttingen, 1972).

35. Peter Domann, *Sozialdemokratie und Kaisertum unter Wilhelm II: Die Auseinandersetzung der Partei mit dem monarchischen System, seine gesellschaftlichen und verfassungspolitischen Voraussetzungen* (Wiesbaden, 1974). See also Werner K. Blessing, 'The Cult of Monarchy. Political Loyalty and the Workers' Movement in Imperial Germany', *Journal of Contemporary History*, vol. 13, no. 2 (Apr. 1978), pp. 357-76.

36. Hans-Josef Steinberg, *Sozialismus und deutsche Sozialdemokratie. Zur Ideologie der Partei vor dem Ersten Weltkrieg* (Bonn-Bad Godesberg, 1972), pp. 129-42; Dieter Langewiesche and Klaus Schönhoven, 'Arbeiterbibliotheken und Arbeiterlektüre im Wilhelminischen Deutschland', *Archiv für Sozialgeschichte*, vol. XVI (1976), pp. 135-204.

37. Dieter Groh, *Negative Integration und revolutionärer Attentismus. Die deutsche Sozialdemokratie am Vorabend des Ersten Weltkrieges* (Berlin/Frankfurt, 1973).

38. Dieter Dowe, 'The Workers' Choral Movement before the First World War', *Journal of Contemporary History*, vol. 13, no. 2 (Apr. 1978), pp. 269-76.

39. Horst Ueberhorst, *Frisch, frei, stark und treu. Die Arbeitersportbewegung in Deutschland 1893-1933* (Düsseldorf, 1973).

40. Klaus Tenfelde, 'Mining Festivals in the Nineteenth Century', *Journal of Contemporary History*, vol. 13, no. 2 (Apr. 1978), pp. 377-412; Gerhard A. Ritter, 'Workers' Culture in Imperial Germany: Problems and Points of Departure for Research', *Journal of Contemporary History*, vol. 13, no. 2 (Apr. 1978), pp. 175-6.

41. Ulrich Linse, 'Arbeiterschaft und Geburtenentwicklung im Deutschen Kaiserreich von 1871', *Archiv für Sozialgeschichte*, vol. XII (1972), pp. 205-71; R.P. Neumann, 'The Sexual Question and Social Democracy in Imperial Germany', *Journal of Social History*, vol. 7, no. 3 (Spring 1974), pp. 271-86; Jean Quataert, 'Feminist Tactics in German Social Democracy: a Dilemma', *Internationale Wissenschaftliche Korrespondenz zur Geschichte der deutschen Arbeiterbewegung*, no. 1 (1977), pp. 48-65.

42. Thus even authors critical of the present-day SPD conform to the general pattern, e.g. Georg Fülberth, *Proletarische Partei und bürgerliche Literatur. Auseinandersetzungen in der deutschen Sozialdemokratie der II. Internationale über Möglichkeiten und Grenzen einer sozialistischen Literaturpolitik* (Neuwied, 1972). General surveys include Helga Grebing, *Geschichte der deutschen Arbeiterbewegung. Ein Überblick* (Munich, 1966); Willi Eichler, *Hundert Jahre Sozialdemokratie* (Bielefeld, 1963); Hans Mommsen (ed.), *Sozialdemokratie zwischen*

Klassenbewegung und Volkspartei (Frankfurt, 1974); Heinrich Potthoff, *Die Sozialdemokratie von den Anfängen bis 1945* (Kleine Geschichte der SPD, vol. I, Bonn-Bad Godesberg, 1974).

43. Cf. the critique advanced in Georg Fülberth and Jürgen Harrer, *Kritik der sozialdemokratischen Hausgeschichtsschreibung* (Pahl-Rugenstein Hefte zu politischen Gegenwartsfragen, 22, Frankfurt am Main, 1975). Unfortunately the same authors' attempt to provide a general account of Social Democratic history in no way fulfils the promise of their critique of other historians' work (see Georg Fülberth and Jürgen Harrer, *Arbeiterbewegung und SPD. Band 1. Die deutsche Sozialdemokratie 1890-1933* (Darmstadt, 1974)).

44. Hans Mommsen (ed.), *Sozialdemokratie zwischen Klassenbewegung und Volkspartei* (Frankfurt, 1975), p. 7.

45. See especially Klaus Saul, *Staat, Industrie, Arbeiterbewegung im Kaiserreich. Zur Innen- und Sozialpolitik des Wilhelminischen Deutschland 1903-1914* (Düsseldorf, 1974).

46. Gerhard A. Ritter, 'Workers' Culture in Imperial Germany: Problems and Points of Departure for Research', *Journal of Contemporary History*, vol. 13, no. 2 (Apr. 1978), pp. 165-89.

47. Cf., for example, Jochen Loreck, *Wie man früher Sozialdemokrat wurde. Das Kommunikationsverhalten in der deutschen Arbeiterbewegung und die Konzeption der sozialistischen Parteipublizistik durch August Bebel* (Schriftenreihe des Forschungsinstitut der Friedrich-Ebert-Stiftung, vol. 130, Bonn – Bad Godesberg, 1977), a study of worker autobiographies which explicitly regards itself as providing no more than further illustrations of Roth's theses.

48. The classic example of this is of course the almost entirely static picture of society in Imperial Germany portrayed by Hans-Ulrich Wehler, *Das Deutsche Kaiserreich 1871-1918* (Göttingen, 1973).

49. This theory of 'negative integration' indeed is the main respect in which the SPD features in overall characterisations of the social and political system of Imperial Germany by present-day West German historians. See for example not only Groh, *Negative Integration* and Wehler, *Sozialdemokratie*, but also, for a particularly clear formation ('artificially whipped-up fear of socialism...[as] a relatively effective means of...uniting all non-socialist forces'), Peter Christian Witt, 'Innenpolitik und Imperialismus in der Vorgeschichte des 1. Weltkrieges' in Karl Holl and Günter List (eds.), *Liberalismus und imperialistischer Staat* (Göttingen, 1975), p. 16. Cf. also Siegfried Mielke, *Der Hansa-Bund für Gewerbe, Handel und Industrie 1909-1914* (Göttingen, 1976), p. 20 – all of these general characterisations of the Wilhelmine state which conform to this rule.

50. See F.L. Carsten, *Revolution in Central Europe 1918-19* (London, 1972); Gerhard A. Ritter and Susanne Miller (eds.), *Die deutsche Revolution 1918-1919 – Dokumente* (Frankfurt am Main, 1968); see also the critique by Brian Peterson, 'Workers' Councils in Germany 1918-19: Recent Literature on the Rätebewegung', *New German Critique*, vol. 4 (1975), pp. 113-23.

51. For this see Geoff Eley, 'The Wilhelmine Right: How it Changed' in Richard J. Evans (ed.), *Society and Politics in Wilhelmine Germany* (London, 1978), pp. 112-35.

52. Rosemarie Leuschen-Seppel, *Sozialdemokratie und Antisemitismus im Kaiserreich* (Bonn – Bad Godesberg, 1978), a study which concludes that 'the workers' culture of the nineteenth century, despite its emancipatory claims, was helplessly at the mercy of the dominant culture in both form and content.'

53. Cf. note 36, above; also Roth, *Social Democrats*, pp. 232-43.

54. Georg Lukács, *History and Class Consciousness: Studies in Marxist Dialectics* (London, 1971).

55. S.S. Prawer, *Karl Marx and World Literature* (Oxford, 1977).

56. Quataert, 'Feminist Tactics', pp. 48-65; on the general question of

'embourgeoisement', see Hermann Bausinger, 'Verbürgerlichung – Folgen eines Interpretaments' in Günther Wiegelmann (ed.), *Kultureller Wandel im 19. Jahrhundert. Verhandlungen des 18. Deutschen Volkskunde-Kongresses in Trier vom 13. bis 18. September 1971* (Studien zum Wandel von Gesellschaft und Bildung im Neunzehnten Jahrhundert, 5, Göttingen, 1973), pp. 24-49.

57. So at least I have attempted to argue in my book *Sozialdemokratie und Frauenemanzipation im Deutschen Kaiserreich* (Bonn-Bad Godesberg, 1979).

58. Dowe, 'Workers' Choral Movement', p. 293.

59. Cf. Wehler, *Sozialdemokratie*, pp. 124-31; Christa Berg, *Die Okkupation der Schule. Eine Studie zur Aufhellung gegenwärtiger Schulprobleme an der Volksschule Preussens (1872 bis 1900)* (Heidelberg, 1973); Folkert Meyer, *Schule der Untertanen. Lehrer und Politik in Preussen 1848-1900* (Hamburg, 1976).

60. Erhard Lucas, *Märzrevolution 1921, Bd. 2: Der bewaffnete Arbeiteraufstand im Ruhrgebiet in seiner inneren Struktur und in seinem Verhältnis zu den Klassenkämpfen in den Regionen des Reiches* (Frankfurt am Main, 1973), pp. 63-95.

61. See the quotations above, pp. 18-22, for these assertions.

62. See Erhard Lucas, *Zwei Formen von Radikalismus in der deutschen Arbeiterbewegung* (Frankfurt am Main, 1976); and Dick Geary, 'Radicalism and the Worker: Metal-workers and Revolution 1914-23' in Richard J. Evans (ed.), *Society and Politics in Wilhelmine Germany* (London, 1978), pp. 267-86.

63. See Chapter 2, pp. 54-79, below.

64. Ralf Lützenkirchen, *Der sozialdemokratische Verein für den Reichstagswahlkreis Dortmund-Hörde* (Dortmund, 1970), pp. 51-70. In this case, of course, the stress laid by the functionalist sociological tradition's originators on bureaucratisation was correct and is certainly much more helpful than the attempt by Roth to stress instead the isolated position of the party's intellectuals. However, the formation of a reformist party bureaucracy should be seen not as the mere expression of an 'iron law' of sociology, valid at all times and in all places, as Michels asserted, but rather in the context of wider social changes taking place within the working class, and as a response to specific historical circumstances. Again, the role of the bureaucracy in the German Communist Party in the 1920s was clearly very different to that of its counterpart in the pre-1914 SPD: see Hermann Weber, *Die Wandlung des deutschen Kommunismus – Die Stalinisierung der KPD* (Frankfurt am Main, 1969).

65. Quoted above, p. 19.

66. Stephen Hickey, 'The Shaping of the German Labour Movement: Miners in the Ruhr' in Richard J. Evans (ed.), *Society and Politics in Wilhelmine Germany* (London, 1978), p. 236.

67. See, for example, the essays collected in Jürgen Reulecke and Wolfhard Weber (eds.), *Fabrik, Familie, Feierabend: Beiträge zur Sozialgeschichte des Alltags im Industriezeitalter* (Wuppertal, 1978).

68. 'Workers' Culture': Special Issue of *Journal of Contemporary History*, vol. 13, no. 2 (Apr. 1978); expanded versions and additional contributions in Gerhard A. Ritter (ed.), *Arbeiterkultur* (Königstein, 1979). A shorter but similar collection is to be found in Jürgen Kocka (ed.), 'Arbeiterkultur im 19. Jahrhundert', *Geschichte und Gesellschaft*, vol. 5, no. 1 (1979).

69. As pointed out in the unpublished paper by David Crew cited above, note 1.

70. E.g. Heilwig Schomerus, *Die Arbeiter der Maschinenfabrik Esslingen: Forschungen zur Lage der Arbeiterschaft im 19. Jahrhundert* (Stuttgart, 1977); Peter Borscheid, *Textilarbeiterschaft in der Industrialisierung* (Stuttgart, 1978). An exception is Hartmut Zwahr, *Zur Konstituierung der deutschen Arbeiterklasse* (East Berlin, 1978).

71. See note 67 above.

72. Reulecke and Weber, *Fabrik, Familie, Feierabend*, p. 10.

73. More promising in this respect are the essays in *Sozialwissenschaftliche Informationen für Unterricht und Studium*, vol. 6, no. 4 (1977); for example, Franz Brüggemeier, 'Bedürfnisse, gesellschaftliche Erfahrung und politisches Verhalten: Das Beispiel der Bergarbeiter im nördlichen Ruhrgebiet gegen Ende des 19. Jahrhunderts', ibid., pp. 152-9.

74. Reulecke and Weber, *Fabrik, Familie, Feierabend*, p. 7.

75. See the extended critique of *Alltagsgeschichte* along these lines in the paper by David Crew, cited above, note 1.

76. See especially Gerhard Huck (ed.), *Sozialgeschichte der Freizeit* (Wuppertal, 1980).

77. See in this context the remarks of Gareth Stedman Jones, 'Class Expression versus Social Control? A Critique of Recent Trends in the Social History of "Leisure" ', *History Workshop: a Journal of Socialist Historians*, Issue 4 (Autumn 1977), pp. 163-70.

78. These remarks are conceived as a response to Geoff Eley and Keith Nield, 'Why does Social History Ignore Politics?', *Social History*, vol. 5, no. 2 (1980), pp. 249-71, criticising an earlier version of this introductory essay.

79. Quoted above, p. 21.

80. Particularly strong emphasis is laid on the 'traditional' aspects of working-class culture by Klaus Tenfelde, *Sozialgeschichte der Bergarbeiter an der Ruhr in 19. Jahrhundert* (Bonn-Bad Godesberg, 1977), and his contributions to the various collections cited above, note 68.

81. Cf. the discussion of this point in the paper by David Crew, cited above, note 1.

82. For some of the complexities of this term, see Raymond Williams, *Keywords* (London, 1977), 'Culture'.

83. Cf. the essay on similar institutions in Britain by Gareth Stedman Jones, 'Working-class Culture and Working-class Politics in London, 1870-1900: Notes on the Remaking of a Working Class', *Journal of Social History*, vol. 7 (1973-4), pp. 460-505.

84. For the argument that the history of the Wilhelmine period as a whole has been structured too much by the perspective of '1933', see Geoff Eley, 'The Wilhelmine Right: How it Changed' in Richard J. Evans (ed.), *Society and Politics in Wilhelmine Germany* (London, 1978), pp. 112-35.

85. Thus the volume is, among other things, conceived of as a corrective to the collections cited above in notes 67, 68 and 76.

86. Gerhard A. Ritter, introduction to the special issue of the *Journal of Contemporary History* cited above, note 68.

87. Pages 80-107 below.

88. James Wickham, 'Working-class Movement and Working-class Life' (paper delivered to the fourth meeting of the SSRC Research Seminar Group in Modern German Social History, University of East Anglia, July 1980).

89. Pages 54-79 below.

90. Pages 108-41 below.

91. Saul, *Staat, Industrie*; also Klaus Saul, 'Der Staat und die "Mächte des Umsturzes" ', *Archiv für Sozialgeschichte*, vol. XII (1972), pp. 293-350; Alex Hall, *Scandal, Sensation and Social Democracy* (Cambridge, 1978); Alex Hall, 'The War of Words: Anti-Socialist Offensives and Counter-propaganda in Wilhelmine Germany 1890-1914', *Journal of Contemporary History*, vol. 11, nos. 2-3 (1976) pp. 11-42; Alex Hall, 'By Other Means: the Legal Struggle Against the SPD in Wilhelmine Germany 1890-1900', *Historical Journal*, vol. 17, no. 2 (1974), pp. 365-86.

92. Raymond B. Fosdick, *European Police System* (New York, 1915), pp. 27-8.

93. Pages 142-73 below.

94. Regine Schulte, *Sperrbezirke. Tugendhaftigkeit und Prostitution in der bürgerlichen Welt* (Frankfurt am Main, 1979), pp. 181-2. More generally, see my

article, 'Prostitution, State and Society in Imperial Germany', *Past and Present*, vol. 70 (February, 1976), pp. 106-29, and Abraham Flexner, *Prostitution in Europe* (New York, 1914).

95. Alfred Urban, *Staat und Prostitution in Hamburg vom Beginn der Reglementierung bis zur Aufhebung der Kasernierung* (Hamburg, 1927), pp. 34-40.

96. Flexner, *Prostitution in Europe*, pp. 147-57.

97. Erhard Lucas, *Zwei Formen von Radikalismus in der deutschen Arbeiterbewegung* (Frankfurt am Main, 1976), pp. 109-18.

98. See Robert Roberts, *The Classic Slum* (Manchester, 1971), pp. 75-7, for vivid details of the role of the police in an English working-class community before the First World War.

99. There is a large sociological literature on street gangs: see, for example, Herbert A. Block, *The Gang: a Study in Adolescent Behavior* (Westport, Conn., 1976); Albert K. Cohen, *Delinquent Boys: the Culture of the Gang* (Glencoe, Ill., 1955).

100. Karl Marx and Friedrich Engels, *The Communist Manifesto* (Seabury Press, New York, 1967, Commentary by Harold Laski), p. 146.

101. Karl Marx, *The Eighteenth Brumaire of Louis Bonaparte* (Internl. Pub. ed., New York, 1951), p. 65.

102. Louis Chevalier, *Labouring Classes and Dangerous Classes in Paris during the First Half of the Nineteenth Century* (London, 1973).

103. See the article cited in note 110 below.

104. Besides the contributions in this volume, see also (for example) Stephen Hickey, 'The Shaping of the German Labour Movement: Miners in the Ruhr' in Richard J. Evans (ed.), *Society and Politics in Wilhelmine Germany* (London, 1978), pp. 215-40.

105. Fritz Lang's celebrated film *M*, made under the Weimar Republic, with its portrayal of a criminal underworld outraged by a child murderer, tracking him down and trying him in a 'court of thieves', is perhaps the best known illustration of this point.

106. Cf. the demonstration in Hickey, 'The Shaping of the German Labour Movement', that trade unions in the Ruhr failed to stop wildcat, localised strikes even though these were often highly damaging to the labour movement.

107. See below, pp. 199-201.

108. For illustrations of this, see my essay 'Politics and the Family: Social Democracy and the Working-Class Family 1891-1914' in Richard J. Evans and W.R. Lee (eds.), *The German Family: Essays in the Social History of the Family in Nineteenth and Twentieth Century Germany* (London, 1981).

109. Wickham, 'Working-class Movement'.

110. Though bourgeois commentators maintained vehemently that all three were profoundly subversive of moral, social and even political order, through their alleged destruction (for example) of the family, which was regarded as the foundation of society and indeed the state, through its supposed function in keeping the working-class male happy and contented and therefore immune to the blandishments of Social Democracy. See also Richard J. Evans, ' "Red Wednesday" in Hamburg: Police, Social Democrats and Lumpenproletariat in the Suffrage Disturbances of 17 January 1906', *Social History*, vol. 4, no. 1 (Jan. 1979), pp. 1-31.

111. *Protokoll des Parteitags der Sozialdemokratischen Partei Deutschlands 1906*, p. 409.

112. See James Wickham, 'Social Fascism and the Division of the Working Class Movement: Workers and Political Parties in the Frankfurt Area 1929/30', *Capital and Class*, no. 7 (Spring 1979).

113. It should also be said that we have no intention of implying that lawbreaking was confined to the working class. Evasion and contravention of the law was (and is) characteristic of all social classes; it would be naive to suppose that

the bourgeoisie conformed to their own moral standards, especially after all that has been written about the role of hypocrisy in the life of the nineteenth-century middle class. Another book could be written about middle-class deviance; not just embezzlement, corruption and 'white-collar crime', but about violence, drunkenness, transgression of laws on morality (e.g. concerning child prostitution) and so on. None of this, however, invalidates in my view the legitimacy of investigating working-class contraventions of bourgeois morality and law as well.

114. See the remarks in Geoff Eley and Keith Nield, 'Why does Social History Ignore Politics?', *Social History*, vol. 5, no. 2 (May 1980), pp. 249-69.

115. Ibid., p. 256.

2 WORKING-CLASS CRIME AND THE LABOUR MOVEMENT: PILFERING IN THE HAMBURG DOCKS 1888-1923

Michael Grüttner

I

In *The Condition of the Working Class in England*, written in 1844/5, Frederick Engels divided the development of the labour movement into three phases which for him were at the same time three different stages in a collective learning process.[1] Crime, and in particular theft, was regarded by him as the 'earliest, crudest and least fruitful form' of social rebellion:

> The workers soon realised that crime did not help matters. The criminal could protest against the existing order of society only as a single individual; the whole might of society was brought to bear upon each criminal and crushed him with its immense superiority.

According to Engels it was in the second phase that the working class began to express itself as a class, through the practice of Luddism. But mere protests against new technology could not produce fundamental change, so workers finally moved on to the third, decisive phase, and sought to represent their interests through the formation of their own organisations and through use of the strike weapon.

It is unlikely that the merchants, businessmen and shipping magnates who dominated the political and economic life of Hamburg in the decades before the First World War had read Engels' remarks. It is even more unlikely that they would have recognised Engels' three-stage model of workers' behaviour as applicable to the problems which they themselves encountered in dealing with the working class. For them, theft was in no way an 'early industrial phenomenon' that was pushed into the background by the development of working-class organisations and numerous strikes. It was a fundamental and ever-present problem that was debated continually and at great length. Indeed, even today the problem of theft at work remains acute.

In Hamburg during the period of industrialisation and in the revolutionary crisis following the war (1919-23), as today, theft at work was not so much a matter of spectacular outbreaks of criminal activity as, in reality, a more or less everyday occurrence in the lives of dockers and their families.

Numerous documents attest to the fact that pilferage has been a problem in the Hamburg docks for centuries. At the end of the eighteenth century, the local authorities had formed a dockside police force whose main task was simply to combat theft from the docks. There was great hostility between them and the workers from the start.[2] For most of the nineteenth century this situation continued more or less unaltered. However, towards the end of the 1880s complaints from the ranks of shipowners and merchants suddenly underwent a massive increase. All agreed that the incidence of theft had grown by a considerable amount. Similar complaints continued in the following years. In 1891, one of the leading Hamburg shipowners, Carl Laeisz, complained that on every sailing 'the shipowners have to pay large sums in compensation for stolen goods'.[3] After the turn of the century it seemed for a while as if the business community and the police had managed to stem the tide. But from 1907 the complaints increased again. They reached a new peak in the inflation of 1920-3. In these years, indeed, it was maintained that 'there was more stolen from the Hamburg docks than from anywhere else in the world.'[4]

The business community itself argued that the major reason for the increase in theft in the 1880s was the fundamental restructuring of dock work that had taken place shortly before. The seventies and eighties witnessed the transition from sail to steam along with corresponding changes in the organic composition of shipping capital, which had turned the attention of the shipowners and businessmen towards the problem of increasing the efficiency of the docks. As a general rule in the 1870s it took a week or longer to load a ship; within twenty years this time had been halved. This was achieved not only by increasing workers' productivity (for example by the introduction of steam-operated winches) and by the intensification of the work process, but also by increasing the length of the working day. Night work became the rule at the Hamburg docks. During the day, work could be constantly overseen by ships' officers; but the loading and unloading of ships during the night remained more or less unsupervised. So, for the dockers, the extension of their hours of work, combined with the intensification of the labour process itself, was bound up with a decrease in supervision. The consequences were soon visible: 'If people work all night alone and without supervision', wrote the *Hamburg Stock Exchange Journal (Hamburgische Börsen-Halle)*, 'is it then any wonder that one or the other of them gains a few pounds in weight during the night and that this extra weight consists in fact of coffee?'[5]

II

Who were these workers whose behaviour gave rise to so many complaints, conferences and newspaper reports? Did pilfering occur equally in all parts of the docks? What was the significance of the stratification of the dock workers? Were unskilled workers more frequently transgressors than skilled ones? The material available to answer these questions systematically is less than satisfactory. However, there does exist a police list of proceedings taken against offenders accused of theft in the docks between the years 1906 and 1910. On the whole it deals with small groups of workers who came before the courts accused of a common offence.[6] An analysis of this data gives some insight into the involvement of the three most important groups of dock workers; the stevedores (*Schauerleute*); the lightermen (*Ewerführer*); and the wharfmen (*Kaiarbeiter*). Unfortunately the list only contains details (such as job description) of a few of the accused. The following summary, then, is of those whose profession is given and who were convicted of the alleged offences.

Table 2.1: Dockers Convicted of Pilfering, Hamburg 1906-10

Year	Stevedores	Lightermen	Wharfmen	Other Dock Workers	Others
1906	20	13	3	15	18
1907	35	12	1	14	17
1908	16	6	3	1	25
1909	25	9	4	6	16
1910	20	11	1	6	13
Total	116	51	12	42	89

To evaluate the significance of these figures, more information on the total number of people employed in each category is necessary. Unfortunately, the extant statistics are extremely scanty. The large number of small concerns and the rapid turnover of employees have always hindered the compilation of a precise statistical picture of the dock labour force. Detailed information on the numbers employed exists only for 1895/6 and 1913. In 1896 there were on average 1,700 stevedores, 2,000 wharfmen and 1,500 lightermen employed daily. In the following years, the number of wharfmen in particular increased sharply, while the numbers of lightermen were only gradually augmented. In 1913 on average 4,900 stevedores, 6,300 wharfmen and 2,300 lightermen were employed daily.[7] Comparing these figures with the figures given in Table 2.1 produces a surprising result. The largest group of dock workers, the wharfmen, were obviously only marginally involved in the pilferage. The theory that it was the unskilled workers in particular who were most heavily involved in crime is not confirmed. The lightermen, the only large group of skilled dock workers, were clearly more heavily involved in the stealing than were the unskilled wharfmen, although they were apparently less heavily involved than were the unskilled stevedores.

An explanation of this situation is only possible in the light of a more detailed description of the work process in the Hamburg docks. The lightermen worked on small, flat-bottomed boats (barges or lighters) on which they transported goods from the ships to the warehouses. Usually there were only one or two workers on each boat. Their work was therefore relatively isolated, autonomous and, above all, unsupervised. It was impracticable to keep these workers under constant surveillance. In contrast, the work of the stevedores was carried out in gangs under the supervision of a deputy (*Vize*), although some of the stevedores worked inside the ship and were thus out of sight. In addition, it was impossible for one deputy constantly to oversee all the stevedores working at the different hatches, so that here as well, in particular at night, there was always an opportunity for goods to change hands illegally. But the wharfmen were in a very different situation. They received the goods at the quayside and transported them on carts into the warehouses, where they were stamped and later collected by the transport firms and merchants. The incoming goods were registered and sorted by a host of warehouse officials, loading supervisors and clerks. The chances of opening one of the cases, removing the goods and wiping out all traces of the offence were minimal under such circumstances, 'as the sheds, which open out on to the waterside, are supervised during the day by a host of officials, and both the ships' personnel and passersby contribute to controlling theft'.[8] This short description of the working situation indicates that the incidence of theft was, above all, a result of the impossibility of subjecting all sectors of the docks to constant, comprehensive surveillance. Whether a worker engaged in theft or not depended apparently less on whether he was a qualified, skilled worker than on the opportunities which his work afforded him to supplement his income illegally without any great risk.

Some statistics from 1921/2 put this statement further into perspective. Here as well it is necessary to make a few prefatory remarks about the organisation of work. As a result of the great Hamburg dock strike of 1896/7 and a series of work stoppages in 1906/7, the managers had begun to restructure the system of casual labour.[9] Thus in all sectors of dock work there developed a core of permanent workers whose living and working conditions were reasonably secure. At the same time the casual workers who, for a long time, had formed the majority of the work-force, were more and more pushed to the fringes. After the First World War there developed — at times against considerable resistance from those concerned — a three-tier hierarchy of dock workers. Apart from the dock workers permanently employed by specific firms, there were the so-called 'short-term workers' (*Kurzarbeiter*), who were the most significant group of workers. Like the permanent workers (*Feste*) they were employed on a more or less regular basis, but, unlike these, were sent hither and thither between the different firms according to demand. Then, if these workers were insufficient in number to cope with the work, further casual workers were engaged to help out. In 1921 the Hamburg 'Federation of Dockside Firms' (Hafenbetriebsverein), an association of all the firms concerned with port business, employed on average over the year 7,500 permanent workers, 6,300 'short-term' workers and 7,700 casual labourers. In the same period the firms reported 1,842 thefts by casual labourers but only 539 by 'short-term' workers. In 1922 the Federation employed on average over 9,900 permanent workers, 7,500 short-term workers and 8,600 casual labourers; 3,844 thefts by casual labourers and 1,486 by short-term workers were recorded.[10]

In order to analyse these figures more closely, we must note the fact that casual labourers, in contrast to the majority of dock workers, spent most of the year unemployed or seeking work in other occupations. If the proportion of the casual poor to the overall number of workers who were daily employed at the docks was very much lower than the above figures suggest, then their over-proportional involvement in theft is that much more remarkable. But it is also surprising that the number of 'short-term' workers discovered in the act of theft in 1922 had both absolutely and relatively increased. Obviously the worsening inflation of the period led even the better-positioned workers to resort to methods of ensuring their survival which had previously been employed mainly by the lower strata of the dock proletariat. So although, in the first instance, the ability of the management to provide effective surveillance of the work-force appears to account for the frequency or absence of theft, these later figures indicate that the stratification of the dock workers is no less important as an explanatory factor. The large numbers of casual labourers who engaged in pilfering throw into sharp relief the situation of a stratum of workers for whom long periods of unemployment were a common experience. Petty crime for these workers had long been one of many methods of survival. The process of stratification which began in 1897 and the corresponding marginalisation of casual labour had aggravated an already bad situation. It was these strata of the working class which provided the basis for the bourgeois public image of the 'drunken, work-shy docker' which became such an important negative symbol of the working class for the power elite of the big city.

The large number of people in Table 2.1 who were convicted of theft but who were not dock workers must also be explained. In fact, for some sections of the population, in particular for women, youths and children, the Hamburg docks exerted a considerable attraction; an attraction which had little to do with the romance of seafaring and much more to do with concrete material needs. In particular, in all areas of the docks where coal was loaded, groups of women and youths, equipped with prams, would gather to wait for an unguarded instant in order to collect some of the valuable fuel. After the war this activity grew to such proportions that in 1919 the dock area was closed to the public altogether.[11] Often children and youths were sent to the docks by their parents expressly to supplement the family income. Others did so on their own initiative and in conscious contravention of the moral precepts of their elders. The worker-writer Ludwig Turek described the situation later in his autobiography:

I went to the docks almost every day. I was irresistibly drawn there; it ruined my shoes . . . but it was worth it, for there was often something or other to be had. Of course, the good citizens of Hamburg didn't pop it into your pocket — you had to do part of the work yourself. I learnt a lot from others. It was in the forbidden areas that there was most to collect. This principle made us (we seldom worked alone in this field) the bane of all sorts of officials . . . My mother was astounded at my good luck which manifested itself at the most critical moments and allowed her son such a 'lucky find'. My mother called it luck; she never lost her faith in it. She really did a lot for the education of her children. Almost always as I went out with my sack and pickaxe she would say 'Don't ever take anyone else's property. Son, don't bring shame upon us.'[12]

III

The figures quoted above indicate the effect of the internal stratification of the work-force on the readiness of workers to take part in criminal activity. Despite internal divisions, the dock workers remained in general a close-knit community, unapproachable to the employers. In 1889 and 1891 the shipowners attempted to increase the number of informers by posting placards all over the dock area offering rewards of up to 200 marks — more than the average dock worker would earn in two months — for those who offered information leading to the capture of the thieves. This proved to be a complete fiasco. Not one dock worker, as the chamber of commerce later confirmed, had come forward. All they got were a few policemen demanding the reward.[13] Thus working-class solidarity was expressed and maintained not only through strikes and great conflicts, but was carried through to the grey area of petty crime, and greatly hindered attempts to control it. The workers fought for the maintenance of this solidarity in a decisive and uncompromising manner. For instance, in December 1904 all the lightermen of one of the larger dockside firms stopped work without informing their union beforehand. Their sole demand was the dismissal of a worker who had talked of his acquaintance with a police officer who was reported to have said that it was possible to earn some easy money by informing for the police.[14]

Here norms and values can be discerned which seemed alien and dangerous to the bourgeoisie. A report by the chamber of commerce stated that almost all workers regarded it as 'their right' to acquire some of their food through pilfering.[15] Their behaviour towards colleagues who had been arrested for or convicted of theft corresponded with this attitude. There was no observable ostracism or exclusion of delinquents. When the lighterman Heinrich Cardinahl, an activist in the dock workers' union, was convicted in 1893 of serious theft and sentenced to eighteen months' imprisonment and after his release was unable to find employment, his colleagues supported him with considerable sums of money. A little while later the lightermen, who were organised in trade unions, elected him as a delegate to the general assembly of the federation of dock workers. Finally Cardinahl was appointed auditor for the Hamburg branch of the union.[16] That a worker who had been convicted of a serious crime against property could be elected by his colleagues to a position of such trust underlines the assertion that theft from employers or large firms was not regarded as illegitimate. It also highlights the specific, discrete nature of dockyard pilferage as an activity. Obviously, for these workers the fact that a colleague had stolen goods was no grounds for assuming that he would steal from them or their organisation. And this was by no means an isolated case. The long-standing treasurer of the central committee of the dock workers' union had also been convicted of theft and served a six-month sentence;[17] and the list can be extended by further examples.

These findings compare well with more recent data gathered by Gerald Mars in the 1960s in the docks of St John's, Newfoundland. Mars reported that nearly all the dock workers were involved in pilferage (the only exceptions were members of religious sects), but that a sharp distinction was drawn between stealing from shipowners and firms on the one hand and theft from individuals' luggage on the other. The latter was taboo; the few workers who stole from individuals had to face the contempt and disdain of their colleagues.[18] Against this background the phenomenon of theft can be seen in bolder outline. Beyond the barren crime statistics and the innumerable complaints about the immorality of the working classes, a differentiated framework of norms and rules becomes visible. It emerges that pilferage from the docks was also a form of social conflict, a form of struggle between workers and employers, which precipitated – as will be shown below – certain changes on both sides in the configuration of power structures.

IV

The alarming increase in theft at the end of the 1880s resulted in a number of conferences between the employers and the authorities, in which methods of control were discussed at length. The conferences concluded with regret that it was not possible to set up a comprehensive system of inspection of workers leaving the docks at the end of their day's work. Such a system existed, it was true, in the London docks; but it could not be employed in Hamburg because the geographical lay-out of the docks prevented them from being sealed off and provided with a few exits. Thus increased surveillance remained the most promising method. The large shipping concerns instituted a system of increased protection for particularly valuable goods. The Hamburg Senate and citizens approved a strengthening of the dock police force. The employers concentrated on persuading the judiciary of the need for more severe measures against offenders. In particular, the fact that courts tended to treat the theft of food very leniently (regarding it as being undertaken for immediate consumption) gave rise to vehement complaints. These complaints eventually succeeded to the extent that in June 1890 the judiciary advised the public prosecutor (Oberstaat-sanwalt) that thefts from the docks should be dealt with more severely in future.[19]

No less important were the measures introduced by individual employers aimed at the better control of the hiring of labour. In May 1890, during a wave of strikes and lock-outs which brought not only the docks but the entire economy of Hamburg to a halt, the owners of the lighter transport concerns instituted a system of work permits which from the beginning excluded from employment not only strike leaders and trade union activists, but also workers convicted of theft.[20] Like-wise from 1890 onwards, workers employed on a permanent basis on the quays (owned by the state) were regularly investigated by the police before being taken on. Workers who had previously been convicted of theft or who were registered as a result of political or trade union activity had no chance of finding employment.[21] Finally, also on the state-owned quays, a reimbursement fund was instituted. The employers created this fund by regular deductions from the workers' wages and used it to cover costs arising from the theft or damaging of goods. Only the 'permanent' workers had to contribute to this fund, and they were thus forced into a position of surveillance over the casual quayside workers.

However, the limited success of these and other measures confirmed the sceptics in their opinion that no lasting improvement could be expected from acting in a purely 'repressive manner'.[22] Through such insights a problem that had concerned clerics, publicists and education-alists as far back as the eighteenth century was brought to the employers' notice; namely, as Michael Foucault has said, it was about the need to erect a 'barrier to separate delinquents from all the lower strata of the population from which they sprang and with which they remained linked'.[23] In other words, it required the destruction of those values and structures of solidarity that have been described above. The employers believed that they had discovered in the newly founded trade unions an institution that would play an essential role in this. All the employers' protective measures, so stated the 'Union of Hamburg Shipowners' (Verein Hamburger Reeder) in 1889,

> will not achieve a thorough-going success as long as the dock workers themselves, in particular the lightermen and stevedores, are not seriously attempting to eradicate the criminal elements amongst themselves, in the realisation that this state of affairs shames their entire class. The unions that have been formed by these workers

offer an effective instrument, and here have the opportunity to show that their sole aim is not to fight the employers, but, as they are always emphasising, to aim at the improvement of their whole class and of the industry in general.[24]

V

The workers' union represented in the Hamburg docks ran into an obvious dilemma through such initiatives. Their attempts to present themselves to the shipowners as a respectable negotiating partner were bound in this situation to conflict with their efforts to win broadly based support from the workers. This became clear when the shipowners sent the placards offering rewards to informers to the unions as well, and demanded that they distribute them. At a meeting of the stevedores' union, the chairman's report that the executive had sent these placards to the bars and pubs frequented by dockers provoked serious criticism from the ranks of union members. They felt the behaviour of the union executive condoned 'denunciation', with the result that each worker would 'act as a policeman to his neighbour'.[25] Likewise, though the employers' federation urged the unions to exclude workers who had been convicted of theft from membership, this plea met with a luke-warm reception and had, as the chamber of commerce confirmed, little success apart from 'a few placatory noises'.[26] When, a little later, the warehousemen who worked at the docks formed their own union, a similar attitude was revealed. At the first members' meeting, during the discussion of the statutes, a clause to the effect that 'only workers without a criminal record' could become members was struck out. One speaker defended the decision on the grounds that 'in these times people are sentenced to punishment who, in the eyes of the members, are in no way at fault'. Similarly at the founding of the federation of dock workers the members voted that the 'possession of civil respectability' should not be made a condition of membership in the union.[27]

For the trade union leaders, there was nothing else to do under such circumstances but to balance, with more or less elegance, the demands of the shipowners and the expectations of the workers. When, in 1891, the employers again offered rewards for informers and demanded support from the federation of dock workers, the union leaders decided simply to ignore the problem. The distribution of placards was refused, ostensibly on the following grounds:

Only organised workers belong to the union, and these workers have freely and openly declared that their wages are insufficient. Thus they have turned, again freely and openly, to the employers, seeking an improvement in their wages, and have never attempted to increase their income through theft etc. If coffee and similar is really being stolen from the Hamburg docks, then this must be the handiwork of those who have till now remained aloof from workers' unions.[28]

Thus the federation of dock workers retreated behind a somewhat shaky line of argument. It was not unusual for workers convicted of theft to be members or even, as we have seen, officials of the union. The bourgeois press was not slow to point out this fact and to conclude from it that the trade unions were clearly not prepared to combat theft seriously.[29] However, to some extent the position of the trade union leaders was justified. For the group of workers who were most actively involved in stealing, the casual workers, were at the time clearly underrepresented in the federation of dock workers. Continuous trade union activity was at that time basically the affair of the better-situated minority whose living standards were relatively secure.[30]

The position of the federation of dock workers remained ambivalent in the following years. On the one hand the 'immorality' of stealing was condemned, and the counter-measures of the employers condoned. Thus one of the most important trade union leaders declared to the Senate in 1890 that he had 'nothing to say against the temporary exclusion of people who had been convicted of theft from employment in lighter transport concerns'.[31] The general practice of the state-owned quays of refusing to employ workers previously convicted of theft was agreed to because, as one of the leading figures in the Hamburg SPD, Otto Stolten, declared, 'there are mounds of goods stored there and one must have trustworthy people'.[32] On the other hand, representatives of trade unions tried to negotiate a relaxation of the employers' measures. After the employers had founded their 'federation of dockside firms' in 1906 and centralised the employment of stevedores, they had for the first time an instrument in this central area of dock work which made the exclusion of offenders a real possibility. At the same time an appeals tribunal was set up, consisting of representatives of both employers and unions. The stevedores whose right to work had been removed could appeal against the decision to this tribunal, and the union representatives on the tribunal did all they could to prevent both the prosecution and exclusion from dock work of those who had been caught stealing. The employers' press accused them of being a 'protection racket for thieves'.[33] The trade union leaders justified their position on the grounds that the thefts were simply a consequence of material need. The low wages of the casual labourer were almost 'a provocation to steal' — so ran an article in one of the trade union papers.[34] Thus the thefts could only be ended by the realisation of trade union demands: 'If the workers were paid better wages', explained one of the trade union leaders, 'the stealing would stop.'[35]

VI

The statistical material on the incidence of pilferage which would provide information on the effect of union policies and economic fluctuations is very unsatisfactory. The only usable figures which exist are of thefts reported to the criminal and dock police from the turn of the century up to the First World War and for 1922/3.

Table 2.2: **Thefts of Goods in Transit** (*Güterberaubungen*), **Hamburg, 1900-13**

Year	Number of Thefts	Year	Number of Thefts
1900	906	1907	1,120
1901	815	1908	1,266
1902	760	1909	1,449
1903	712	1910	2,455
1904	660	1911	2,733
1905	654	1912	3,468
1906	884	1913	3,217

Source: Annual reports of the Hamburg police, 1900-13.

The significance of these figures is limited in several respects. For a start one must assume a relatively high number of undetected thefts. Many thefts were carried out so skilfully that the theft was only discovered at the point of delivery and it was impossible to trace back where it had taken place. Furthermore, one can assume that numerous small thefts of food for immediate consumption were never reported to the police at all.[36] In addition the statistics do not list thefts of goods in transit through the docks separately from thefts of goods on railway trains, carts and other forms of transport. The above figures include thefts which took place at other points along the line of delivery. The main place of theft remained, however, the docks. The principal problem is that hardly any usable figures on the numbers of employees exist. Thus the statistics can only be used to sketch out crudely some of the main trends. It is known that the number of dock workers employed daily rose from 7,200 in 1896 to 17,000 in 1913 on average.[37] Overall, then, the number of their thefts rose faster than the number of employees. What is particularly surprising is the fact that the period 1900-13 falls neatly into two quite distinct phases. A continual decrease in the number of thefts until 1905 — which in reality was very much more impressive than the figures suggest at first glance as the numbers of dock workers rose dramatically in those years — is contrasted with completely the opposite trend from 1906/7 onwards.

There are difficulties in finding a convincing explanation of this surprising change of direction. A brief look at economic fluctuations in these years offers very few clues. It is surely safe to assume that the economic collapse which began in 1907 and lasted until 1909 contributed to the increase in theft. But the explanatory power of this circumstance should not be overestimated, as after 1909 the increase in the number of reported thefts continued unabated. In addition, a second look at the table reveals that in the crisis years 1901/2 the number of reported thefts even decreased. Nor was there any official redefinition of theft during the period which could have influenced the statistics. The increase in employees only very partially accounts for the massive increase in thefts from 1906 — between 1907 and 1913 the number of stevedores employed daily increased on average only by 30 per cent.[38] At any rate the thesis that an over-proportional increase in casual workers could be responsible for the increase in theft is not confirmed.[39]

Probably more significant is the rapid increase in the cost of living which followed the adoption of a new customs tariff in 1906. In 1912 the average working-class family — assuming an unchanged standard of living — had to pay 20 per cent more for food than in 1905. The rent for a room in a small flat rose between 1905 and 1910 by some 16 per cent.[40] For heat and lighting the costs increased between 1905 and 1912 by 23 per cent. In the same period, however, the income of workers also rose faster than before. Thus the wages for lightermen and piece workers on the state-owned quays increased by 23 and 22 per cent respectively. This did not apply to all groups of workers. The wages of stevedores — which increased by about 16 per cent — clearly lagged behind the increased cost of living. The same was true for other groups of workers. One can assume that this set of circumstances strengthened the inclination of part of the dock work-force to improve their wages in an alternative manner. However, it is unlikely that this alone can adequately explain an increase of more than 500 per cent in the number of reported thefts.

One further explanation seems plausible. The period from 1897 to 1906 witnessed the golden years of trade unionism in the Hamburg docks. During the great strike of 1896/7 almost all the workers had joined the federation of dock workers and few of those later left, although the struggle had ended with a defeat. Thus the events of 1896/7 were the starting-point of the development of a relatively strong trade union organisation with broad-based support and a considerable number of officials. Although the federation of dock workers remained un-recognised as a 'negotiating partner' in most sectors of dock enterprise at first, it managed during this period to bring portions of the employment market under its control and to become a mediator of increasing significance in the numerous conflicts at shop-floor level. In 1906 large sections of the Hamburg docks had become 'closed shops'; non-trade-union workers were unable to find employment. The zenith and at the same time the end of this period of growing trade union power was marked by a wave of strikes and lock-outs, which from January 1906 to April 1907 brought all groups of workers represented in the docks into action for the first time in a decade. At the end there was a lock-out of about 5,000 stevedores. These struggles provoked the employers into undertaking a complete restructuring of the organisation of the work-force. With the foundation of the employers' union (the federation of dockside firms) they created for themselves not only an instrument that strengthened their power in relation to the employment market, but also made possible the creation of a new, privileged stratum of workers whose interests were bound up with those of the employers.

At the end of the stevedores' lock-out, which by and large ended successfully for the employers, some of the imported strike-breakers were settled in Hamburg and employed on long-term contracts. These 'contract workers' — from now on the hard core of Hamburg stevedores — were differentiated from the majority of dock workers by higher wages, regular employment, a month's notice and obligatory member-ship of a savings and insurance fund. The fund, the central core of the contract worker system, was formed by deductions from wages and contributions from the employers' union. The contract workers could claim maintenance in case of illness or accident and also received money if a birth or death occurred in the family. If the worker left the employ-ment of the employers' union 'in a regular fashion' then he received the money he had saved. If he left without leave, refused to work, was 'rebellious', behaved in an 'unfit manner' or was guilty of drunkenness or theft, the money paid in was forfeit. The employers, following the example of other large firms, had created with the 'savings and insurance fund' an instrument with which to ensure 'good behaviour' on all levels. It was indeed largely successful in preventing strikes by the contract workers. The effects of this new institution were far-reaching. The stevedores, traditionally the most militant group of workers, were from now divided into, on the one hand, a group of workers whose interests were closely bound up with those of the employers, and on the other, the mass of former stevedores who were forced to the margin as supplementary workers. Work stoppages by stevedores which had previously been a common occurrence disappeared almost completely. In the following period the employers' union gradually extended its control of the employment market in all sectors of the docks, and the contract system was extended to other groups of workers.

Overall the net effect of the unrest of 1906/7 was a considerable change in the power constellation to the advantage of the employers. At the same time the dock workers' union, also affected by the economic depression of 1908/9, experienced the greatest crisis in its history. The dissatisfaction of its members with the way events had been developing since 1907 manifested itself in massive complaints of betrayal by the union's officials. In 1907 the dock workers' union in Hamburg had 11,100 members. Only two years later, a mere 6,100 remained.[41] Even later, as the number of trade union members gradually increased again, the relationship between the 'masses' and the 'leaders' remained tense, and latent mistrust was all-pervasive. However, the predominant feeling was a general one of powerlessness against the newly consolidated employers' camp. The reports of the political police in particular bear witness to this — they regularly sent plain-clothes men to workers' pubs to report the content of conversations overheard (*Wirtschaftsvigilanzberichte*): 'The employers' union does just what it wants and we can do nothing about it,' went a conversation between two stevedores for example. 'A strike at the docks is old hat, and these days it would be daft to try,' said another resignedly.[42]

This short sketch of the changes in the relationship between labour, capital and the trade unions offers some insight into why theft increased so dramatically after 1906/7. The extension of trade union power from 1896/7 had resulted in the dissemination of a specific labour movement culture: the formalisation of conflict and the development of new norms and values, but also the rejection of traditional forms of proletarian insubordination. One of the workers questioned by Adolf Levenstein on the influence the Social Democratic movement had had on his life answered:

I state with satisfaction that the trade union and political movement exerted a great moral influence on my life. Before my acquaintance with the trends and ultimate aims of our party I had been in continual conflict with the police (theft, disturbing the peace) and was for two years an inmate of the Rhineland penitentiary. Since I joined the above mentioned movement I have not committed a single crime. I am proud of my moral success.[43]

The decrease in stealing in the first few years after the turn of the century shows that the working-class movement could have a significant reforming effect even in the Hamburg docks. However, these successes seem to have lasted only as long as the efficiency and effectiveness of the trade union strategy was not called into question. The trade union leaders preached tirelessly for years that the sole means of improving workers' living and working conditions lay in strengthening their organisation. But 1907 clearly demonstrated that, despite an undeniable growth in strength on the part of the working-class organisation, the employers had made very much more rapid headway on the same terrain. The crisis of the trade unions after 1907, resulting from the new *status quo* achieved by the employers' offensive, was at the same time, as the increase in pilferage clearly shows, a crisis of the labour movement culture. Thus during these years the old forms of social conflict were resorted to as other possibilities of representing the workers' interests effectively began to lose significance and credibility for the workers. At the same time this apparently offered the possibility of expressing aggression and protest against the new power of the employers, because the articulation of this aggression in more open and direct ways was hindered by the new state of affairs.

Overall, then, an analysis of the development of pilferage in the Hamburg docks before the First World War provides a number of clear indications that petty crime at work cannot simply be evaluated in terms of need,[44] but was also the expression of tensions between employers and employees, of insubordination and power structures; it was not only an index of social misery but also of changes in the relation between labour and capital.

VII

Compared with the massive increase in theft in the years after the First World War, developments before 1914 appear rather harmless. In 1922

the police recorded 6,726 reports of theft. In 1923 it was 5,958. Thus
the incidence of pilferage had approximately doubled in comparison
with the situation before the First World War, while the number of
dock workers had risen by only about 20 per cent.[45] The rapid increase
in pilferage after the end of the war began with the arrival of the first
cargo ships carrying provisions. As early as May 1919 one trade union
representative complained that there were many workers 'who have
only come here to steal'.[46] In 1922 the chamber of commerce even
registered some refusals to work on the loading of certain goods, which
the workers expressly justified on the grounds that they 'couldn't use
any of that stuff'.[47] The merchants and shipowners were particularly
helpless in this situation because it was bound up with the collapse of
all those structures of supervision and authority which before 1914 had
ensured that some areas at least of the docks remained more or less free
of thefts. Thus many of the deputies (*Vize*), whose job it was to oversee
the stevedores, stopped reporting pilferages for fear of being beaten up
by the workers.[48] Above all, the fact that the supervisors, quay officials
and even small businessmen were also involved in the thefts is clearly
evident. The agent of a Magdeburg insurance company who had been
sent to the Hamburg docks to investigate the disappearance of large
quantities of sugar reported succinctly to his chief that 'if one wanted
to seek out the guilty party one would have to lock up the entire staff
including the manager.'[49]

As in the years before 1914, 'by far the greatest part' of these post-
war thefts consisted of the necessities of life, in particular coffee, flour
and bacon.[50] In addition, however, there also developed organised
crime rings, at the head of which stood substantial Hamburg merchants.
The black market developed in the post-war years into a blooming
branch of the local economy.[51] Although, as the Pilferage Committee
of the British Chamber of Shipping confirmed, an increase in theft took
place in all the ports of the world at this time, the phenomenon was
particularly marked in Hamburg. It went so far that in 1922/3 the
larger trading companies began to fear for their overseas trade. In particular in 1923 growing numbers of Scandinavian firms refused to allow
their goods to be transported via Hamburg. Even the largest Hamburg
shipping company, the Hamburg-America line, began to unload its
imported coffee in Antwerp rather than in Hamburg.[52]

The history of this escalation of petty crime begins during the First
World War. As early as February 1915 the shortage of foodstuffs was
making itself felt in Hamburg and in the following years it became the
single most important problem for Hamburg's inhabitants. For many

the illegal acquisition of foodstuffs through theft, the black market or hoarding had become a question of survival and moral scruples disappeared. The collapse of public order, which affected the great majority of the middle class as well, coincided with the erosion of state authority and the evident powerlessness of the local authorities. In August 1916 and February 1917 food shops were looted, in particular by women and youths, in some working-class districts. Such examples of militant self-help were sharply criticised by the Social Democratic press, but they were interpreted by some left-wing radical groups as the expression of a growing desire for peace and, as such, were condoned.[53] The November revolution of 1918 and the concomitant radicalisation of large sections of the working class were, on the one hand, foreshadowed by these developments and, on the other, forced their continuance. However, the decisive cause of the high amount of pilferage was the unparalleled impoverishment of the mass of people as a result of the rapid fall in the value of real wages. If, in the following years, the well-off sections of the bourgeoisie sought to minimise the effects of the inflation by their 'retreat into material assets' (*Flucht in die Sachwerte*), then the increase of thefts from the docks should be seen in the first instance as an illegal proletarian variant of the same phenomenon, a reintroduction of wages in kind on the workers' own initiative.

Counter-measures on the part of the employers and authorities remained largely without effect. Demands to alleviate the problem by introducing more severe punishments were refused by the judiciary on the grounds that pilferage from the docks was already punished more severely than other forms of property crimes. Apart from this, as the regional court's president Ipsen continued, the prisons at that time 'were so packed full with serious offenders . . . that [the judiciary] must think twice before passing longer, more severe sentences'.[54] The employers' repressive control of the employment market had diminished in effectiveness as well. Plans to exclude all workers convicted of theft from employment were unrealistic because, as the Hamburg chamber of commerce stated, 'there would not be enough workers left.'[55] In addition the attitude of the workers themselves had changed. Up till the First World War the closing of ranks in the face of the powers above had manifested itself in a solidarity of silence. After 1919 an active solidarity developed which expressed itself loudly and clearly, sometimes even violently. Bound up with this was the politicisation of lower-class criminality. The new activism expressed itself not only in violent retributions on informers: the arrest of workers who had been found with stolen goods on their person was no longer an orderly proceeding but often led to violent struggles with the police and customs officials. The Communist Party organised the looting of grocery shops in order to test 'the militancy of the mass of unorganised workers'.[56] Employers who sacked a worker for stealing had to reckon with strikes.[57] In June 1919, after a violent confrontation between police, troops and dock workers who had been caught in the act of stealing, there was a three-day strike by the stevedores.[58]

While the conflicts escalated at the docks, the position of the trade union leadership had changed dramatically. Theft was now no longer simply condemned but actively combated in co-operation with the employers. Since 1919 the trade union leaders had been included in conferences of shipowners, merchants, jurists and police officials called to discuss measures aimed at reducing the amount of pilferage. The other side of the power which the trade unions won after 1916 (with the passing of the law on patriotic auxiliary labour service – *Gesetz über vaterländischen Hilfsdienst*) now showed itself as they began to participate in the control of the workers on the factory floor. They clearly risked losing the trust of their membership through this. As early as 1919, one trade union representative complained that attempts to control his colleagues had resulted in physical attacks.[59] By the end of 1922 the Hamburg branch committee of the General German Trade Union Confederation (Allgemeiner Deutscher Gewerkschaftsbund – ADGB) had to confirm that 'all the admonition from our side and all the security measures taken by the state and representatives of the trade unions' had been unable to prevent 'the thefts from the dock area reaching catastrophic proportions'. The branch committee referred to the fact that 'large foreign shipping companies are seriously considering banning their ships from docking at Hamburg'. The report ended with the demand that 'no more mercy' should be shown:

> Anyone who steals, illegally opens packing cases, sells on the black market, plans robberies in conjunction with sailors etc. in the Hamburg docks is to be reported without delay to the security forces. This is not 'informing', but a measure that can only improve the image of our Hamburg working class. Anyone who, out of a false sense of solidarity, silently allows the stealing to carry on is also guilty if the end result is to be the crippling of our shipping industry.[60]

Thus the silent coexistence of lower-class petty crime and the values and norms embedded in the labour movement culture came to an abrupt end. The precise effect of such declarations cannot be judged with any accuracy in view of the dearth of usable evidence. The incidence of theft did decrease slightly in 1923, the year when the inflation reached its height, and this could be seen as a result of the hard line taken by the trade unions. However, it is more likely that such a policy further increased the distance between a considerable section of the dockers and the trade unions. The strong position gained by the syndicalist/left-wing radical groupings at the beginning of the 1920s in all the great German ports and the mass desertion of the membership of the Free (Social Democratic) trade unions between 1922 and 1924[61] can possibly be traced back to such experiences. A significant decrease in the number of thefts did not come in the wake of trade union initiatives; only after the inflation had ended did the number of thefts decrease significantly. In 1924 only 2,354 thefts were reported to the police. Pilferage remained, however, an everyday phenomenon in the Hamburg docks; for the employers it was an evil that appeared ineradicable, but from now on it remained within bounds and no longer threatened the future expansion of Hamburg trade.

VIII

It is clear, then, that behind the phenomenon of pilfering a variety of different causes is hidden. In the post-war years, thefts from the docks — as is shown by the rapid decrease in stealing in 1924 — were primarily a means of escaping the consequences of the drastic fall in real wages caused by the inflation. Material deprivation by itself is, however, insufficient to explain petty crime in the working class. In particular the developments in the years before the First World War show that theft was potentially a vehicle for articulating protest which under other circumstances would perhaps have been expressed in a number of alternative ways.[62] Both aspects justify an interpretation of lower-class petty crime as a component of working-class culture — providing of course that 'working-class culture' is taken to encompass more than the subculture of the organised labour movement.[63] Pilferage from the docks formed an illegal aspect of everyday life for the working classes, one of the means the workers had at their disposal to solve their material problems. Fundamental to this behaviour were forms of class solidarity, which, despite all the differences, united all the differing strata and subgroupings within the working class. Values and norms which stood in direct contradiction to the dominant culture formed the basis of this petty crime. 'Working-class culture' was here simultaneously 'contraculture'.[64]

The question as to how far the conclusions of this chapter can be generalised to other groups of workers is debatable. There is some evidence that the docks comprised a branch of economy where traditionally the boundaries between the *classes laborieuses* and *classes dangereuses* were particularly fluid.[65] Whether theft in a particular industry was an everyday occurrence or a more marginal problem was clearly dependent on several factors: the usefulness of the product and materials with which the worker came into contact, for instance, or the composition of the work-force, or the opportunities available to the employer to keep the workers under control. However, it seems as if in wide sections of the working class, petty crime on the shop floor has long been an integral component of securing a living wage. Many workers clearly regarded it as a customary right, which was sometimes exercised as a matter of course and which was violently defended against the encroachments of employers and the state.

A spectacular example of this is afforded by one of the great strikes of the 1870s, when, in Königshütte, Upper Silesia, 3,000 miners went on strike under extremely difficult conditions. The sparking point for this strike was the proposed introduction of security measures by the owners of the mines which, amongst other things, were specifically aimed at reducing the large amounts of coal appropriated by the miners. The strike was broken by massive military intervention, but the mine-owners retracted the plans which had caused the trouble under the influence of events.[66] Generally it seems realistic to assume that for large sectors of the working class during industrialisation it was no uncommon fate to come into conflict with the law or spend part of one's life behind bars. The quantitative data available to support such assumptions are admittedly fragmentary and insufficient,[67] and more detailed studies on the subject have yet to be published.

It would seem that we are dealing here with an aspect of working-class life that until now has received scant attention from German historians; in so far as it has been studied at all, it has been too hastily settled by the notion of a *Lumpenproletariat*. This study has shown that the analysis of petty crime affords an opportunity to reconstruct one of the hidden fronts in the everyday battle between the classes. In doing this the outlines of a proletarian 'contraculture' have become visible, a culture which is clearly different from that of the labour movement. It seems to me therefore of some interest not only to work out the gap between working-class culture and the culture of the labour movement, but also to investigate more closely the confrontation between these two value systems. If in Germany it is often maintained

— and also bemoaned — that working-class culture did not differ essentially from the form and content of bourgeois culture, then perhaps this is a consequence of the fact that until now German historians have concentrated almost entirely on the culture of the Social Democratic working-class movement.

Notes

This chapter was first given as a paper to the fourth meeting of the SSRC Research Seminar Group in Modern German Social History, held at the University of East Anglia in July 1980. I would like to thank David Blackbourn, Richard Evans and Klaus Saul for their discussions, criticisms and encouragement. Unless otherwise indicated, all documents cited are from the Staatsarchiv Hamburg.

1. F. Engels, *The Condition of the Working Class in England* (Panther Books, London, 1969).
2. Gustav Roscher, *Grossstadtpolizei. Ein praktisches Handbuch der deutschen Polizei* (Hamburg, 1912), p. 18. The newspaper of the chamber of commerce in Hamburg commented that only those 'who came into close contact with the dock workers of today and who have the chance to observe the intentional rudeness and insolence which these people steeped in socialism display at every opportunity to the dock officials can understand the difficult task of the dock police . . . If one of these chaps is finally reported, there are enough friends ready to swear him innocent . . ., and he usually gets off with a very light sentence' (*Hamburgische Börsen-Halle*, 90, 23 Feb. 1891).
3. Protocol of the Senate Commission meeting on the adoption of measures to combat pilfering, 25 Feb. 1891; Senatsakten Cl.VII Lit.Me. no. 2, vol. 13, appendix to no. 54.
4. Thus a representative of the chamber of commerce in a protocol on the discussions on combating pilfering in the Hamburg docks, 23 Jan. 1923, p. 5; Senatskommission für die Justizverwaltung (abbreviated: SKJV), IIDb3d, vol. 1, appendix to no. 83.
5. *Hamburgische Börsen-Halle*, 92, 24 Feb. 1891.
6. From SKJV IIDb3d, vol. 1.
7. Figures from: *Bericht der Senatskommission für die Prüfung der Arbeitsverhältnisse im Hamburger Hafen* (Hamburg, 1898), p. 111; *Jahresbericht des Hafenbetriebsvereins in Hamburg* e.V. (abbrev. *HBV*) for 1913, p. 65.
8. Quay director Hedler to Senator O'Swald, 18 Oct. 1889; Deputation für Handel, Schiffahrt und Gewerbe (abbrev. DHSG) II Spezialakten VIII D.7.1.
9. Michael Grüttner, 'Mobilität und Konfliktverhalten. Der Hamburger Hafenarbeiterstreik 1896/7' in Klaus Tenfelde and Heinrich Volkmann (eds.), *Streik. Zur Geschichte des Arbeitskampfes in Deutschland während der Industrialisierung* (Munich, 1981), pp. 143-61; Albert Haas, 'Les Grèves dans les ports européens et la situation des armateurs', *Revue économique internationale*, vol. 5, no. 1 (1908), pp. 41-61.
10. Figures from *Jahresbericht des HBV* (1922), p. 4. The figures on numbers employed were calculated from the data on p. 9. There are no figures on the thefts committed by the 'permanent' workers.
11. *Jahresbericht des HBV* (1914-19), p. 8.
12. Ludwig Turek, *Ein Prolet erzählt. Lebensschilderung eines deutschen*

Arbeiters (Cologne, 1972), 9.16. Such strict moral tenets did not, however, prevent Turek's mother from regularly smuggling chocolates out of the storerooms of the chocolate factory in which she worked (p. 10).

13.   The Hamburg Chamber of Commerce to the deputation for trade and shipping, 2 Apr. 1897; DHSG II Speziakakten VIII D.7.1. no. 38.

14.   Politische Polizei (abbrev. PP) V 485-9, vol. 4. Überwachungsbericht 8 Jan. 1905.

15.   Report from the Hamburg regional court's president to the SKJV, 10 Jul. 1923; SKJV IIDb3d, vol. 1.

16.   PP V 485-9, vol. 1, Aktennotiz 11 Aug. 1893, Überwachungsbericht 3 May 1896 and 5 Oct 1898. PP.V 485-1, vol. 1. Überwachungsbericht 11 Aug. 1898, 17.

17.   PP S 2267.

18.   Gerald Mars, 'Dock Pilferage. A Case Study in Occupational Theft' in Paul Rock and Mary McIntosh (eds.), *Deviance and Social Control* (London, 1974), pp. 209-28. Here pp. 224f in particular.

19.   Report of the Executive Committee of the SKJV, 31 Oct. 1910; SKJV IIDb3d, vol. 1, no. 38.

20.   The unpublished annual reports of the Verein der Hamburg-Altonaer Ewerführer-Baasse vom 1874, 1890 ff.; Archiv des Hafenschiffahrtsverbandes Hamburg.

21.   DHSG II Spezialakten VIII F.1.191. In this the fear of the thieves was greater than the fear of 'Social Democratic agitators'. Quay director Hedler to senator O'Swald, 4 Apr. 1893, as above.

22.   Thus the public prosecutor Hirsch in a letter to Senator Hertz, 30 Dec. 1898; Senatsakten Cl.VII Lit.Me. no. 2, vol. 13, no. 18a.

23.   Michael Foucault, *Discipline and Punish. The Birth of the Prison* (Penguin Books, Harmondsworth, Middlesex, 1977), p. 285.

24.   *Jahresbericht des Vorstandes des Vereins Hamburger Reeder* (1889), p. 4.

25.   PP V 141 Überwachungsbericht, 11 Aug. 1889.

26.   The Hamburg Chamber of Commerce to the Deputation für Handel und Schiffahrt, 16 Apr. 1890, DHSG II Spezialakten VIII D.7.1, no. 25.

27.   PP V 139 Überwachungsbericht 18 May 1890; PP V 327-41, Überwachungsbericht 2 Jan. 1890.

28.   The correspondence was printed in the paper of the dock workers' union; *Gerechtigkeit*, 2, 24 Jan. 1892.

29.   Thus the *Hamburgische Börsen-Halle*, 50, 30 Jan. 1892, on the tariff negotiations of 1888 between the lightermen and the chamber of commerce. It continued: 'How very much the lightermen's union. . .condemns the pilfering can be seen from the fact that of the six representatives it sent to the negotiations with the chamber of commerce three had been convicted of crimes against property, and it was only after this had been pointed out that one, who had been convicted of a serious crime, remained away from further negotiations.'

30.   Grüttner, *Mobilität*, p. 153.

31.   *Protokolle der Senatskommission für die Prüfung der Arbeitsverhältnisse im Hamburger Hafen über die Vernehmung vom Arbeitgebern und Arbeitnehmern* (Hamburg, 1898), p. 106. This trade union leader was by the way the abovementioned Johann Will, a former lighterman who had himself been imprisoned for six months for serious theft.

32.   PP V 485-3 vol. 4, Überwachungsbericht 28 Mar. 1903.

33.   Courier no. 44, 30 Oct. 1910.

34.   As above.

35.   PP V 485-1, vol. 2. Überwachungsbericht 15 Aug. 1902.

36.   The police were also convinced that the number of thefts was in reality much higher than the number reported. See Polizeisenator Hachmann to Bürgermeister Petersen, 12 Dec. 1889; Senatakten Cl. VII Lit.Me. no. 2, vol. 13, no. 17.

37. *Bericht der Senatskommission*, 111, *Jahresbericht des HBV* (1913), p. 65.
38. Calculated from information in Carl von Düring, *Die Organisation der Arbeit im Hamburger Hafen* (Hamburg, 1925), p. 40. There were no figures on the lightermen.
39. Ibid., p. 43.
40. The definition of a small flat is here a flat with up to two heatable rooms. On the rise in the cost of living see Raphael E. May, 'Kosten der Lebenshaltung und Entwicklung der Einkommensverhältnisse in Hamburg seit 1890' *Schriften des Vereins für Sozialpolitik*, vol. 145, no. IV (Munich/Leipzig, 1915), pp. 259-524. Information on the rise in wages from the *Jahresberichte des HBV* and the trade unions.
41. Verband der Hafenarbeiter und verwandten Berufsgenossen Deutschlands (Mitgliedschaft Hamburg-Altona), *Jahresbericht der Ortsverwaltung für das Geschäftsjahr 1909*, p. 74.
42. PP S 15350-22 report of the policeman Noroschat, 8 Jan. 1908; PP S 16600-19 report of policeman Szymanski, 4 May 1909.
43. Adolf Levenstein, *Die Arbeiterfrage* (Munich, 1912), p. 293.
44. Both the older studies on petty crime in the nineteenth century – in so far as they are of interest today – and the few more recent German publications on this theme have interpreted petty crime primarily as the expression of material deprivation in the lower classes. See in particular Herbert Schwarz, 'Kriminalität und Konjunktur. Eine kausalstatistische Untersuchung über die deutsche Vermögenskriminalität 1882-1936', *International Review of Social History*, vol. 3 (1938), pp. 335-97, in particular pp. 347ff and 385; Dirk Blasius, *Bürgerliche Gesellschaft und Kriminalität. Zur Sozialgeschichte Preussens in Vormärz* (Göttingen, 1976), pp. 34ff, and *Kriminalität und Alltag* (Göttingen, 1978), pp. 47ff. Blasius sees a form of social protest in petty crime as well. Zehr's theory of 'modernisation' of crimes against property in the second half of the nineteenth century stands in opposition to this: Howard Zehr, *Crime and the Development of Modern Society. Patterns of Criminality in Nineteenth-century Germany and France* (London, 1976), pp. 43ff and 80ff.
45. *Jahresbericht der Verwaltungsbehörden der Freien und Hansestadt Hamburg* (1925), p. 387. Average number employed on work days: 1913: 17,000; 1922: 20,100; 1923: 20,500. Calculated from information given in the *Jahresbericht des HBV* (1923), p. 2.
46. Protocols of talks between representatives of the wharfmen and the DHSG, 22 May 1919, DHSG II Spezialakten VIII F.1.194.2.
47. The Hamburg Chamber of Commerce to the DHSG, 19 Aug. 1922 (copy) SKJV IIDb3d, vol. 1, no. 67.
48. Protocol of a talk on the thefts at the docks in the chamber of commerce, 14 May 1920, p. 8, SKJV IIDb3d, vol. 1, appendix to no. 45.
49. Letter from the agent of the Wilhelma-Versicherungs AG to the management in Magdeburg, 24 Jul. 1922 (copy); SKJV IIDb3d app. 3 to no. 67. On the collapse of control structures: *Bericht der Polizeibehörde Hamburg*, Abteilung II, Kriminaloberinspektion Hafen, 14 Oct. 1920 (copy); SKJV IIDb3d, app. 1 to no. 56, and the above-mentioned protocols of discussions.
50. Thus wrote the regional court's president Ipsen in a report to the chamber of commerce, 7 June 1922, SKJV IIDb3d, app. to 51.
51. Report by the regional court's president to the SKJV, 10 Jul. 1923, and the report of the public prosecutor (Generalstaatsanwalt) Lang to the SKJV, 17 Dec. 1924; both letters in SKJV IIDb3d, nos. 104 and 117.
52. A loss of 2 per cent was underwritten in advance by the insurance firms when coffee was being transported. Hamburg chamber of commerce to the DHSG, 12 Jun. 1923 (copy), and the report of the regional court's president, 10 Jul. 1923, SKJV IIDb3d, nos. 100 and 104.

53.   Volker Ullrich, *Die Hamburger Arbeiterbewegung vom Vorabend des ersten Weltkrieges bis zur Revolution 1918-19* (Hamburg, 1976), vol. 1, in particular pp. 268f and 353f; Jürgen Kocka, *Klassengesellschaft im Krieg. Deutsche Sozialgeschichte 1914-1918* (Göttingen, 1978), pp. 132ff.

54.   The regional court's president Ipsen to the Hamburg chamber of commerce, 7 Jun. 1920 (copy), SKJV IIDb3d, vol. 1, appendix to 51.

55.   As above, 10 Jul. 1923, SKJV IIDb3d, vol. 1, no. 104.

56.   Jan Valtin (i.e. Richard Krebs), *Out of the Night* (Alliance Book Corporation, New York, 1941) pp. 26 and 50. This book is one of the many reports by former Communists that appeared in the forties and fifties. The first half contains some interesting information on the milieu of the Communist dock workers and seamen during the Weimar Republic. On the role of the docks as a centre of working-class radicalism in the post-war years see Richard A. Comfort, *Revolutionary Hamburg. Labor Politics in the Early Weimar Republic* (Stanford, California, 1966), pp. 91f. Unfortunately, some of Comfort's conclusions lack conviction and precision mainly because he fails to distinguish between dock and shipyard workers, although the composition of the work-force was very different in these two separate branches of the economy.

57.   Sackings were often not carried out so that the industrial peace would not be endangered. See the Protokoll der Besprechung über Hafendiebstähle in der Handelskammer, 14 May 1920, p. 10f; SKJV IIDb3d, vol. 1, appendix to 45.

58.   Jahresbericht des HBV 1914-19, 8.

59.   Protokoll der Besprechung zwischen Vertretern der Kaiarbeiter und der DHSG, 22 May 1919, p. 4; DHSG II Spezialakten VIII F.1.194.2.

60.   *Die Freie Gewerkschaft. Offizielles Mitteilungsblatt des ADGB, Ortausschuss Gross-Hamburg*, no. 45, special supplement of the *Hamburger Echo*, no. 524, 7 Dec. 1922.

61.   The Social Democratic trade unions lost almost two-thirds of their members in the docks during these years. See Johannes Ehrhardt, 'Die Arbeitsverhältnisse im Hamburger Hafen', Diss.jur. MS., Hamburg, 1926, appendix, Table 3. Overall the losses of the 'Free' trade unions were clearly smaller. Their membership fell from 7.8 million in 1922 to 4.0 million in 1924. Cf. Helga Grebing, *Geschichte der deutschen Arbeiterbewegung* (Munich, 1970), p. 179.

62.   Cf. the notes in Blasius, *Bürgerliche Gesellschaft*, pp. 31 ff on the correlation between crimes against property and political misdemeanours.

63.   More recent German publications also point out the need to distinguish between 'working-class culture' and the 'culture of the labour movement'. This, however, does not alter the fact that generally these publications, in so far as they are concerned with Germany, concentrate mainly on the culture of the Social Democratic working-class movement, in particular Gerhard A. Ritter (ed.), *Arbeiterkultur* (Königstein/Ts., 1979). Most of the articles in this collection appeared earlier, often in abbreviated form, in the *Journal of Contemporary History*, vol. 13, no. 2 (1978). Also the edition of *Geschichte und Gesellschaft* (vol. 5, no. 1, 1979) on 'Arbeiterkultur im 19. Jahrhundert', edited by Jürgen Kocka.

64.   J. Milton Yinger, 'Contraculture and Subculture' in David O. Arnold (ed.), *Subcultures* (Berkeley, 1970), pp. 121-34, in particular pp. 126 ff.

65.   Louis Chevalier, *Labouring Classes and Dangerous Classes in Paris during the First Half of the Nineteenth Century* (London, 1973), pp. 366ff; Fritz Sack, 'Stadtgeschichte und Kriminalsoziologie' in Peter Christian Ludz (ed.), *Soziologie und Sozialgeschichte. Aspekte und Probleme* (Opladen, 1973), pp. 357-85, in particular pp. 374ff.

66.   I am referring here to Lothar Machtan, ' "Arbeiterbewegungen" in der Konjunktur des Klassenkampfs. Studien und Dokumentation zur Streikbewegung im deutschen Kaiserreich 1871-1875', unpubl. ms., Bremen, 1981. The acquisition

of substantial amounts of coal was apparently regarded as completely legitimate by the miners, as it was the product of their own labour.

67.   Thus an investigation by the authorities revealed that of 1,750 miners convicted after the great strike of the Ruhr miners in 1912, 35 per cent had previous convictions (Zentrales Staatsarchiv Potsdam, Reichsministerium des Innern, no. 6841. B1.73ff).

3 DRINK AND THE LABOUR MOVEMENT: THE *SCHNAPS* BOYCOTT OF 1909

James S. Roberts

I

At its 1909 party Congress in Leipzig, the Social Democratic Party of Germany (SPD) launched what was in some respects its most ambitious national political protest – it called on German workers to renounce the use of *Schnaps*. The immediate occasion of this extraordinary protest was the reform of Imperial finances completed that summer amidst a storm of political controversy.[1] The reform was necessary chiefly because the nation's ambitious naval programme, the keystone of Kaiser Wilhelm's world-political ambitions, was plunging the government deeper and deeper into debt. Despite Chancellor Bernhard von Bülow's efforts to base the nation's finances for the first time at least partially on substantial direct taxation, the combined strength of the conservative and Catholic Centre parties forced the Chancellor to abandon this approach. In the end, Germany's rulers left the burden of taxation where it always had been, on the mass of German consumers. Altogether some four-fifths of the Reich's fiscal requirements were to be met through indirect taxes. The items affected by the new legislation were central to the little that German working men enjoyed of the good life, including beer, spirits and tobacco. This blow to accustomed standards of living came at a time when rising prices, partly the result of government tariff policies, were already putting pressure on working-class budgets.

The events of 1909 brought the SPD an opportunity to combine in a single and creative form of protest its roles as political opposition movement, defender of popular living standards and cultural vanguard of the working class. But the results of this novel form of political protest were unhappy. The SPD's efforts to recast working-class drinking patterns were unsuccessful, and the *Schnaps* boycott ended in failure. This chapter explores the reasons for this failure, some of them of general significance for understanding the relationship between the labour movement and its working-class constituency in the years before the First World War.

80

II

In Germany, as in the other industrialising countries of Europe and North America, the Drink Question — the discussion of the causes, consequences and control of popular drinking behaviour — had become a matter of serious public concern by the middle of the nineteenth century. Industrialisation and urbanisation made alcoholic beverages more accessible, altered the contexts in which they were consumed and created a new and highly visible class of consumers, the industrial proletariat. At the same time, the number of people with a material and moral stake in sobriety was increasing. Undoubtedly there were alarmists whose exaggerated claims about the consequences of popular drinking behaviour were as grossly distorted as their simplistic understanding of its origins. But there were few serious social and political commentators in late-nineteenth-century Germany who would have denied that alcohol consumption could be a source of serious problems in working-class life. This was not primarily a question of habitual drunkenness or alcoholism in the modern medical sense. The alcohol problem was the cumulative effect of everyday patterns of consumption that were socially acceptable and widely practised.[2] Such drinking could not only undermine the health and sap the resources of German working men but could also retard their material and cultural expectations. The magnitude of these problems — or potential problems — cannot be defined with quantitative precision, but they were not merely the products of the bourgeois imagination. No socialists who wrote on the Drink Question ever disputed that the alcohol problem had a real existence in working-class life. Their discussion revolved not around whether there was a drink problem but around its fundamental causes and ultimate solution. The *Schnaps* boycott was not the labour movement's first confrontation with the Drink Question. By 1909, German socialists had discussed the issue for nearly two decades, but they had not produced a clear and decisive policy. In retrospect, this is not surprising, for the SPD was forced to perform a delicate balancing act on the Drink Question, seeking a middle ground between competing interests and conflicting tactical imperatives. Several factors forced the SPD, and with it many individual trade unions, to take a stand on the Drink Question, but these same factors, taken together, actually operated to retard decisive action.

Several factors constrained the labour movement's approach to the alcohol problem, making any sort of direct appeal to German workers to alter their drinking behaviour unlikely. The first of these factors, paradoxically, was the very strength of the working class's attachment to drink. As far as most German workers were concerned, there was no drink problem. Working men regularly consumed alcohol in a variety of everyday contexts — as a meal-time beverage, as a source of refreshment on the job, and as a means of diversion and escape. Styles of popular alcohol consumption undoubtedly varied widely within the working class, but there can be no doubt that most working men regarded the beverages they drank as an integral part of their standard of living, something to be defended rather than curtailed.[3] A decisive anti-alcohol policy would therefore run the risk of alienating the very people it was meant to influence and thus also of cutting into the labour movement's organisational strength and electoral support.

Another constraint on the labour movement's response to the Drink Question lay in its own dependence on the tavern. In the first place, the meeting rooms provided by co-operative publicans were the organisational prerequisites of virtually all of the labour movement's activities.[4] Tavern keepers, consequently, played a prominent role in the labour movement's local affairs, and a few, like Friedrich Ebert, won positions of national prominence.[5]

The labour movement's dependence on socialist publicans for meeting rooms naturally inhibited the development and implementation of a decisive anti-alcohol stance, but this was only one aspect of the relationship between the labour movement and the drink place. As the principal centres of popular social life, the taverns of the working class also had a less visible political significance. Tavern life nourished the social networks among working men from different neighbourhoods and occupations that provided the labour movement's hidden infrastructure. Writing in 1891, Karl Kautsky called the tavern an indispensable bulwark of the socialist labour movement and warned that a successful temperance movement in Germany, by forcing working men out of the taverns and into the privacy of their own miserable homes, could destroy the social ties that bound the socialist labour movement together.[6] The connection between the labour movement and the tavern loosened somewhat after the expiration of Germany's repressive anti-socialist laws in 1890, but Kautsky's observation remained valid even two decades later. Given these views, and the realities they reflected, the SPD was bound to look upon moderate drinking with favour.

By the time the SPD first seriously considered the Drink Question in the early 1890s, popular drinking behaviour had already become a matter of public controversy, the terms of which were largely defined by middle-class temperance reformers and their allies in government and the Protestant church. The Drink Question was thus pre-empted by the labour movement's enemies. As a result, the SPD's public posture on the Drink Question — at least until 1909 — was fundamentally defensive, designed more to counter criticisms of popular drinking behaviour than to alter it.[7]

Critics of the working class and the socialist labour movement often blamed excessive drinking and other 'moral' failings for the misery and discontent so evident around them. This view of the Social Question was sometimes accompanied by the belief that the labour movement itself encouraged heavy drinking and attracted men little better than common drunkards to its cause. The SPD did not let these claims go unchallenged.[8] But to counter the argument that alcohol consumption was at the root of the modern social problem, the SPD simply reversed the causality and insisted that the drink problem was not a cause but a consequence of the evils of industrial capitalism. And in response to the suggestion that the labour movement itself was saturated with alcohol, the party's spokesmen insisted that the drink problem afflicted not the organised, class-conscious proletariat affiliated with the labour movement but the hopeless masses outside it. The party's early response to the Drink Question thus combined a defence of indictment of the social and political *status quo*.

The formulation of the Drink Question by critics of popular drinking behaviour forced leading socialists to respond in highly charged polemical terms. Their conception of the Drink Question in turn helped shape the labour movement's response to the alcohol problem. If the source of the drink problem lay with the shortcomings of industrial capitalism rather than the choices of individual drinkers, there could be no solution within the confines of the existing social order. The only adequate way to address the Drink Question was therefore to attack the social, economic and political conditions at its root. Given this theoretical framework, it made little sense to encourage workers to alter their drinking behaviour. Such efforts were not only bound to fail; they could divide the labour movement, divert energy from more pressing tasks, and — perhaps most important — muddy the distinction between the proletarian and bourgeois conceptions of the Social Question.

Given the tactical constraints under which the labour movement operated, it is not surprising that only a minority of German socialists took an active interest in launching a temperance campaign within the working class. The German labour movement never fully accepted the view that the fight against alcohol could be an integral and necessary part of the class struggle. In virtually every other European country, leading figures of the labour movement — men like Emile Vandervelde in Belgium and Viktor Adler in Austria — lent their influence to this cause.[9] German socialists of similar stature were not found in the vanguard of the fight against alcohol. The alliance with the tavern, cemented during the period of the anti-socialist law, and the rigidity of ideological fronts in Germany prevented it. Nevertheless, the Drink Question was an issue that could not be avoided by the central institutions of the labour movement.

A movement against alcohol had originated in predominantly middle-class, Protestant circles during the 1880s.[10] By the early nineties, interest in the Drink Question had spread. A few voices within the labour movement were now heard arguing that alcohol was an obstacle to the class struggle and urging an energetic anti-alcohol campaign within the working class.[11] These early demands from within the labour movement for a proletarian anti-alcohol campaign were put to rest by a series of articles written by Karl Kautsky in 1891.[12] It was Kautsky who established the orthodox position on the Drink Question. He insisted that the alcohol problem was an inevitable outcome of the conditions of industrial capitalism and warned against efforts to 'smuggle' anti-alcohol agitation into the labour movement. The Drink Question was discussed sporadically at subsequent party congresses, but those who wanted to see the issue on the agenda for a full-scale debate were repeatedly disappointed.[13] After 1903, however, the relatively few socialists determined to make an issue of the Drink Question acquired a new and more potent voice. In that year the League of Abstinent German Workers (Deutscher Arbeiter Abstinenten Bund — DAAB) was founded in Bremen.[14] The DAAB's principal goal was to convince the socialist labour movement to endorse teetotalism and to carry on an active propaganda on its behalf. The abstinent socialists believed that even the organised working class still had a good deal to learn about alcohol and its potential dangers to the individual, the community and the labour movement itself. In their view, the party's quietism in the face of the modern alcohol problem was inconsistent with its responsibilities as the moral and cultural vanguard of the working class.[15] Like Emile Vandervelde, the leader of Belgian socialism and a champion of working-class abstinence, the DAAB insisted that the SPD 'must have the courage to tell the world-conquering proletariat what it needs to be worthy to rule the world'.[16] By 1907, the DAAB had succeeded in winning a place for the 'Drink Question' on the agenda of a socialist party congress, but it remained an isolated minority within the labour movement, unable to alter the party's fundamentally defensive position.

Despite the unpopularity of the abstinent socialists, their agitation did help bring the Drink Question to the labour movement's attention at the local level. Perceptions of the potential ill effects of alcohol consumption were often clearer at the grass roots, and local-level party leaders and trade union functionaries had a freer hand in dealing with alcohol's potentially disruptive consequences. After the turn of the century, the Drink Question was discussed with increasing frequency in the labour movement press and at occasional local meetings of working-class organisations. In this way, at least, the potential dangers of alcohol consumption were brought home to many workers and the ideal of genuine moderation extolled. But even at this level there were significant constraints that forced the labour movement to treat the Drink Question with caution when it treated it at all.

The SPD's definitive statement of policy on the Drink Question came at the 1907 party congress in Essen.[17] The party executive appointed the Reichstag deputy Emanuel Wurm to give the report. Wurm's address was a polemic against critics of popular drinking behaviour who continued to see in alcohol consumption a major source of the contemporary social problem. Wurm countered these arguments in the course of his two-and-a-half hour address. At the same time, he developed a position on the Drink Question that could only be congenial to the working-class drinkers.

Wurm began from the premiss that alcoholic beverages were not intrinsically harmful if consumed in moderation. But under the conditions of modern industrial capitalism, excesses were inevitable, especially among those workers most vulnerable to economic exploitation, poverty and hopelessness. Responsibility for the alcohol problem therefore lay not with its individual victims but rather with the system of industrial capitalism and the social groups which supported it. The best way to combat the alcohol problem, therefore, was to attack the social and economic conditions that underlay it. In the meantime, the party could help workers learn about the potential ill effects of alcohol consumption. Ultimately, however, the decision of whether, what and how much to drink had to be left up to each individual.

The party Congress at Essen unanimously adopted a resolution based on these principles and thus established a formal position on the Drink Question.[18] Both tolerant of popular drinking behaviour and fatalistic about its sometimes untoward consequences, it attacked the evils of industrial capitalism while asserting the essential respectability of the labour movement. The resolution adopted at Essen was not a call to action but rather a reaffirmation of the *de facto* position long since established. The Drink Question remained a matter of individual choice and conscience. The labour movement's task was not to reform drinking behaviour but to root out the causes of its abuse.

III

Just two years after the congress at Essen, the SPD called resoundingly on all German workers to renounce the use of *Schnaps*. The SPD thus abandoned, at least temporarily, the cautious approach to the Drink Question established in the years since Kautsky first wrote on the subject in 1891. For the first time, the SPD seized the initiative on the Drink Question, linking it creatively to the labour movement's larger concerns and goals. Such an approach, much feared by some middle-class temperance reformers, had always been a possibility.[19] The Imperial fiscal reform and the new indirect taxes were the catalysts of this sudden change of direction.

The socialist Reichstag delegation had fought hard in 1909 to give the Imperial fiscal reform a more progressive shape.[20] Once they were defeated, however, the socialists could only welcome and encourage the widespread popular indignation which the new taxes evoked. Having suffered a serious electoral setback in 1907, they now hoped to give political voice to the discontents of German consumers. The SPD's agitational leaflets sought to display in graphic terms what the new tax increases would mean. In one leaflet preserved in Amsterdam, working-class consumers were confronted with drawings that compared the cigars, beer mugs and *Schnaps* glasses they had enjoyed before the tax increases with the shrunken delights of the coming era. It left no doubt about who was to blame for the new taxes and to what dangerous military purposes they would be put.[21]

Popular disenchantment with the fiscal reform focused first on the new tax on beer and the efforts of the brewers who actually paid the tax to introduce a general increase in prices. In many areas, tavern keepers and other retailers also announced price increases that would have more than compensated for the new taxes.

The price of beer had long been a sensitive issue in Germany. One of the bloodiest civil disturbances in the history of the Empire erupted in Frankfurt a/M in 1873 when brewers there attempted to raise their prices.[22] Fearing the political consequences of pushing up the cost of beer, successive Reichstags had refused the government's not infrequent requests to increase the tax on beer.[23] Even in 1906, when taxes affecting beer were increased for the first time since 1871, the Reichstag tried to ensure that the tax increase would not be passed on to consumers in the form of higher prices.[24] But in 1909 this caution was abandoned. In fact, a contrary approach was taken. In order to win the support of the German brewing industry for this second tax rise in three years, the government's draft, which passed the Reichstag with only minor modifications, envisioned a tax on beer structured both to favour existing breweries against new competitors and to make it easy to pass the new tax on to consumers. To the same end, the Reichstag also legalised the use of smaller beer glasses in the retail trade, a stratagem not likely to fool many beer-drinking working men.[25]

In the summer of 1909, working men throughout north Germany demonstrated vigorously against the impending increases in the cost of beer.[26] Similar protests occurred in Baden and Bavaria in the following summer, when the tax increases were due to take effect there. Popular indignation often resulted in boycotts, dubbed 'beer strikes' in the working-class press, designed to prevent brewers and tavern keepers from raising their prices more than was warranted by the new tax law. In Brunswick, for example, a 'gigantic popular demonstration ... of a kind never before seen in Brunswick' gathered to protest against the efforts of brewers and middlemen to up their prices. The crowd was estimated at 6,000 to 7,000 strong and resolved to drink no beer at increased prices.[27] Similar actions were reported in Frankfurt, Leipzig, Breslau, Essen, Dortmund and at least a score of other north German cities and towns. The boycotts were often successful, at least in the short run. Tavern keepers and their associations rolled back their prices. Brewers also felt the consequences of the 'Beer War' and were forced to come to terms with popular pressures. In some places, as in Duisburg and Gera, the local labour movement negotiated settlements with producers and distributors to hold down the price of beer.[28]

The 'Beer War' demonstrated vividly the working class's determination to defend its standard of living — including customary levels of alcohol consumption — against the new indirect taxes. The labour movement supported and sometimes guided this popular movement. Its response to the new tax on spirits, however, was markedly different. There was nothing like the 'Beer War' to protest the impending increase in the cost of spirits, partly because beer rather than *Schnaps* was the real staple beverage of most German working men, especially in urban areas. But the labour movement's response to the new tax on spirits was shaped less by consumer protests than by the political and cultural issues that surrounded the production and consumption of *Schnaps*.

In the first place, *Schnaps* production and taxation had a very special political significance. As Frederick Engels suggested in the 1880s, the production of raw spirits was one of the material foundations of the anachronistic social and political order of the Empire.[29] And the peculiar system by which spirits production was taxed was central to the nexus of special fiscal privileges developed by Bismarck during the agricultural depression of the 1870s and 1880s to maintain the financial viability of the estates of the East Elbian Junkers.[30] Despite the growing opposition to these arrangements, the fiscal reform of 1909 perpetuated the lucrative bounty, or *Liebesgabe*, paid out to the agricultural producers of raw spirits. The sums involved were considerable. The various benefits accruing to producers at the expense of both consumers and the Imperial treasury amounted to at least 960 million marks between 1887 and 1912.[31] The names of those who benefited from this bounty remained a closely guarded secret, but there was no question that the Junkers were its main beneficiaries.[32]

In addition to the special political sensitivity of the spirits tax, the cultural stereotypes that surrounded the use of *Schnaps* also help to explain why this beverage, rather than beer, became the object of the labour movement's wrath in 1909. For most spokesmen of the labour movement, *Schnaps* consumption was somehow *déclassé*, a symptom of that cultural and material backwardness characteristic of the most disadvantaged segments of the working class. This attitude was expressed, for example, in the autobiography of M.W.T. Bromme, whose vivid description of a great cultural 'gulf' in the working class drew on familiar images of the degraded *Schnaps* drinker:

> on the one side there is the cultivated and refined portion of the working class, seeking the highest treasures of humanity and equality with the ruling classes; and on the other, the *Lumpenproletariat*, depraved through *Schnaps*, ignorance, misery and want, the dregs of human society, which knows only base, animal instincts and wastes away without the least spiritual or intellectual involvement.[33]

The *Schnaps* drinker was thus pictured as degraded and solitary, interested primarily in drowning his sorrows and hence as demoralised, hopeless and politically apathetic. Beer drinking, on the other hand, was implicitly seen as a more social activity, an activity not at all incompatible with the needs of the labour movement.

The idea of turning popular revulsion against the new taxes into a boycott against distilled liquor was discussed first in the *Volkswacht* of

Breslau, an SPD newspaper in one of the most important industrial areas of eastern Germany.[34] By the eve of the socialists' party congress, scheduled for Leipzig in mid-September, just before the new taxes were to take effect, the party and trade union press was full of similar-sounding appeals urging workers to smash their brandy flasks and renounce the use of *Schnaps*. Boycotts had already begun on local initiative in some places, and Breslau, Bielefeld-Wiedenbruck, Hamburg and Bunzlau all addressed motions to the party Congress calling for the SPD's endorsement of a nation-wide *Schnaps* boycott.

The party Congress convened in Leipzig on 13 September. Paul Löbe of Breslau introduced the *Schnaps* boycott resolution, which won the assembly's unanimous endorsement amidst stormy applause from the rostrum, the floor and the galleries. Despite the unanimity and enthusiasm of the congress's endorsement, however, there remained an ambiguity about the boycott's real purpose that would provide the seeds of later disagreements.[35]

Löbe made clear that he was motivated by political concerns and that he intended the boycott to achieve political ends. In his view, the boycott's primary purpose would be to keep the inequity of the government's fiscal reform in the eye of a working-class public prone to forget too quickly. By actively engaging the working population in some form of continuing protest, the boycott would keep the issue alive until the next Reichstag election and thus help the socialists recoup their losses of 1907. But at the same time, even for Löbe, the *Schnaps* boycott was inextricably bound up with the fight against alcohol consumption *per se*. For Löbe, as for many others, this was no doubt a secondary motivation, but he none the less made clear that the 'favourable economic and hygienic by-products that a boycott of spirits would call forth are naturally very welcome'.[36]

Other voices only added to the ultimate confusion about the real purposes of the boycott. Luise Zietz spoke for the Party Executive Committee and urged that the resolution be unanimously endorsed. The party's leadership, she announced, supported the boycott not only as a tax protest but also because its members expected from it an 'extraordinary moral victory'.[37] She expressed confidence that the labour movement's adherents would make the boycott effective, and she suggested that agitation for the boycott could be used to reach the men and women not yet actively involved in the collective struggle of the working class.

The exuberance that greeted Zietz's announcement of the party executive's support for the *Schnaps* boycott was echoed in the party and trade union press. The Leipzig resolution evoked a sense of pride, enthusiasm and confidence.[38] The moral dimensions of the action, moreover, were as much in the foreground as were the political. 'The boycott strikes two enemies', wrote the Berlin *Vorwärts*, the party's leading daily newspaper, 'the external and the internal, the exploitation and repression of the Junkers and the apathy and ignorance in our own ranks.'[39] The boycott would not only undermine the social and material foundations of Junker rule by striking directly at the vulnerable bounty system (*Liebesgabe*), it also promised the 'proletariat's liberation from chains of its own making'.[40] The party's confidence that this great moral and political mission would succeed, the newspaper suggested, was founded on the close relationship between the proletariat and the labour movement established over the course of many years. As the paper's editorial put it:

> The party can count on the fact that its moral influence in the proletariat is stronger than the evil customs of the past and the tremendous force of habit. Social Democracy can count on this fact because its educational work in the working class has gone on for decades and because it has succeeded in bringing the masses of its followers to the realisation that the individual has to make sacrifices in the interests of the whole. This resolution is therefore a living testament to the inner strength of the party, to the fact that it is one with the forward striving proletariat.[41]

Vorwärts was joined by the *Correspondenzblatt* of the General Commission of German Trade Unions and a host of lesser lights in the working-class press in calling for energetic agitation in all branches of the labour movement to ensure the boycott's success.[42]

As the statements at the Party Congress and the editorials in the party press reveal, the *Schnaps* boycott was the product of a variety of motives. It was not launched, as the Party Executive Committee would later claim, exclusively out of narrowly defined political motives, for in fact there was no single end in view, indeed, no definite way of knowing if and when the boycott's objectives had been achieved. The agitation was to be open-ended. The proletariat was being asked to renounce spirits not temporarily, to achieve a specific goal, but forever. An action made possible by political events and intended, to be sure, to produce political consequences was thus also conceived as an end in itself. This was true in two senses, for the boycott was meant both to reduce alcohol consumption and to broaden political education by involving workers directly in a concrete form of class struggle.

The party, followed spontaneously by the 'Free' trade unions, had thus embarked upon a path it had long eschewed in its previous confrontations with the Drink Question. It had, in Ludwig Frank's terms, committed its moral capital with the working class in the hopes of reaping both moral and political rewards.[43] The older view that the individual drinker was powerless in the face of insurmountable environmental forces was decisively abandoned and, with it, the notion that the organised, class-conscious proletariat had abandoned the taste for hard liquor. The Leipzig Resolution was addressed to the *whole* working class. Organised workers were expected to support the boycott as a matter of course, and their example was to spread to the unorganised masses. The risks in this course of action were considerable. Kautsky had long before warned that the Drink Question could seriously fragment the labour movement. And, as Franz Mehring now observed, from one point of view the *Schnaps* boycott placed the party in a double bind.[44] If the boycott brought about a dramatic reduction in *Schnaps* consumption, the old caricature of the red-nosed socialist that the party had long sought to dispel would be embarrassingly confirmed. On the other hand, if the boycott failed to produce a substantial decline in consumption, the enemies of the labour movement could ridicule its tenuous hold on the masses and continue to propagate the image of the drunken and irresponsible worker.

IV

Despite the enthusiasm that accompanied the adoption of the Leipzig resolution, dissension over the interpretation and implementation of the boycott was soon rampant in the German labour movement. It is difficult to determine what went on in the local meetings at which the *Schnaps* boycott was discussed and debated, but inevitably differences of opinion arose about how it should be carried out and by what means it should be enforced. Conflicting interests within the labour movement produced local tensions. A headline appearing in *Vorwärts* in early November — 'Is Cognac Schnaps?' — was indicative of the confusion.[45]

In response to this chaos, the party executive issued a clarification of the Leipzig resolution that was published in the working-class press on 20 November.[46] Its purpose was both to quell dissent about the boycott and to provide guidelines for its further implementation. The party's leadership interpreted the *Schnaps* boycott in extremely narrow terms, focusing exclusively on its political origins and purposes. The economic and social motives behind the Leipzig resolution were ignored, and there was no mention of the 'extraordinary moral victory' Luise Zietz, the executive's spokeswoman at Leipzig, had foreseen. The party's leaders called for the boycott's continuation, but they warned that it could be conducted only by means of 'moral influence' and that there could be no question of intra-party disciplinary measures for those who failed to comply with the Leipzig Resolution. The party executive insisted, moreover, that the *Schnaps* boycott had not altered the position on the Drink Question adopted at the 1907 Essen congress, which emphasised the socio-economic roots of the alcohol problem and condoned the moderate use of alcohol.

If the party executive's declaration sought to recast the boycott in a narrower mould, the comments of the influential socialist publicist Franz Mehring, appearing a week later in *Die Neue Zeit*, the party's most prestigious theoretical journal, cast doubt on the wisdom of the whole enterprise.[47] Mehring's article was a lucid restatement of the arguments that in the past had prevented the SPD from seizing the initiative on the Drink Question. According to Mehring, the Leipzig Resolution was based on faulty assumptions and was thus unlikely to achieve its political goals; in the end, therefore, it could only embarrass the party. In the first place, Mehring argued, the resolution's appeal to organised workers seemed to suggest to the German public that the labour movement was 'more or less saturated with alcohol'.[48] Yet the assumption that party and trade union members could bring about a drastic reduction in spirits consumption, Mehring contended, was not only unflattering; it was false. It was the hopeless masses not yet touched by the working-class movement who accounted for the level of spirits consumption in Germany, and these segments of the working population were unlikely to heed the party's call. But since the resolution could have little real effect on consumption, the boycott was bound to fail in its political objective, and – what apparently seemed equally troubling to Mehring – the party would be open to the derision of its enemies as a result. Mehring's remarks seem to betray a certain insecurity about whether the boycott would be supported even within the organised working class. Nevertheless he concluded with bitter irony: 'It is a tricky business to pass resolutions that can only be carried out on the condition that the party is more underdeveloped than it actually is.'[49]

Taken together, Mehring's article and the party executive's clarification raised important questions not only about the wisdom of the Leipzig Resolution and the way it was being executed but also about the cultural differences between the organised and unorganised segments of the working class, the extent of the labour movement's influence beyond – indeed, even within – its own membership, and the possibility that that influence could be extended by an action like the *Schnaps* boycott. About these issues there were now serious disagreements.

In the working-class press, there was an immediate and for the most part negative reaction to the cautionary note sounded by Mehring and the party executive.[50] Resentment against the *Flaumacherei*, the defeatism, of both Mehring and the party leadership was the dominant theme. Editorial writers naturally agreed that there could be no question of disciplinary action against those who continued to drink *Schnaps*, but this sentiment appeared so obvious as to go without saying. To advocate caution so soon after the boycott was launched seemed to provide a ready excuse for local leaders and rank and file socialists to evade the demands the party had made on itself at Leipzig. Such evasions were intolerable to many socialists whose views now appeared in the party press. For the boycott's most enthusiastic supporters, the decision of the Party Congress, in this as in other matters, established the guidelines socialists should be expected to follow. To be sure, the deeply ingrained character of drinking habits required some flexibility, but fundamentally, the principles of the party and the discipline of its members were at stake. The socialist *Volksblatt für Anhalt*, for example, conceded that 'external measures of coercion' were out of the question but insisted that the 'full force of moral criticism' should be levelled against those who continued to drink *Schnaps*.[51] Attitudes such as these, however justifiable in principle, were bound to produce conflict and resentment in the labour movement's local organisations.

Mehring was taken to task for other reasons as well. Most significant was the criticism, repeatedly voiced, that Mehring simply had no conception of the realities of working-class life. 'Such *naïveté* and pedantry', wrote the Breslau *Volkswacht*, 'we had not thought possible.' Mehring's ' "class-conscious" worker' was 'about as far removed from the real German worker as the idealised goddess of liberty is from the real proletarian housewife'.[52] Mehring had asserted that the boycott was bound to fail because organised workers did not consume *Schnaps* and because the labour movement had no influence on those who did. These propositions were roundly disputed in both theoretical and empirical terms. In the first place, it was argued, the level of *Schnaps* consumption in Germany was determined neither by the drunken *Lumpenproletariat*, nor by the numerically declining agricultural labour force, but by the mass of moderate drinkers, among them many socialists and trade unionists. It was a delusion, Mehring was repeatedly told, to believe that organised workers had abandoned the taste for hard liquor:

> The author can never have been even once in one of the thousands of proletarian taverns in Berlin, not to mention East Elbia, in which organised workers gather, if he does not know how it is with the *Schnaps* consumption of our workers.[53]

This line of attack was not to suggest that socialist working men were a lot of hopeless drunkards, but it was the linchpin of the boycott's more realistic supporters' argument that the *Schnaps* boycott, culturally necessary, could be politically effective. If, as one supporter argued, the greater part of the millions of marks expended each year on *Schnaps* 'is composed of the individual pennies, which respectable and sober working men spend one after the other', then it would be possible to make the boycott a success.[54] It was not a question of reforming drunkards or curing alcoholics but of appealing to class-conscious workers to make a small personal sacrifice. Surely, the class-conscious proletariat would respond to an appeal endorsed by the highest party authority and designed not only to move the labour movement closer to its political goal but also to enhance the cultural and material quality of working-class life. The key was to give the boycott energetic and consistent leadership. The boycott's supporters were under no illusions that they could eliminate the use of spirits from working-class life altogether. But any decline was an improvement in cultural terms, and even a moderate reduction could affect the Reich's treasury and the financial resources of the Junkers.

The boycott's proponents took issue just as strongly with the second part of Mehring's pessimistic argument. In those segments of the proletariat in which drinking really was excessive, Mehring had suggested, *Schnaps* consumption was an inevitable response of workers to the hopelessness of their objective situation. The boycott, as a moral appeal, could have no impact where such hopelessness and apathy were so deeply rooted in basic material conditions. Numerous editorials, particularly in the trade union press, took exception to this line of reasoning and offered an interpretation of the *Schnaps* boycott at once more optimistic and more ambitious. Mehring's premiss was often accepted, but not his fatalistic conclusion. Economic exploitation, cultural degradation and the psychology of hopelessness were surely conducive to excessive alcohol consumption, but Mehring, his critics argued, left the autonomous force of the alcohol problem out of his historical question. As one rebuttal insisted:

the consumption of *Schnaps* is not only rooted in the hopeless condition of the modern proletariat; it also helps to prevent the worker
from freeing himself from this hopelessness. For thousands of workers,
a determined decision to renounce the use of *Schnaps* would make it
possible for the first time to begin the fight for better conditions.[55]

If this were so, then it was necessary to take the fight against alcohol
well beyond the confines of the organised working class and to use the
agitation for the *Schnaps* boycott as a way to reach and win over those
workers previously outside the influence of the labour movement. Luise
Zietz had made this argument at the Leipzig congress, and it was
repeated now in much of the working-class press.[56] The proponents of
this broader strategy were to be disappointed.

Thus far, the abstinent socialists have been treated only in passing.
In fact, the genesis of the SPD's *Schnaps* boycott owed very little to
their efforts. At Leipzig, the abstinent socialists sought to make themselves inconspicuous, recognising that the boycott would have a better
chance of gaining the party's endorsement if, in Simon Katzenstein's
words, it was not allowed to seem the product of the still unpopular
'water fanatics' (*Wasserfanatiker*) within the party.[57]

The adoption of the Leipzig Resolution thus presented the abstinent socialists with a new situation, but it by no means constituted a
victory for their principles. Although the years of growing concern with
the Drink Question, fuelled by the agitation of the abstinent socialists,
no doubt paved the way for the *Schnaps* boycott, its immediate source
was the peculiar constellation of political and economic forces brought
to public consciousness by the Imperial fiscal reform. The abstinent
socialists harboured no illusions on this point, but they believed the
boycott could be cast in terms that would reduce working-class alcohol
consumption generally. Katzenstein announced a wait-and-see policy,
hoping that the party would take its self-imposed task seriously but
warning that the abstinent socialists were ready 'to defend the party
energetically against its leaders' if the execution of the boycott proved
unsatisfactory.[58] In the months following, they found much to criticise.

By the beginning of 1910, the *Schnaps* boycott had ceased to attract
much attention in the party press. Interest rose only slightly with the
approach of each year's Party Congress; the boycott was renewed at the
congresses held in Magdeburg (1910), Jena (1911) and Chemnitz
(1912).[59] Otherwise, the periodic exhortations which continued to
appear from time to time in random issues of the working-class press
provided the only outward sign that the boycott was still in force.

Despite the demand, heard fairly frequently early on, that the party organise and lead the boycott, its execution was ultimately left up to local editors and labour movement functionaries. The *Schnaps* boycott thus meant different things in different places, but it appears that nowhere was it followed — or enforced — very strictly.

Although there is no way of knowing how typical their examples were, the abstinent socialists made it their mission to point up the laxity of the boycott's execution. This not only stiffened the opposition of the action's detractors but also delighted the labour movement's critics. Opposition to the Leipzig Resolution showed itself in a number of small gestures. To order a 'Leipzig Resolution Shot' became a standard joke in the labour movement. Placards supporting the boycott were ripped from walls. The party's agitational pamphlet was left undistributed. Excuses for evasion were readily at hand. Not rum or arak, the recalcitrant told themselves, but the Junker's rot-gut *Schnaps* was banned by the Leipzig Resolution. The boycott was meant not for upstanding and moderate drinkers like us, they said in Berlin or Hamburg or Munich, but for the wretches of East Elbia or the Ruhr. More serious was the fact that union halls continued to offer the boycotted *Schnaps* for sale, while the working-class press continued to advertise it.

Individual inertia, conflicts of interest and temperament, and the caution of the central institutions of the labour movement all contributed to the movement's stagnation. By the beginning of 1910, the DAAB was convinced, despite subsequent efforts to revivify it, that the *Schnaps* boycott was dead. In a lead article in its April number, the DAAB's official organ, *The Abstinent Worker*, suggested that the party had failed to provide the energetic leadership necessary to counteract the public's natural tendency to lose sight of the purposes and importance of the boycott and become absorbed in other issues.[60] An action born of momentary discontents, the memory of which was constantly eroded by the succession of equally aggravating events, was bound to lose its impetus unless given a larger meaning and goal that would focus the public's discontents and keep the issue in the public eye. Such a strategy, explicit in Löbe's Leipzig speech, would have made the boycott a political success and provided a useful agitational vehicle in the struggle against the ruling class and the militarist state. But the early disagreements within the party, rooted, the DAAB believed, in the economic interests of influential party circles in the drink trade, had led to both active and passive resistance to the boycott. Instead of serving to expand the party's influence, the boycott threatened to undermine it; the moral conquests made by the resolution would be more than undone by the party's inability to execute it.[61]

The *dénouement* of the SPD's *Schnaps* boycott was played out in 1912. Agitation on behalf of the Leipzig Resolution was stepped up, at least temporarily, after the government was forced to modify the spirits tax once again. This time the bounty for privileged producers was formally abolished, but the massive subvention of the East Elbian distillers was to continue under the new law. Junker producers were rid of the odium but not of the benefits of the *Liebesgabe*, and the power of the Spiritusring, the cartel of major East Elbian producers, to limit production and control prices remained unbroken.[62]

The abstinent socialists saw the events of 1912 as a final opportunity to win the party over to a more energetic and meaningful execution of the Leipzig Resolution. At that year's Party Congress at Chemnitz, Georg Davidsohn, the DAAB's spokesman, put a direct challenge to the assembled delegates: either carry out the boycott in a way befitting the reputation of German Social Democracy or rescind the Leipzig Resolution.[63] Asking the Party Congress to support a more radical and energetic approach to the boycott, Davidsohn introduced a resolution calling for more active leadership from local party functionaries, an end to liquor advertisements in the party press, and a ban on the sale of the boycotted beverages in union halls and Social Democratic meeting houses.

Davidsohn's plea was rejected. He was answered, among others, by Paul Löbe, the 'father' of the Leipzig Resolution. Löbe's argument, which was apparently accepted by the overwhelming majority of the delegates present, showed that the party had come full circle from the position of aggressive moral and cultural leadership implicit in the Leipzig Resolution. Löbe had proposed the boycott principally as a political weapon. Now that the weapon was backfiring, Löbe's tactical sense changed accordingly. In response to Davidsohn, Löbe warned that by prohibiting the sale of *Schnaps* in the labour movement's establishments, the party would only drive away the people it most hoped to influence, not only on the question of the *Schnaps* boycott but on the whole range of Social Democratic concerns.[64] Löbe's caution suggests that little remained at Chemnitz of that glowing faith in the proletariat's willingness for self-sacrifice that had resounded through the Leipzig meeting hall three years before.

By now the boycott was little more than a face-saving operation. Unable to admit defeat, the party's spokesmen resorted to familiar images of proletarian virtue and heroism, insisting that the *Schnaps* boycott was a great success. Löbe, who only moments before had warned that the boycott could cut into the labour movement's support, now provided its eulogy. Löbe attributed the decline in consumption since 1909 to the efficacy of the boycott and the self-sacrificing idealism of the proletariat. Behind this reduction, Löbe suggested, were 'hundreds of thousands of our functionaries who used to drink *Schnaps* as they went off in the early morning cold to distribute leaflets [but who] now say: enough of that, my party discipline forbids it'. Thanks to the Leipzig Resolution, he went on, there were now 'hundreds of thousands of families in which the children no longer see their fathers drinking *Schnaps*, [and] in which the money that previously went to rot-gut liquor is now devoted to more refined and useful amusements'.[65]

V

Löbe had thus proclaimed a great victory where Davidsohn saw only defeat. Disagreement was built into the logic of the situation. The abstinent socialists, stressing the moral and cultural side of the boycott, undoubtedly set higher standards than most of their party comrades; no matter what was achieved, it could always be bettered. The party leadership, on the other hand, was in a position to be too complacent. Consumption was bound to decline simply because the new taxes would raise prices. The party was quick to claim this reduction as evidence for the boycott's effectiveness. The boycott undoubtedly did have some effect on consumption, but judged in relationship to the expectations raised in Leipzig and echoed in the party and trade union press, the SPD's *Schnaps* boycott must be called a failure.

The *per capita* consumption of spirits declined 25.9 per cent between 1908 and 1912.[66] This reduction was sufficient to upset the government's revenue calculations. The spirits tax of 1909 was supposed to bring in 230 million marks annually, 100 million more than the total garnered in 1906. During the first year of its operation, revenues were actually down, and in subsequent years, even after further adjustments in the system of taxation in 1910 and 1912, this target was never reached.[67]

But the tax's failure is not necessarily an argument for the boycott's success. The magnitude of the decline is not in dispute. What can be questioned is whether the SPD's boycott contributed substantially to this decline. Certainly, there were workers who abandoned *Schnaps* in response to the Leipzig Resolution. Adolf Levenstein surveyed working-class opinion on a variety of issues between 1907 and 1911 and shed some light on this issue. Of the 5,040 organised miners, metalworkers and textile workers he questioned about their drinking habits, 617 said they had given up *Schnaps* because of the boycott.[68] Another 187 working men claimed to be teetotalers, though 34 of these admitted to lapses of up to six pulls on the brandy flask per day.[69]

Levenstein's survey suggests that the boycott did find supporters within the working class, but it tells us nothing about their contribution to changing consumption patterns. But there are other indications that the decline in *per capita* consumption after 1909 cannot be attributed primarily to the boycott. In the first place, spirits were not the only item of mass consumption to decline after 1909. The consumption of coffee, for example, a working-class staple affected by the new taxes but not by the SPD's boycott, experienced a decline of similar magnitude, falling 22.8 per cent between 1909 and 1912.[70] Second, the decline in *per capita* spirits consumption after 1909 only continued a trend evident since the turn of the century. Between 1899 and 1909, the *per capita* consumption of spirits had fallen 13.6 per cent, from 4.4 to 3.8 litres of pure spirits per annum.[71] The rate of decline did accelerate after 1909, but that was probably less a direct result of the boycott than of the rising cost of drinking *Schnaps*. Consumption had also declined on previous occasions when tax increases had appreciably affected prices. Between 1887 and 1888, for example, *per capita* consumption fell by 23.6 per cent in response to tax-related price increases.[72] Finally, although the *per capita* consumption of spirits declined almost 26 per cent between 1908 and 1912, the total amount of money spent on spirits *per capita* was much less elastic, declining only 11.5 per cent.[73] In aggregate terms the disparity is even more striking. Aggregate consumption declined 22.0 per cent, but the reduction of expenditure amounted to only 4.0 per cent.[74] All of these factors suggest that the decline of consumption between 1908 and 1912 was less the result of the boycott than of rising prices. The boycott may have reinforced the tendency of working-class drinkers to cut back their consumption as prices increased, but it apparently created no fundamental shift in drinking behaviour.

If the *Schnaps* boycott was not an unmitigated failure, it was hardly a genuine success. The hopes with which the boycott was begun remained unfulfilled. The Leipzig Resolution had neither significantly reduced consumption nor mobilised the political energies of the working class. The outcome of the *Schnaps* boycott belied the assumptions of its supporters no less than its critics. Both had conceived the relationship between the labour movement and the larger proletariat in terms that proved to be highly unrealistic. Franz Mehring and those who shared his views on the boycott were confronted with an outcome that challenged their flattering assumption that the class-conscious proletariat had outgrown the taste for *Schnaps* and that there was somehow a clear-cut cultural division between the labour movement's adherents and those who remained outside it. The grass-roots resistance to the Leipzig Resolution from within the labour movement itself flew in the face of that assumption. But this same resistance also belied the central assumption of the boycott's supporters: that the class-conscious proletariat would alter its drinking behaviour in response to the party's call and thus make the boycott a cultural and political success. Both errors stemmed from an unrealistic evaluation of the labour movement's working-class constituency. As it turned out, the working class, even the organised working class, was neither so virtuous nor so willing to sacrifice as the party's contending spokesmen supposed. In the end, Mehring was right, but for the wrong reasons. The *Schnaps* boycott was a failure not because it had been unable to reach the unorganised masses, but because the labour movement itself had failed to close ranks behind it.

Why had workers failed to support the boycott? Certainly part of the explanation must lie with the party's refusal or inability to organise and lead it. Once the *Schnaps* boycott's potential for creating disagreement had become clear and the unanimity of the Leipzig congress hall had evaporated in the crucible of local debate, the party executive retreated. Perhaps this was inevitable, given the party's previous treatment of the Drink Question. The *Schnaps* boycott, as we have seen, was an unexpected reversal which naturally created doubt and confusion. Had the ground been better prepared, however, a firm lead by the party at this juncture might have stopped the early haemorrhaging of support that proved fatal to the SPD's ambitious national political protest. As it was, the party's half-hearted leadership only increased dissension, allowing the recalcitrant to evade the Leipzig Resolution while provoking the self-righteous to try to enforce it.

But the inability or unwillingness of the central institutions of the labour movement to provide a firm lead is only part of the story of the *Schnaps* boycott's failure. The SPD had called on German workers clearly and unequivocally to alter their drinking behaviour. How is the refusal of so many of them to heed this call to be interpreted?

In the first place, there is some indication that many workers simply considered what they drank to be an individual, private affair. No doubt the discussion of the Drink Question within the labour movement raised the level of awareness among many working men of the potential ill effects of alcohol consumption and expenditure. This made it all the more likely that they would respond to the rising costs of alcoholic beverages by reducing their consumption, especially since the cost of more basic necessities was increasing as well. But if many workers participated in a long-term learning process to which the labour movement undoubtedly contributed, they were still unlikely to respond to overt attempts to alter their drinking behaviour. Adolf Levenstein provides some of the most striking evidence for this view. In the course of his investigation of working-class attitudes, Levenstein discovered that the question he posed about alcohol consumption was the one most often left unanswered. Moreover, personal encounters with working men sometimes turned hostile over just this issue.[75]

The Leipzig Resolution, despite the political terms in which it was cast, apparently failed to alter this tendency to regard habits of consumption as a matter of personal choice and individual preference. Most workers were apparently no more likely to follow the recommendation of the labour movement in this matter than they were the injunctions of their employers or the pleas of German temperance reformers. Even those workers most under the sway of the labour movement, in other words, appear to have maintained a considerable independence from it, at least as far as their intimate, private lives were concerned. The culture of the working class – or of German workers – was never precisely equivalent to the values and standards of behaviour espoused by the labour movement's local and national spokesmen, often, as in the case of the Drink Question, to defend themselves and their constituents against the scurrilous moral attacks of the labour movement's enemies.[76]

A related point was suggested earlier. Most workers considered what they drank to be an integral part of their standard of living. As incomes increased, they spent more on alcohol, not less. Drinking was something to be defended rather than curtailed. When workers looked to the labour movement to protect their living standards, the quantity and the quality of the alcohol they consumed was one of the things they had in mind. The 'Beer War', which the labour movement generally supported, was ample evidence of this inclination. But for critics as well as defenders of the *Schnaps* boycott, it was axiomatic that a distinction could be drawn between beer and *Schnaps*. The same cultural evaluations of these two beverages were apparently not shared by many German working men. From their point of view, the labour movement's effort to defend the consumption of beer and condemn the use of *Schnaps* was ultimately an inconsistent policy. It was not possible to capitalise on the workers' sense of deprivation and encourage the spirit of self-sacrifice simultaneously.

But this last point still leaves open the question of why workers considered beer and *Schnaps* such an integral part of their way of life and standard of living. This is not the place for a complete review of the role of alcohol in working-class life. But even after the turn of the century, when *per capita* consumption trends took a downward turn in Germany, working men continued to use alcohol in a wide variety of everyday contexts, none of which would have been quite the same without drink. Beer and *Schnaps* continued to meet a variety of legitimate needs in the working class, as a dietary supplement, as a thirst quencher and stimulant on the job, and as a means of escape from everyday cares. In addition, alcohol was a crucial ingredient of working-class sociability and the drink place a principal institution of working-class social life. In short, German workers, whether organised or unorganised, found an important source of satisfaction in drink and the activities of which it was conventionally a part. Drinking was by no means the only source of such satisfactions by the early twentieth century, but drink and the tavern still held their own — especially as a source of social satisfactions — against the available alternatives: the family, the churches and the multiplicity of organisations and programmes affiliated with the labour movement itself. Even for workers who took advantage of these alternatives, drink remained one of the good things in life, something to be enjoyed and defended rather than curtailed.

What was the significance of this attachment? I would argue that the working class's devotion to drink was not primarily a manifestation of alienation *from* the existing order but rather a form of attachment to it. Despite the efforts of middle-class temperance reformers and their allies, the cult of sobriety was never as deeply ingrained in German society as it was in Great Britain or North America. Drink was thus not something that set workers apart, but rather an element of the social and material world that linked German workers to a broadly based popular culture in which many of their social superiors also participated.

The working class's attachment to drink did not imply perpetual intoxication and was by no means incompatible with participation in the socialist labour movement or even with conventional standards of respectability. Indeed, the labour movement skilfully exploited the tavern and the social ties that centred there and turned popular discontent over the price of alcoholic beverages to political advantage. Its defence of popular living standards was a major factor in the SPD's 1912 electoral victory, which left it the strongest party in the German Reichstag.[77] But at the same time that the labour movement drew strength from its foundations in popular culture, it was also constrained by them. As the eminent bacteriologist and social hygienist Max Gruber argued, alcohol was one of the indispensable foundations of the modern social order. Without it, contemporary social and political conditions would long since have become intolerable.[78] The satisfactions drink and the tavern provided were bound to dull the edge of discontent, lower expectations and ease frustrations with the existing order. For a variety of reasons, the labour movement found it easier to defend this part of the working class's culture than to transform it.

Notes

1.   On German fiscal policy and its political context in this period, see Wilhelm Gerloff, *Die Finanz- und Zollpolitik des Deutschen Reiches, nebst ihren Beziehungen zu Landes- und Gemeindefinanzen von der Gründung des Norddeutschen Bundes bis zur Gegenwart* (Fischer, Jena, 1913), pp. 440-76; Peter-Christian Witt, *Die Finanzpolitik des Deutschen Reichs von 1903 bis 1913: Eine Studie zur Innenpolitik des wilhelminischen Deutschland*, Historische Studien, no. 145 (Matthiesen, Lübeck, 1970).

2.   Among the best contemporary discussions of the Drink Question are the works of the socialist physician Alfred Grotjahn, a pioneer in the field of public health. See his *Der Alkoholismus, nach Wesen, Wirkung und Verbreitung* (Wigand, Leipzig, 1898); and *Alkohol und Arbeitsstätte* (Mässigkeitverlag, Berlin, 1903). For more recent discussions, see Utz Jeggle, 'Alkohol und Industrialisierung' in Herbert Cancik (ed.), *Rausch-Ekstase-Mystik. Grenzformen religiöser Erfahrung* (Patmos, Düsseldorf, 1978), pp. 78-94; and James S. Roberts, 'Der Alkoholkonsum deutscher Arbeiter im 19. Jahrhundert', *Geschichte und Gesellschaft*, vol. 6, no. 2 (1980), pp. 220-42.

3.   For a discussion of the patterns of expenditure on alcohol revealed in contemporary family budget surveys, see James S. Roberts, 'Drink and Working Class Living Standards in Late Nineteenth Century Germany', forthcoming in an as yet untitled collection to be edited by Werner Conze and Ulrich Engelhardt and published in 1981 by the Ernst Klett Verlag (Stuttgart) as part of the Industrielle Welt series.

4.   This point is discussed by Grotjahn, *Alkoholismus*, pp. 230-9. See also James S. Roberts, 'Wirtshaus und Politik in der deutschen Arbeiterbewegung' in Gerhard Huck (ed.), *Sozialgeschichte der Freizeit. Untersuchungen zum Wandel der Alltagskultur in Deutschland* (Hammer, Wuppertal, 1980), pp. 123-39.

5.   Robert Michels, *Zur Soziologie des Parteiwesens in der modernen Demokratie. Untersuchungen über die oligarchischen Tendenzen des Gruppenlebens* (Klinkhardt, Leipzig, 1911), pp. 271-4.

6.   Karl Kautsky, 'Der Alkoholismus und seine Bekämpfung', *Die Neue Zeit*, vol. 9, pt. 2, nos. 27-30 (1890/1), pp. 1-8, 46-55, 77-89, 105-16; here pp. 107-8.

7.   For an example of this orientation, see 'Beiträge zur Alkoholfrage', *Sozialdemokratische Partei-Correspondenz*, vol. 2, no. 34 (1907), pp. 537-40.

8.   The most important response to the Drink Question came from Karl Kautsky and will be discussed more specifically below. See his 'Der Alkoholismus', *passim*.

9.   Ernest Gordon, *The Anti-Alcohol Movement in Europe* (Revell, New

York, 1913), pp. 157-208; F. Hanauer, 'Die sozialistischen Parteien und die Alko-holfrage', *Die Neue Zeit*, vol. 29, pt. 2, no. 49 (1910/1), pp. 828-33; P.E. Prest-wich, 'French Workers and the Temperance Movement', *International Review of Social History*, vol. 25, no. 1 (1980), pp. 35-52; Brian Harrison, *Drink and the Victorians: the Temperance Question in England, 1815-1872* (University of Pitts-burgh Press, Pittsburgh, 1971), pp. 395-405, *passim*.

10.   An anti-spirits movement had developed in Germany under American and British influence in the 1830s, but after the Revolution of 1848 it all but vanished. New organisations were founded in the 1880s and 1890s. A general survey of these developments can be found in Johannes Bergmann and Reinhard Kraut, *Geschichte der Nüchternheitsbestrebungen* (2 vols., Neuland, Hamburg, 1923/4). The temperance movement is treated briefly in Wolfgang Krabbe, *Gesellschaft-sveränderung durch Lebensreform. Strukturmerkmale einer sozialreformerischen Bewegung im Deutschland der Industrialisierungsperiode* (Vandenhoek & Ruprecht, Göttingen, 1974), pp. 37-47. See also James S. Roberts, 'Drink, Temperance and the Working Class in Nineteenth Century Germany', unpublished PhD disserta-tion, University of Iowa, 1979.

11.   See especially Ferdinand Simon, 'Zur Alkoholfrage', *Die Neue Zeit*, vol. 9, pt. 1, no. 15 (1890/1), pp. 483-90.

12.   'Der Alkoholismus', *passim*. The discussion continued with rebuttals and re-rebuttals. See Simon's 'Herrn Kautsky zur Entgegen', *Die Neue Zeit*, vol. 9, pt. 2, no. 36 (1890/1), pp. 309-15; and Kautsky's 'Noch einmal die Alkoholfrage', *Die Neue Zeit*, vol. 9, pt. 2, no. 37 (1890/1) pp. 344-54.

13.   Wilhelm Schröder (ed.), *Handbuch der sozialdemokratischen Parteitage* (Birk, Munich, 1910), pp. 26-31; *Protokoll über die Verhandlungen des Parteitages der Sozialdemokratischen Partei Deutschlands* (1900), pp. 181-3; (1901), pp. 306-7; (1904), pp. 190-8; (1905), pp. 359-60; (1906), pp. 224-7.

14.   By 1911, the last year for which membership figures are available, the DAAB claimed 2,600 members in 109 organisations throughout Germany; Deutscher Arbeiter Abstinenten Bund, *Protokoll der IV. ordentlichen General-Versammlung des Deutschen Arbeiter Abstinenten Bundes zu Berlin, 5. bis 8. April 1912* (Michaelis, Berlin [1912]), p. 12.

15.   The DAAB's leading spokesman was Simon Katzenstein, a lawyer by training who served the labour movement in a variety of capacities. He joined the staff of the SPD's party school in Berlin in 1905 and lectured on trade unionism, the co-operative movement and communal politics. For his views on the Drink Question, see 'Die deutsche Sozialdemokratie und die Alkoholfrage', *Sozialistische Monatshefte*, vol. 11, no. 9 (1907), pp. 760-7. *Moderne Jugendbewegung und Alkoholfrage*, Deutscher Arbeiter Abstinenten Bund Veröffentlichungen, no. 14 (Michaelis, Berlin, n.d.); 'Die Sozialen Beziehungen des Alkoholismus', *Sozial-istische Monatshefte*, vol. 11, no. 6 (1907), pp. 463-71; *Wofür Kämpfen Wir?* Deutsche Arbeiter Abstinenten Bund Veröffentlichungen, no. 8 (Michaelis, Berlin, n.d.).

16.   Emile Vandervelde, 'Die oekonomischen Faktoren des Alkoholismus', *Die Neue Zeit*, vol. 20, pt. 1, no. 24 (1901/2), p. 750; cf. Katzenstein's speech at the SPD's 1903 party congress; *Verhandlungen* (1903), p. 191.

17.   *Verhandlungen* (1907), pp. 345-66, 375-6.

18.   Despite their reservations and some strong words by Wurm against their organisation, members of the DAAB supported the resolution in the interest of establishing a united front on the Drink Question. (*Verhandlungen*) (1907), pp. 366-9; Simon Katzenstein, 'Die Alkoholfrage auf dem Essener Parteitag', *Inter-nationale Monatsschrift zur Erforschung des Alkoholismus und Bekämpfung der Trinksitten*, vol. 17, no. 11 (1907), pp. 331-9.

19.   See, for example, Carl. C.H. von Strauss und Torney, 'Die Alkoholfrage und die Sozialdemokratie', *Mässigkeits-Blätter*, vol. 21, no. 10 (1904), pp. 156-7.

20. Witt, *Finanzpolitik*, Ch. 4, *passim*; Carl. E. Schorske, *German Social Democracy, 1905-1917: the Development of the Great Schism* (Harvard University Press, Cambridge, Mass., 1955; rpt. Harper and Row, New York, 1972), pp. 147-62.

21. Agitational leaflets emphasising these themes are preserved in the Friedrich Ebert Stiftung, Archiv der sozialen Demokratie, Flugblätter Sammlung, 1908-10; International Institute for Social History, Iconographic Department, Deutscher Arbeiter Abstinenten Bund, 1909.

22. Charles Tilly, Louise Tilly and Richard Tilly, *The Rebellious Century, 1830-1930* (Harvard University Press, Cambridge, Mass., 1975), p. 311.

23. *Handwörterbuch der Staatwissenschaften*, 3rd ed, s.v. 'Bier, Bierbrauerei und Bierbesteuerung', by Emil Struve.

24. Gerloff, *Finanz- und Zollpolitik*, pp. 431-2.

25. Ibid., p. 469; SPD, *Handbuch für sozialdemokratische Wähler. Der Reichstag 1907-1911* (Vorwärts, Berlin, 1911), pp. 270-1, 273.

26. The progress of the 'Beer War' was reported in short notices in the working-class press beginning in late August. This account is based on reports in *Der Abstinente Arbeiter* and *Vorwärts*.

27. 'Vom Bierkrieg', *Vorwärts*, 27 Aug. 1909.

28. 'Vom Bierkrieg', *Vorwärts*, 8 Sept. 1909.

29. 'Preussischer Schnaps' in *Marx-Engels-Werke* (Dietz, East Berlin, 1962), 19:37-51.

30. Witt, *Finanzpolitik*, pp. 44-54, *passim*; Hans Rosenberg, *Grosse Depression und Bismarckzeit: Wirtschaftsablauf, Gesellschaft und Politik in Mitteleuropa* (de Gruyter, Berlin, 1967; reprint edn, Ulstein, Frankfurt, 1976), pp. 169-91, *passim*; Hans Ulrich Wehler, *Das Deutsche Kaiserreich, 1871-1918*, Deutsche Geschichte, no. 9, 2nd 3dn, Vandenhoek & Ruprecht, Göttingen, 1975), pp. 142-6.

31. Witt, *Finanzpolitik*, p. 46.

32. SPD, *Handbuch*, pp. 261-2.

33. *Lebensgeschichte eines modernen Fabrikarbeiters* (Diederichs, Jena, 1905; reprint edn, Athenäum, Frankfurt a/M, 1971), pp. 360-1.

34. On the genesis of the *Schnaps* boycott, see 'Vorpostengefechte', *Der Abstinente Arbeiter*, vol. 7, no. 16 (1909), pp. 133-5; 'Zum Schnaps-Boykott', ibid., pp. 143-4; 'Vom Bier-und Schnapskrieg', ibid., pp. 150-1.

35. *Verhandlungen* (1909), pp. 283-6.

36. Ibid., p. 283.

37. Ibid., p. 286.

38. The following discussion is based primarily on excerpts published in various issues of *Der Abstinente Arbeiter*. The opinions of every working-class newspaper were obviously not recorded there, but the selections included did represent both positive and negative points of view and therefore seem to provide a good cross-section of labour movement opinion.

39. 'Zwei Kulturaufgaben', *Vorwärts*, 15 Sept. 1909.

40. Ibid.

41. 'Die Leipziger Tagung', *Vorwärts*, 19 Sept. 1909.

42. 'Pressestimmen', *Der Abstinente Arbeiter*, vol.7, no.19 (1909), pp. 159-61.

43. *Verhandlungen* (1909), p. 285.

44. See below, pp. 23-4.

45. *Vorwärts*, 7 Nov. 1909.

46. 'Der Branntweinboykott', *Vorwärts*, 20 Nov. 1909.

47. 'Der Schnapsboykott', *Die Neue Zeit*, vol. 28, pt. 1, no. 9 (1909/10), pp. 289-91. See also his reply to critics of his initial article: 'Gegen den Sektenfanatismus', ibid., vol. 28, pt. 1, no. 12 (1909/10), pp. 385-8.

48. Mehring, 'Schnapsboykott', p. 289.

49. Ibid., p. 291.

50. 'Der boykottierte Schnapsboykott und die Arbeiterpresse: V', *Der Abstinente Arbeiter*, vol. 8, no. 11 (1909), pp. 91-2.

51. 'Der boykottierte Schnapsboykott und die Arbeiterpresse', *Der Abstinente Arbeiter*, vol. 7, no. 24 (1909), p. 203.

52. Cited in 'Zum Schnapsboykott', *Metallarbeiter-Zeitung*, vol. 27, no. 50 (1909), pp. 399-400.

53. Ibid.

54. R. Darf, 'Wirkt der Schnapsboykott?', *Die Neue Zeit*, vol. 28, pt. 1, no. 11 (1909/10), pp. 380-1.

55. Ibid., p. 380.

56. The socialist *Volkswacht* in Bielefeld, for example, emphasised the potential agitational value of the *Schnaps* boycott:

If there were a clear boundary line between the class-conscious proletariat, between the workers who have joined the modern labour movement and those under the influence of the bourgeois world-view, then the effectiveness of the *Schnaps* boycott would be very doubtful. But such is not the case; everywhere there are points of contact, and precisely the *Schnaps* boycott is a means of gaining influence over those workers who do not yet count themselves among the members of our party and to draw them over to our side.

Cited in 'Der Passionsweg einer Resolution', *Der Abstinente Arbeiter*, vol. 7, no. 23 (1909), p. 193.

57. 'Der Parteitag', *Der Abstinente Arbeiter*, vol. 7, no. 19 (1909), pp. 157-9.

58. Ibid., p. 158.

59. *Verhandlungen* (1910), pp. 393-5, 475-6; (1911), p. 401; (1912), pp. 274-81.

60. 'Die "Wirkung" des Schnapsboykottbeschlusses', *Der Abstinente Arbeiter*, vol. 8, no. 7 (1910), p. 57.

61. The labour movement was in fact held up to considerable ridicule in the German press as a result of the dissensions revealed by the *Schnaps* boycott. Critics found it easy to cite the DAAB for evidence against the party. For a sampling, see: Zentrales Staatsarchiv, Reichslandbund 2613 and 2614, 'Pressearchiv', vol. 1, 1905-10; vol. 2, 1910-14.

62. Gerloff, *Finanz- und Zollpolitik*, pp. 502-3; *Handwörterbuch der Staatswissenschaften*, 3rd edn, s.v. 'Spiritusring', by Behrend; *Verhandlungen* (1912), pp. 120-1.

63. *Verhandlungen* (1912), pp. 274-6.

64. Ibid., p. 280.

65. Ibid., pp. 279-80.

66. Calculated from Walter G. Hoffman *et al.*, *Das Wachstum der deutschen Wirtschaft seit der Mitte des 19. Jahrhunderts* (Springer, Berlin, 1965), pp. 172-4, 652.

67. Witt, p. 314.

68. *Die Arbeiterfrage* (Reinhard, Munich, 1912), pp. 13, 246. Note that Levenstein's findings provide only a very rough approximation of the extent of the boycott's support since his respondents were not asked directly to comment on the boycott. Moreover, some of Levenstein's information was gathered before the Leipzig party congress took place.

69. Ibid., p. 243.

70. Calculated from Hoffman, *Wirtschaft*, pp. 172-4, 652.

71. Ibid.

72. Ibid.

73. Ibid., pp. 172-4, 657.

74. Ibid., pp. 652, 657.

75.   Levenstein, *Arbeiterfrage*, pp. 6-7, 243.

76.   On the distinction between labour movement culture and workers' culture, see Jürgen Kocka, 'Arbeiterkultur als Forschungsthema', *Geschichte und Gesellschaft*, vol. 5, no. 1 (1979), pp. 5-11; Gerhard A. Ritter, 'Workers' Culture in Imperial Germany: Problems and Points of Departure for Research', *Journal of Contemporary History*, vol. 23, no. 2 (1978), pp. 165-90.

77.   Schorske, *Social Democracy*, pp. 226-35; Beverly Heckart, *From Bassermann to Bebel: the Grand Bloc's Quest for Reform in the Kaiserreich, 1900-1914* (Yale University Press, New Haven, Conn., 1974), pp. 186-92.

78.   'Der österreichische Gesetzentwurf zur Bekämpfung der Trunkenheit', *Archiv für soziale Gesetzgebung und Statistik*, vol. 1, no. 2 (1888), pp. 293-320, here p. 306.

4 STEEL, SABOTAGE AND SOCIALISM: THE STRIKE AT THE DORTMUND 'UNION' STEEL WORKS IN 1911

David F. Crew

Scenes from the strike

On the tram.
Conductor: 'The machinists are still on strike.'
Passenger (who appears, from the way he acts, to be a 'Christian')
says that it is the strikers' own fault.
Conductor: 'And then there was that terrible accident.'
Passenger: 'The man was burnt to death on purpose!'
A second passenger: 'You are a nasty sort of fool!'
First passenger: 'I'm not talking to you.'
Second passenger: 'But I *am* talking to you, mate!'

Arbeiter-Zeitung, 27 March 1911

I

The strike at the Dortmund 'Union' steel company which began on 22 March 1911 was not one of the major industrial disputes of the Wilhelmine period. It involved no more than 379 of the almost 7,000 men working there, primarily the machinists and stokers employed in the workshops producing the electricity and steam that powered most of the machinery in this steel mill.[1] The strike lasted only fourteen days and it achieved none of the workers' demands. Yet this brief episode, and others like it, have recently been endowed with considerable significance by Karl-Heinz Roth and Eckard Brockhaus, who have attempted a radical re-interpretation of the history of the German working class. The reason for this is that on the first day of the 'Union' strike there allegedly took place what Brockhaus has called a 'spectacular act of sabotage'.[2] The National Liberal and big-business oriented newspaper, the *Dortmunder Zeitung*, offered the following graphic description:

[The fitter, Friedrich] Schröder. . .was working on the blowing

apparatus with the machinist Werner, who has since fled. The blowing machine stood in the machine shop and its function was to direct
air through the converter in the 'Thomaswerk'. Under the machine, in
the cellar, there were two electric pumps, only one of which was in
use. These electric pumps, which Werner was supposed to look after,
provided power for the crane and the converter in the 'Thomaswerk'.

At about seven a.m., the first machinist, Jansen, started to make
coffee. Werner said to Schröder that he would now stop the blowing
apparatus and told him to go down into the cellar and stop the pump.
Schröder obeyed and shortly afterwards Werner came down to check
that he had done it correctly. . .

Switching off the machine had, however, caused a terrible accident. Converter No.4 toppled as it was deprived of power. Some of
the molten iron flowed over the central crane which was located
nearby. And while everyone else was able to get out of the way in
time, the crane driver, Wiscozyl, was badly burnt by the splashes of
molten iron. A doctor reported today that shreds of charred skin
were hanging from the unfortunate man's body and his face, teeth
and hands were almost completely carbonized. The man died three
hours after the accident in dreadful pain.

A representative of the firm estimated that the damages caused by
this sudden work stoppage would come to about 700 marks in all,
600 of this being for iron and rolling machinery which was now
useless.[3]

Karl-Heinz Roth and Eckhard Brockhaus view such incidents as the
symptoms of a major transformation of the German working class that
began in the two decades before the First World War. But this transformation was scarcely reflected in the structures and the policies of the
'official' working-class organisations, the Social Democratic Party and
its 'Free' trade unions. Indeed, for Karl-Heinz Roth, the tragedy of the
working class in Germany since the late nineteenth century can be
summed up in this fundamental contradiction: 'upheaval of the social
structure [of the working class] and stagnation of the processes of political organisation'.[4] Both the party and the unions were, in Roth's view,
built upon the skilled workers' special position in capitalist production.
Until the late nineteenth century, he contends, the relationship between
capital and labour in Germany was determined by the heavy dependence of German capital upon the 'specialised worker' (*Facharbeiter*).
After 1890, this economic and technical *status quo* produced and was
in turn supported by a political *modus vivendi*:

The workers of the optical and light engineering industries of Saxony and Württemburg, and the tool-making and precision engineering industries of Berlin sold their labour as dearly as possible. In many firms they managed to wring from the capitalists considerable concessions with regard to wages, an eight-hour day, free Saturdays, etc., long before the November Revolution. They were able to do this because the division of labour was written into the framework of the *status quo* by means of continual political pressure.[5]

But although Wilhelmine capitalism paid dearly for the services of the 'specialised worker', it gained a good deal more than simply his labour power. Precisely because they were able to force significant concessions from capital, the highly skilled workers became the 'pillar[s] of support for and the motivating force behind Wilhelmine working-class reformism'.[6] And reformism clearly did not constitute a fundamental challenge to the capitalist ownership of the means of production or to the capitalist state.

However, when employers in certain industries — coal-mining, the iron and steel industry and, eventually, engineering — began to rationalise production, the privileged position of the 'specialised worker' was undermined. Now skilled workers increasingly were replaced by a new class of unskilled and semi-skilled workers, many of them women and youths, who experienced none of the conditions of work or of life that had given rise to the peculiar mentality of the 'specialised worker':

> In contrast with the metal workers and the officials of the German Metalworkers' Union (Deutscher Metallarbeiter-Verband) this class does not identify itself with the course and content of the production process. It is barbarically uncivilised, it attends no workers' educational associations, it is incapable of making a questionable *status quo* the starting point for a 'socialist' strategy for accelerated economic development. It is the 'mob', erratic, aggressive, inclined to acts of violence and 'apolitical'.[7]

For these new *Massenarbeiter*, in the view of Karl-Heinz Roth, the established forms of trade union and party organisation were wholly inappropriate. Therefore, the new 'mass workers' developed their own, separate 'forms of struggle' against capital, ranging from frequent job-changing to violence against employers and police and even to sabotage. These new forms of resistance, intermittent, spontaneous and geographically dispersed as they were, nevertheless constituted what Roth calls 'the "other" working-class movement [*die "andere" Arbeiterbewegung*]'. Not the product of reformist organisations but of a 'daily bush war fought against the organisation of work and the division of labour', this 'other working class movement', as Roth sees it, possessed a far greater revolutionary potential than the official labour movement.[8] For the Social Democratic Party and the 'Free' trade unions,

> the transition to socialism appeared. . .as a relatively harmonious and harmless operation carried on at the level of society. . .and proletarian revolution a thing to be patiently waited for, to be achieved in small steps. . .a thing completely removed from the disorder of revolutionary violence and armed revolt.[9]

By contrast, the 'other working-class movement' was a form of 'proletarian self-organisation which fought the division between political and trade union institutions at its very roots and [which] conceived of the revolutionary, work-based organisation as starting-point for proletarian revolt'.[10] Between the two movements there was clearly 'an unbridgeable chasm' that was only spanned in the years before the war by the increasing attempts of the trade unions and the SPD to suppress the specific forms of struggle developed by the 'mass workers' (*Massenarbeiter*) who now constituted a growing majority of the German working class.[11]

In the German steel industry, the creation of the new 'mass worker' began, so Eckhard Brockhaus contends, with the introduction of the Bessemer-Thomas process after 1880. With this new technology at their disposal, German employers could rapidly reduce the level of skill required to make steel.[12] Working conditions consequently became even worse than those in the mining industry.[13] The 'Free' trade unions and the SPD were able to do little to protect skilled steelworkers, such as puddlers, against this onslaught. Nor could they later gain any ground in the massive, new, autocratically managed steel mills of the Ruhr. Unable, so Brockhaus claims, fully to comprehend the new technology and the new division of labour within the steel mills, the skilled workers who were the backbone of the German Metalworkers' Union could develop no union strategy in this industry which enabled steelworkers to fight effectively for an improvement in their relationship with their employers in the workplace. 'The trade unions are practically [that is, as a power factor] non-existent in this sector.'[14] They could only fall back upon 'an impotent appeal to the "socially concerned" legislator to awaken the public conscience to take up the cause of these poor, helpless people'.[15] The impotence of the official trade union movement thus prompted rank-and-file steelworkers to develop novel forms of resistance to their employers. The sabotage incident that allegedly occurred during the 1911 Dortmund 'Union' strike provided a spectacular example of this new activity.

II

But closer examination of the Dortmund strike suggests that Karl-Heinz Roth's and Eckhard Brockhaus' understanding of the popular meaning and significance of trade unionism and socialism during this period is much too limited. What is missing from the 'mass worker' hypothesis, indeed, what is totally distorted by it, is the actual political context within which rank-and-file consciousness and behaviour were formed. Because they assume that the experience of rationalised capitalist production necessarily alienated the 'mass worker' from the ideology and the tactics of the 'Free' trade unions and the SPD, they do not bother to consider whether there might have been some connection between such 'exceptional' acts as sabotage and the more 'normal' forms of trade union activity and SPD politics, although there are strong indications that such a connection existed. Moreover, their identification of 'reformism' with only certain forms of behaviour and their assumption that violent acts must in some way have been more 'revolutionary' (or, at least, more 'proto-revolutionary') prevents them from seeing the ways in which an admittedly reformist trade union practice, in the specific context of the steel industry, might well have prepared the way for the incidents associated with the 1911 'Union' strike.

This possibility was, however, not ignored by at least one contemporary observer. In a speech delivered to a meeting of the Verein deutscher Eisenhüttenleute (an association of iron and steel industrialists) in Düsseldorf on 24 March 1911, Professor Ludwig Bernhard, a political economist at the University of Berlin, attempted to establish a direct link between the events in Dortmund and the recent development of the German trade union movement. According to Bernhard, the Dortmund strike demonstrated the degeneration (*Entartung*) of German trade unionism which was being caused by the 'muscling in [on the unions] of the unskilled masses'. Trade unionism in Germany was no longer (if indeed it ever had been) a force for social order and progress.[16]

Bernhard had studied with the liberal political economist and social thinker, Lujo Brentano. But, by the time he gave his Düsseldorf speech, he had clearly moved to the right of Brentano on the 'Social Question'. Indeed, Brentano charged that Bernhard's assertions with regard to the Dortmund strike constituted

> a complete renunciation of your earlier views. . .Formerly, your ideas were close to those who saw the reason for the defects of the present labour/capital relationship in the fact that collective bargaining had no legal recognition and thought that these defects could be remedied by the passing of laws and the existence of legal sanctions. Now you have gone over to the side of those who, for forty years, have fought by means of what you yourself called 'welfare slavery' against negotiating about working conditions with organised workers and who have used their powerful political influence to that end.[17]

Brentano claimed that Bernhard's assertions could only be the result of 'complete ignorance of the facts or. . .ill-will' as it was unclear that there had even been a case of sabotage at the Dortmund 'Union'.[18] But whatever the reasons for Bernhard's conversion 'from a Saul to a Paul, the propagandist for the extreme right', the political implications of his changed opinions were obvious:

> You now see no other means of redressing the damage caused by the present state of anarchy which governs the regulation of working conditions than the use of government force to protect those willing to work, i.e. violence. . .but you will have as little success with this medicine as those who cheered you in Düsseldorf. Force without a remedy for the disease is always the answer given by political incompetents — to use it you need no further investigation of the underlying causes, i.e. no scientific inquiry; all that is required is a belief in the efficacy of the holy power of the police.[19]

Brentano did not deny that there might be some disruptions as trade unionism came to embrace increasing numbers of German workers, but he saw no reason to revise his own views:

> The events of recent years, which on the face of it, seem to contradict my theories and those of the Webbs, in fact constitute a well-known phenomenon, and that which you regard as the 'degeneration' of the trade unions is nothing more than an intermediate stage in the development of working-class organisation which can be found among all categories of workers before they have been educated by the organisation.[20]

Of course, much of the force of Brentano's attack upon Bernhard rested on his assertion that there had in fact not been a case of sabotage during the 1911 strike in Dortmund. But this argument, as A. Voigt pointed out in an article which commented upon the exchange between Brentano and Bernhard, seemed to be based on a complete contravention of Brentano's own scientific rules of method. Brentano had often argued that 'social facts' could not be discovered directly from the testimony of 'interested parties'. Yet in this instance Brentano had based his interpretation solely on a report published in the *Newsletter of the General Committee of the Trade Unions of Germany (Korrespondenzblatt der Generalkommission der Gewerkschaften Deutschlands)* which, as Voigt pointed out, had an obvious interest in hushing up any hint of sabotage.[21] Brentano had committed this obvious error, so Voigt suggested, because 'It is hard for humans to acknowledge facts and truths that contradict their pet theories and plans,' a maxim which, up until then, had been another of Brentano's 'scientific rules'. Bernhard had thus been attacked not because his facts were wrong, but because he had dared to contest the 'pet theory of his teacher. . .according to which trade union organisation and collective bargaining were the best means of ensuring social peace'.[22]

Initially, the national and local Free trade union and Social Democratic Party press did not comment at great length on the incidents of 22 March. The reason for this silence was that the trade union and party leaders saw the Dortmund 'Union' strike not as a symptom of the 'deterioration' of the trade union movement but rather as a substantial breakthrough for organised labour in Ruhr heavy industry. They did not wish to mar or diminish the significance of this development by focusing, as the bourgeois press was doing, on what seemed in reality simply another case of accidental death in the steel industry. Deadly accidents, as the local daily socialist newspaper, the *Arbeiter Zeitung*, pointed out, happened every week in the Ruhr steel mills without attracting any of the attention currently being devoted to this particular instance. Far from representing a new, barbarous phase in industrial and class relations, as some of the bourgeois papers were arguing, the Dortmund 'Union' strike represented a first, progressive step away from the barbarity that had existed until then in the Ruhr steel industry:

It has taken a long time for the enslaved workers of the iron and steel industry to remember their human dignity. All around them, masses of workers have come to life; in all the trades they have sought better wages and working conditions. For a long time, all this passed the steelworkers by without a trace. Behind the walls and doors of heavy industry, the air was leaden and oppressive. . .[But] the raging of the storm has cleansed the thick air. First it was the miners who, through the explosive outburst of their accumulated discontent, came to recognise the value of organisation and who are now consciously and carefully hammering out their own destiny within the Social Democratic movement. And now their brothers from the steel works follow.[23]

Of course it had to be admitted that the strike itself had achieved no concrete gains for the steelworkers at the 'Union'. Yet even in this defeat the local socialist press found a certain kind of victory:

Although the workers' struggle has brought them no direct advantage, it must not be overlooked that in terms of experience this sort of strike can operate in the workers' favour, if the entrepreneur has suffered a significant loss. The 'Union' itself best knows the enormous injury it has had to sustain as the result of its hard-line attitude towards the workers. This loss will however operate from now on in the workers' favour. . .the burnt child keeps away from the fire. The 'Union' will think twice before it brings this sort of harm down upon its head again. . . One cannot judge the effect of the strike simply by the numbers of those who walked out and those who stayed. . . The directors of the 'Union' now know what they formerly did not wish to believe. . . Now the time is drawing near when the long, preparatory work of Social Democracy will finally produce results. . . The old days are gone, and Thyssen, Krupp and Stinnes must reconcile themselves to that fact. If they do not then they must pay the price. In heavy industry too, the worker quite rightly wants to play a part in the determination of his conditions of work. And this 'trend of the times', which is based on the very nature of [modern] technology, can only be somewhat delayed; but no power in the world can force it to a halt.[24]

But this flurry of self-congratulation could not obscure the fact that something quite unusual — whether sabotage or simply an accident — *had* occurred during the first day of the strike, that this incident *had* already assumed a considerable political significance in the contemporary debate on the German labour movement and that it must therefore be examined and explained by the Free trade unions and the SPD.

For even if the SPD and the unions could have afforded simply to dismiss as reactionary and irresponsible the kinds of charges levelled by Bernhard, they could not ignore the responses of liberal voters, of the Christian trade unions and of the Centre Party. Before the war, Dortmund was certainly one of the strongholds of the SPD; the Free trade unions and the party had an important working-class base in the town and the strike at the 'Union' suggested to them the possibility of expanding that constituency. At the same time, Dortmund was the home of the Christian trade union movement and, as was frequently the case in the mixed Protestant/Catholic industrial towns of the Ruhr, the Centre Party also had a considerable political foothold in the working class.[25]

Founded in 1899, the Christian Metalworkers' Union, like the somewhat older and larger Christian Miners' Union (formed in 1894) attempted to offer 'non-socialist' Catholic and Protestant workers an alternative to 'socialist' Free trade unions. Although the German Metalworkers' Union (DMV) had more than 500,000 members nationally by 1911, the national membership of the Christian Metalworkers' Union had reached almost 34,000 by early 1910.[26] Although the DMV normally attempted to deny the importance of the Christian Metalworkers' Union or to brand it as nothing more than a 'tool of the employers', in reality it could hardly afford to ignore the reaction of 'Christian' workers to the alleged sabotage at the Dortmund 'Union'.[27] Local leaders of the Christian Metalworkers' Union refused to join the strike before it began, labelling it an 'illegal walkout'. Predictably, then, the Centre Party press painted an even harsher picture of the events of the first strike day than that presented by Bernhard. Coming, as it did, in the midst of preparations for the 1912 Reichstag elections, the 'Union' strike was interpreted by the Centre Party as nothing more than an attempt to spread socialist electoral influence. The Free trade unions, so the Centre Party newspaper, *Tremonia*, charged, were only 'training camps or, rather, touts for Social Democracy', which had engaged in this strike with no particular concern for its success or failure but rather with a single-minded interest in winning more workers to the SPD camp.[28] For this purpose, a failed strike, so *Tremonia* claimed, was regarded by the socialists as even more valuable than a successful one. A long, bitter and ultimately fruitless labour dispute should convince workers of the need to represent their interests politically through the Social Democratic Party. Indeed, *Tremonia* alleged that a local socialist leader had actually said, 'I prefer a lost strike that lasts 14 weeks to a victory that only takes 14 days.'[29] From *Tremonia*'s point of view, therefore, the responsibility for Wiscozyl's death was not Werner's and Schröder's alone: 'All the operatives at the strike meeting who were in favour of the worthless plan of suddenly stopping work at 7 o'clock the following morning are morally guilty of the poor man's death.'[30]

III

Faced with an open accusation that they were prepared to encourage some workers to endanger the lives of others for the sake of political ends, the SPD and the Free trade unions could not afford to remain silent. But the political responses of the working class in Dortmund and Germany were not all that concerned the party and the unions. By late 1910, as Ralf Lützenkirchen has shown in his admirable study of the Dortmund SPD, the 'radicals' had lost their last centres of strength within the local party organisation. Konrad Haenisch, the radical leader and editor of the Dortmund *Arbeiter Zeitung*, a man who had strenuously argued against electoral alliances with bourgeois political parties, had already left the city. The party had come under a reformist leadership which clearly understood that the 'Union' strike threatened to destroy any possibility of an electoral alliance with Left Liberals and National Liberals in the approaching elections. For this reason, as well as their desire to calm the fears of their working-class constituency, the SPD and the Free trade unions eventually found it necessary to produce a politically effective statement about the events of the first strike day. They could no longer afford simply to ignore the alleged 'sabotage' at the Dortmund 'Union'.[31]

But while this specific political conjuncture required the SPD and the unions to say something about the 'sabotage' at the 'Union', these same political circumstances restricted the kinds of interpretations they could advance. The *Arbeiter Zeitung*, for example, suggested that the trial later held to determine whether Werner and Schröder were guilty of wilful damage to property and 'negligent homicide' served instead only to expose the dangerous practices of the company itself. Schröder, the paper contended, had not been properly trained and instructed. Like many other workers in Ruhr steel works, he had been expected to observe safety regulations which he had not even been allowed sufficient time to read and which he probably would not have understood fully in any case:

The worker perhaps remembers seeing thousands of signatures; the official is in a hurry, because there is no time in the busy works. So the worker signs his name; what he has signed and agreed to he does not know. But in fact he has indicated that he has received and understood various documents. . .[including] a copy of the safety regulations and goodness knows what else.[32]

Ignorance of the appropriate safety measures was, however, not the only problem. Even if the worker did know what the proper procedure was in a given instance, he was seldom allowed to follow it:

> How often has the workers' press pointed out that while the great iron and steel works agree in principle to the various safety regulations, they take little trouble to see that they are properly carried out. Regulations abound. The crane should only be loaded to a certain limit. But if the crane driver were to insist on keeping to that limit he could well fall foul of his masters and become branded as a 'rebellious employee'. . . Another rule states that it is strictly forbidden to oil a machine while it is in use. But the slightest halt in production has to be entered into a control book and woe to the worker who enters a few, idle, profitless moments.
>
> We further maintain that with the present mad rush and the huge numbers of workers it is impossible to follow all the regulations to the letter without bringing production to a halt.[33]

The employers' outcry over the death of Wiscozyl therefore seemed completely hypocritical and self-serving to the editors of the *Arbeiter Zeitung*. Workers were injured or died in the steel mills every week of the year. Yet this careless, day-to-day wastage of human lives was ignored, except in the columns of the working-class press. Ironically, then, the Dortmund 'sabotage trial' was beneficial to the cause of the workers in the steel mills because what began as an attempt by the state and the capitalists to indict the labour movement ended up, at least in the view of the *Arbeiter Zeitung*, as a complete condemnation of capitalist practice:

> In so far as the usual system prevailing at the 'Union' was disclosed, the troublemakers achieved the opposite of what they had intended. The capitalists' drive for increased production and profit has now been exposed to public ridicule.[34]

The SPD could so confidently employ the outcome of the trial as the occasion for an attack upon the big capitalists of the Ruhr because the case against Schröder had to be dismissed. The state could find no firm evidence to prove that he had acted with the intent of destroying property or endangering life.[35] Indeed, the national newspaper of the German Metalworkers' Union argued that Schröder could not really have understood the consequences of his actions because

> his knowledge of the nature of production in the factory was quite deficient. [The trial had shown that] he had only a very rough idea of the relationship between the pressure-pump and the steel works and he had never even seen a converter.[36]

Defending Werner, the machinist who had fled rather than stand trial, was a more difficult proposition since his flight seemed to constitute an admission of guilt. But the party and the unions responded to this challenge by situating Werner's individual case within the larger context of their understanding of social relations in heavy industry and of Prussian 'justice'. In doing so, they presented arguments which had come to form the central elements of trade union and party discourse on the 'labour question' in the Ruhr and other districts of Germany where heavy industry predominated.[37] In regions where smaller factories were more common, so this argument ran, the relationship between capitalist and workers was mediated and its harshness mitigated by the capacity workers had developed to engage in organised, collective resistance under the auspices of the SPD and the Free trade unions. But the iron- and steelworkers seemed peculiarly defenceless. In part, this reflected the low cultural level thought to be characteristic of the workers who were drawn into this industry. Often newly arrived from the eastern provinces where they had been under the yoke of East Prussian Junkerdom, the Catholic church and the general backwardness of rural life, and frequently speaking mainly Polish, these workers could not be expected quickly to attain the more advanced levels of trade union consciousness of their west German comrades. The Dortmund *Arbeiter Zeitung* pointed out, for example, that the strike at the 'Union' had fallen apart after fourteen days largely because 'a proportion of the workers proved to be insufficiently schooled in trade unionism'.[38] Yet even a militant west German worker might find that his trade union consciousness would be dimmed by the peculiarly abject and oppressive conditions of the steel mills. The SPD and the Free trade unions found the most disturbing feature of steel-mill labour, from which many of the other problems seemed to flow, to be the steelworkers' lack of skill and of the independence and self-respect that skill alone was assumed to bestow:

The insufficient education of the worker for responsible positions is not restricted to the 'Union' steel mills. For reasons of profit, there is no real period of apprenticeship at all. In the reports of the factory inspectors for 1909, the following can be found [for the administrative district of Arnsberg];

> The larger steel works, in particular those that have a high turn-over of workers, often shorten the apprenticeship of some workers to a few weeks, even a few days, and allow them to take on even the most difficult tasks after such a short trial period, if they seem to be capable.[39]

This deprivation of skill (in the sense that this term was understood by the SPD and the Free trade unions) stripped the worker of his individual and collective capacity to resist capitalist depradations. Consequently, iron- and steelworkers were subjected to daily physical torment for the sake of ever-increasing profits, a torment which itself further contributed to their collective impotence:

> The extraordinarily hard physical labour and long working hours often destroy the foundry-man before his time, and deaden him mentally, so that far too frequently he allows himself to be misused by his enemies against the interests of his own class.[40]

To this physical devastation were added psychological and social disorganisation. The individual worker's fear, anxiety and suspicion blocked the emergence of any strong sense of collective interest. A report published by the German Metalworkers' Union in 1912 contended that it was not uncommon for workers to be offered bonuses for reporting on the trade union activities of their colleagues.[41] Indeed, the *Arbeiter Zeitung* claimed that in most iron and steel works

> an extensive spy system existed and whoever came under 'suspicion' was quickly denounced and thrown out of work... Often it was only by changing their profession that steel workers could avoid starving to death. Hand in hand with this spy system went the most nauseating toadyism — to ensure one's job it was often useful to have a pretty wife willing to perform the appropriate services [for the foreman]. The iron- and steelworkers knew of many masters and other works officials who reportedly would ensure an extra shift and a good wage packet for this sort of consideration.[42]

Such workers, seemingly crushed in spirit as well as in body, were hardly capable of engaging in so defiant an act as sabotage, or so at least the SPD and the Free trade unions wished to argue. Schröder was indeed acquitted by the court because he had been shown to be incapable, whether from the point of view of technical knowledge or simply initiative, of consciously attempting sabotage.[43] Werner's motives were less easily established since, regrettably, he had fled rather than stand trial; but even his flight was turned to good account by the socialist and trade union press. While deploring Werner's lack of 'manliness' in not staying to fight for 'justice', Franz Scheffel, a union leader who commented at length on the trial in the *Correspondenzblatt*, argued that his cowardice was understandable:

We cannot explain to ourselves exactly why he took flight. Perhaps he felt that as a poor ignorant worker he had no chance against the powerful 'Union'. He was one of those arrested on the morning of the strike and was only released after 36 hours' imprisonment through the good offices of the lawyer Frank. . . It is not impossible that this incident could have destroyed Werner's faith in the German legal system. Perhaps he was unwilling to spend another lengthy period 'behind Swedish curtains' [i.e. in gaol] and pre-empted this by flight. That is certainly not a manly thing to do and we do not defend it. But views and tastes differ in this respect and it's not everyone's cup of tea to allow themselves to be imprisoned for an offence they did not commit.[44]

The socialist and trade union commentators who examined the Dortmund 'Union' strike had really not come much closer to a reconstruction of the actual meaning of the events of the first strike day than had the contributors to the bourgeois press. Indeed, socialist and trade union writers consistently refused even to consider whether or not there had actually been an attempt to sabotage the works and what the conceivable motivations for such an act might have been. Because they clearly recognised the political uses to which charges of sabotage could be put at a time when the government was considering new restrictions of such trade union activities as striking and picketing, socialist and trade union leaders insisted upon depicting Werner, Schröder and their fellow steelworkers as helpless and downtrodden, incapable of any form of resistance to their employers until unions and the party had begun to extend their civilising hand into the steel industry.[45] But it was precisely this desire to prove that the Free trade unions and the SPD were civilising influences among the newly organised and unskilled, despite the charges of degeneration raised by Bernhard and other critics, that prevented union and party leaders from seeing that it was in large measure their own attempts to organise and politicise the Ruhr steelworkers that created the context in which such an incident as the 1911 Dortmund 'sabotage strike' could even be possible.

IV

That the strike occurred in 1911 was surely not unrelated to the fusion in 1910 of the Dortmund 'Union', until then an independent company, with the German-Luxemburg Mining Company (Deutsch-Luxemburgische Bergwerksgesellschaft) owned by Hugo Stinnes, who already had a reputation as a 'rationalising' employer in the coal industry.[46] The 1905 miners' strike, which was directed against the increasing intensification of labour in the coal-mines, began with a local conflict in Stinnes-owned mines in Langendreer.[47] Now Stinnes' profit-maximising activities were also having their effect upon steelworkers:

> In the 'Thomaswerk' there have been scarcely any technological improvements in the last few years. In 1907, 118 workers at the plant produced 448 tons of 'Thomas' steel per shift. Now, 78 workers produce 528 tons. In the steel plate department in 1907, 110 workers processed 400 large plates; now the same number of workers processes 500. In the construction materials department, production has increased since 1907 by 15-20 per cent with the same number of workers and without any technological improvements taking place.[48]

Not only had the pace of work increased but, in the months just before the strike, wages were cut. The strikers therefore demanded that all categories of workers involved in the strike receive either specified wage increases or a 15 per cent pay rise and that a definite wage scale be adopted. The strikers argued that '[i]n the face of continually rising prices, the present wage cut means that the wages paid are completely insufficient. The wages which are being demanded are in some instances lower than those paid formerly.'[49] But the striking 'Union' workers were not interested simply in restoring old wage levels or even getting more money for more work; they also demanded that the working day be limited to a 12-hour shift, that overtime be avoided when possible and if overtime was necessary it should be paid at between 25 and 33 per cent more than the usual rate. Any work performed on Sundays or legal holidays must be paid at time and a half. The 'Union' strikers also demanded improvements in working conditions. Wooden shoes and protective suits were to be provided by the company when workers had to clean the boilers and gas pipes or engage in especially dirty repair work. Machinists were no longer to be required to perform work outside the machine house. There were to be sufficient washing and bathing facilities and adequate ventilation in the gas works.[50] Finally, a workers' committee (*Arbeiterausschuss*) was to be formed from among the machinists and boiler personnel 'which must be listened to at all times by the firm's management'.[51]

These were all eminently 'reformist' demands and they were fully supported not only by the Free trade unions but also by the Christian Metalworkers' Union. But what these two different groups of unions could not agree on was the possibility and necessity of achieving these demands by going on strike at that time. The Christian Metalworkers' Union repeatedly argued during the strike that economic struggles must exclude any connection with the broader and necessarily separate field of electoral competition. Electoral politics must not be allowed to dictate the timing and the nature of the economic struggles. Strikes should coincide with economic, not political, conjunctures. And trade union coalitions must be formed without regard for political vendettas: 'common interests are to be jointly represented'.[52]

However, the problem in 1911 was that none of the political conditions for trade union co-operation existed. Indeed, quite the opposite. From the point of view of the Christian trade unions and the Centre Party, the Free trade unions and the SPD had acted in a wholly undemocratic fashion by consistently engaging in a 'policy of exclusion' (*Ausschaltungspolitik*). Although it legitimately represented organised workers at the 'Union', the Christian Metalworkers' Union had been barred from the wage discussions that preceded the strike and for this reason alone it was not prepared to support the walk-out. Beyond this, however, the Christian Metalworkers' Union judged the strike to be stupid and senseless. It had no chance of success and its results were entirely predictable: 'Over 100 operatives, including many older workers, now find themselves on the streets and have not been reinstated. These are the consequences of Social Democratic agitation. . . Social Democracy, your name is betrayal of the workers.'[53]

Yet, behind this economic stupidity, so the Christian trade union leaders thought, lurked political cunning. Although the 1912 general elections lay just in sight, the so-called ' "Free" trade unions. . .are already beginning with their propaganda'.[54] In the eyes of the 'Christian' leaders, the strike was merely one element of this electoral campaign. Whether it was won or lost, the SPD expected to gain many new converts. Indeed the failure of the strike was likely to encourage more workers to vote for the Social Democracy, but also to provide a useful political weapon with which to attack the Christian trade unions and the Centre Party and to attempt to split both from their local constituents: 'putting all reason aside, [the Free trade unions] gave top priority to the battle with the despised Christian trade unions. The Christian Metalworkers' Union. . .had to have the ground cut out from under it at all costs.'[55] But this time, so the local Centre Party newspaper, *Tremonia*, claimed, the socialist tactics had backfired. Although the strike had been lost, workers at the 'Union' did not seem to blame the Christian Metalworkers' Union for not having taken part. In fact:

> [t]his organisation is stronger than ever. . .and the proud local branch of the Social Democratic machinists' union, which did not need the Christian workers, lies in ruins. In Berlin, its chairman, Scheffel, can now raise the same cry as the Emperor Augustus in Rome: Varus, Varus, bring back my legions.[56]

The Catholic *Tremonia* thought it quite unlikely that the SPD and the Free trade unions would learn their lesson from this experience. But German workers could not afford to be so thick-headed. 'In order to serve the propaganda interests of the Social Democratic Party', the Free trade unions were fully prepared 'for hundreds, even thousands of working class families to lose their daily bread'.[57] If 'Christian' and other 'non-socialist' workers wished to prevent this happening again and again in the future, then they must join the Christian trade unions:

> Only in this way can the Social Democratic terror be fought. . .Only if the workers in the Christian trade unions stand firmly together can the filthy handiwork of certain agitators be stopped and the working class saved from another defeat like that at the 'Union'. . . As free workers, organised in Christian trade unions, non-Social Democrats can take a hand themselves in improving their economic position. However, where the power of comradeship rules the trade through Social Democracy there is no longer room for the Christian worker, as the situation in the chemical and engraving trades and many others demonstrates.[58]

As spokesmen not only for the 'Christian' but for other 'non-socialist' workers, the Christian trade unions would try to check the SPD's efforts to dictate trade union policy for its own political ends. But to do that, they must be guaranteed the right to speak out freely within the labour movement:

> Christian workers will only take part in strikes and show their solidarity when the right to participate in decision-making is guaranteed first and foremost. However, where, as in Dortmund at the 'Union', a strike is aimed against the Christian trade unions, then they will refuse to participate in sabotaging their own organisations, as 'only the dumbest calves choose their own butchers.'[59]

The Christian trade unions therefore presented a position which was neither strictly confessional nor *wirtschaftsfriedlich* (economically non-combative). The Christian Metalworkers' Union clearly regarded its natural constituency as more than simply 'Christian' metalworkers; it appealed to all 'non-socialists' who did not wish to engage in strikes just to further SPD electoral aims. That did not, however, mean that the Christian Metalworkers' Union was simply recommending a form of 'yellow unionism'. It was quite prepared to fight the employers when necessary, as the strike at a zinc foundry in Dortmund led by the Christian trade unions that same spring clearly indicated.[60] But strikes could not, so they argued, carelessly be provoked just for the sake of a few more votes at the polls. Thus, despite their initial plea that 'economics' and 'politics' be kept strictly apart, the Christian trade unions came to the conclusion that only a strong commitment to democratic, pluralist, trade union politics could ensure the impartial pursuit of the economic interests of German workers.

The Free trade unions and the SPD also began by arguing that a distinction between 'economics' and 'politics' existed and must be maintained: 'The strike of the "Union" workers is an economic struggle. It is not directed by a political party. The strikers did not consider political questions in their meetings.'[61] But it soon became clear that this argument was either naïve or dissembling. Politics was as much at issue in the 1911 strike for the 'Free' as for the Christian trade unions. The experience of economic struggles, like the 1911 strike, must, so the socialist press argued, progressively educate the German working class to accept that there could be only one party of the working class, the SPD, and only one legitimate form of trade unionism, the Free trade unions. The record of past strikes in the Ruhr had already shown that if workers failed to achieve their material aims this was not the result of the programmatic and tactical shortcomings of the SPD and the Free trade unions but of the 'betrayal' of the German working class by the Centre Party and the Christian trade unions. Little could be expected from a party that

> preferred to sneak around the drawing rooms of the powerful rather than witnessing directly the appalling stench of the latrines, the filthy drinking water of the steel works. That sort of thing is not fitting for a 'respectable, bourgeois' member of the Reichstag; that can be left to the poor suckers, the 'proles' (*Proleten*) of the Social Democratic working class.[62]

Nor could German workers trust a trade union leadership that declared, as the Christian Metalworkers' Union had done the day before the 'Union' strike:

> If the operatives, stokers, crane drivers, etc., of the 'Union' steel works go out on strike over the proposed demand for a 15 per cent wage increase, the members of the Christian Metalworkers' Union will continue to work. As far as the union is concerned, its members are free to fill the jobs that have been deserted.[63]

But the attack upon the Christian Metalworkers' Union contained an important contradiction. The SPD and the Free trade unions were intent on stressing the damaging effects upon the strike of the 'Christians' ' treacherousness. Yet, at the same time, they could not resist pointing out the pitiful weakness of their rivals:

> If the Christians really believe that we needed their three men, then we can only laugh at them (which in fact happened in the meeting) ... It is vain boasting on the part of the Christians. . .Kreil and his little band of pilgrims hold a meeting of four men [*sic*] and then think they can amaze the public with a great fuss about their 'unanimity'.[64]

Although such statements seemed to justify the exclusion of the Christian Metalworkers' Union from the discussions before the strike, they also diminished the credibility of the socialists' claim that the strike eventually failed because of the 'Christian' betrayal. Indeed, one Christian trade union leader took great delight in drawing attention to the inconsistency of arguing that 'the Christian Metalworkers' Union plays no significant role at the "Union" but, on the other hand. . .is responsible for the defeat.'[65]

Since the socialist press could not resolve this contradiction, it simply resorted to increasingly scornful and bitter invective. The Centre Party and the Christian Metalworkers' Union were described not only as 'strikebreakers' but even as the 'hyenas of the economic field of struggle'.[66] Christian leaders were, on one occasion, described as 'shabby and filthy' and it was suggested that when they joined a wage movement 'they start by shouting long and loud, and then secretly inform the management of everything'. One Free trade union leader even claimed that Kreil, the local secretary of the Christian Metalworkers' Union, was urging those of his members who were on strike at the local zinc foundry to 'scab' at the 'Union' because he could no longer find the money to pay them strike benefits.[67]

V

These charges may have helped to obscure the fact that even with the support of the Christian Metalworkers' Union, the strikers would still have had little chance of success. Certainly the management showed no signs of being willing to negotiate collectively with the striking workers. After the strike began, they broke off all discussion with the unions and concentrated their energies upon procuring enough strikebreakers to keep the plant in operation.[68] Striking workers were sent dismissal notices by registered post and those who were living in company housing were evicted.[69] Efforts to involve the state as a mediator failed completely. Near the end of the strike, the national chairman of the Centralverband der Maschinisten und Heizer, Franz Scheffel, along with the union's regional secretary from Cologne, petitioned the Lord Mayor of Dortmund to intercede. The company curtly answered the Lord Mayor by stating that 'it could not consider [his] mediation because of the violent manner in which work had been halted'.[70] If the Dortmund 'Union' was prepared to concede any role to the local authorities in the 1911 strike it was certainly not that of arbitrator. On the first day of the strike, the 'Union' management had allegedly suggested to the local police that they arrest not only the strike committee, which they did, but also all the striking workers.[71]

Faced with this level of intransigence, the SPD and the Free trade unions could only hope that by encouraging the strikers to resist returning to work for yet another day, they might perhaps wear management down to the point at which it would at least recognise their existence. Consequently, the socialist press went to great lengths to stress the indispensability of the striking workers — a remarkable switch from the earlier portrait of the debased and degraded steelworker. On 25 March, for example, it was reported that the 'Union' was already so desperate that it was employing an epileptic on a locomotive. On the 27th, the *Arbeiter Zeitung* suggested that more and more accidents were happening daily and machinery being destroyed because the 'Union' could only obtain inexperienced young workers or disabled old men as strikebreakers. Without their expertise, the striking workers were confidently informed, the company would soon be brought to its knees. As late as 31 March:

> a worker who has joined the strikers caused great amusement at the strike meeting with his description of the capabilities of those prepared to continue working. According to him, 'stokers' are being employed who think a [steam-pressure] gauge is [like] a pocket watch and who have no idea how to service a boiler.[72]

Readers of the SPD daily were also treated to the spectacle 'of engineers running around with oilcans, [while] a couple of strikebreakers [were] sitting peacefully in their corner taking no notice at all'. One of these harried officials was reported to have said that 'It's about time that the older, experienced people came back into the firm.'[73]

At the same time, the SPD and the Free trade unions tried to bolster enthusiasm by presenting melodramatic tales of strikebreakers who had been convinced to see the errors of their ways and to join (or at least not to oppose) their striking comrades. On 27 March, Matthies, another union regional secretary from Cologne, reported that fifteen machinists at the mine 'Tremonia' had been told to go and work at the 'Union', but they refused. The mine took its revenge by demoting a trade union delegate from machinist to haulier.[74] The Dortmund *Arbeiter Zeitung* also reported the following conversation which was supposed to have taken place that same day between an overseer and several fitters sent to the 'Union':

> Ah! There you are at last. Drive that loading crane!
> I was sent to check the crane, not to drive it. There are other people for that job.
> Well then, show [these] other workers how to do it.
> I won't have anything to do with that either.
> Then you're sacked.
> OK. Goodbye!
> (Newspaper report: 17 people arrived, 20 departed.)[75]

Sixty-eight men had also been brought by train from Essen at three in the morning to work at the 'Union'. Having been told that they were destined for Luxemburg, the great majority refused to cross the picket lines even though promised 4 marks a day and free housing. The rest entered the plant but marched out again 'like a platoon of soldiers' that afternoon, once they saw the conditions inside. This act of solidarity seemed particularly heroic to the *Arbeiter Zeitung* because several of the strikebreakers 'could hardly even afford shoes for their feet'.[76] Another strikebreaker was actually gaoled. Refusing to work any longer under the prevailing conditions, he went to one of the factory exits and demanded to be let out. When the porter refused, the strikebreaker hit him and was arrested by the police.[77] Apart from these stories, the strikers were also told that they had the material support of other steel-workers in Dortmund. Workers from the Hösch steel mills were reported to be manning the picket lines alongside the strikers from the 'Union'.[78]

But none of this prevented the strike from coming to an abrupt and inglorious end. Perhaps all it did achieve was to make that ending some-what unexpected and hence all the more debilitating for the rank and file. Certainly, the Centre Party newspaper, *Tremonia*, took great pleasure in reporting that

as was only to be expected, the strike at the 'Union' came to an end after a relatively short time. The only people who will be surprised are the credulous readers of the *Dortmunder Arbeiter Zeitung*, the Social Democrats, who are forbidden to read other papers. As late as the end of the last week, the situation was still being painted in the rosiest colours. The reason given for ending the strike was that in the last few days a large number of strikers are supposed to have broken rank. The readers of the 'workers' paper' must feel as if they have just tumbled out of the clouds.[79]

At least two of the workers at the 'Union' may have been particularly discouraged by the strike's ending. For if Werner and Schröder had in fact engaged in sabotage, then their main reason for doing so would have been in order to enhance the strikers' prospects of success. On 8 April, the German Metalworkers' Union national newspaper indicated this possibility when it suggested:

Perhaps it was the behaviour of the 'Christian' leaders that led to the stokers and machinists stopping work without giving a warning, so that the 'Christians' would not be able to take over their jobs or bring in other strikebreakers during the period of notice.[80]

Werner and Schröder may simply have taken the logic of this action a step further. Walking off the job without giving the prescribed notice might catch the Christian Metalworkers' Union off guard before it had the time to collude with the employers, but sabotage would ensure that 'Christian' strikebreakers had no machinery to run.

Perhaps these precise thoughts never actually ran through Werner's or Schröder's mind, but, in the bitter political context of the 1911 strike, they were certainly not unthinkable. After the strike, when the unions had been publicly accused of sabotage, the Free trade union *Correspondenzblatt* attempted to draw a clear line between fighting the steel capitalists and destroying their machinery:

> If the management is ruthless and stubborn, then the workers can confront this with the power of their solidarity. But the machines, those masterpieces of technology and human ingenuity, should not be destroyed; there is a nobler use for them.[81]

During the strike, however, the Dortmund *Arbeiter Zeitung* made no such distinction. Indeed, it listed the daily disasters within the plant with apparent satisfaction precisely because it seemed that only the prospect of complete ruin might bring the obstinate steel capitalists to the point of seeing reason:

> One of the factory officials said that after a few days everything was in ruins; it couldn't go on for long. Either the plant would have to be shut down or the strikers would win. A shut-down, in view of the large amount of capital involved, was out of the question and production could only continue with the aid of the striking workers.[82]

Admittedly, the newspaper recognised that the destruction that occurred in the firm was the product of the strikebreakers' incompetence more than of sabotage; at no point during the strike had the socialist or trade union press openly advocated sabotage. Yet, a saboteur might well have been excused for reading into such pronouncements a measure of *ex post facto* ratification of his acts.

Nor, certainly, would the willingness to engage in sabotage necessarily have indicated that the saboteur rejected the 'reformist' aims and world-view of the Free trade unions and the SPD. In Dortmund, at least, the Free trade unions and the SPD attempted to distinguish themselves from the Christian Metalworkers' Union and the Centre Party by arguing that they alone consistently pursued a militant course which would serve the workers' material interests. As the *Arbeiter Zeitung* remarked in April 1911, 'In all the years this sub-branch of the Christian Metalworkers' Union has existed, it has only had one strike, while the German Metalworkers' Union in Dortmund has had strikes nearly every year.'[83] It would have been reasonable for a militant worker — and Werner, at least, should be counted a militant — to think that sabotage was a necessary tactic in pursuit of reformist aims within the specific context of the 1911 strike.[84]

VI

The trouble with Karl-Heinz Roth's and Eckhard Brockhaus' 'mass worker' theory is that it does not even begin to confront most of the issues raised in this article. I have suggested that the political context of the 1911 Dortmund strike was extremely important in creating a possibility of sabotage. Brockhaus ignores the political context, tells us little of the relationship between steelworkers on the one hand and the SPD and Free trade unions on the other, and nothing at all about the roles of the Christian trade unions and the Centre Party. I have argued that the events of the 1911 strike were the results of a specific intersection of politics and economics at a definite point in time. Brockhaus regards the 1911 strike as only one symptom of long-term structural developments in the division of labour and of the relationship between capital and labour which began in the 1880s. He cannot explain why the events of the Dortmund strike occurred when they did, nor why 'sabotage' became such an important political issue then and not earlier.

The attempts by Karl-Heinz Roth and Eckhard Brockhaus to reconstruct the relationships among Wilhelmine socialism, trade unionism and the working class are unconvincing because they are simplistic and ahistorical. Rather than being the result of a new form of the relationship between capital and labour which the Free trade unions and the SPD could not penetrate, the Dortmund 'sabotage strike' was a more complex outcome of the efforts of the unions and the party to create a significant presence for themselves in heavy industry while they were simultaneously attempting to block such an entry by the Christian Metalworkers' Union and the Centre Party. Organising the iron- and steelworkers was not a recent concern of the SPD and the Free trade unions that emerged only in 1911. As early as 1893, the importance of this task was outlined by August Bebel at the Social Democratic Party conference of that year:

If Capital managed to achieve in a more widespread fashion the kind of power it has won in such enterprises as Krupp, Stumm, the *Dortmunder Union* and in the coal and iron industry regions of Rhineland and Westphalia, then the game would be up for the trade union movement, and political struggle would be the only path which remained open.[85]

Eighteen years later, Otto Hue, the Ruhr miners' leader, presented the same arguments. The continuing failure of the German Metalworkers' Union to organise the iron- and steelworkers had, in his view, greater significance than simply being 'the weak point which noticeably restricts the effectiveness of the union itself'.[86] Since iron and steel industrialists, along with the coal-owners, were the most important forces resisting the social and political advancement of the German working class, a victory for trade unionism in the steel mills would produce a major shift in the balance of German class relations:

> If these big businessmen were compelled to deal with strong resistance to their arbitrary rule. . . by foundry men [and] if the foundry workers were to force recognition of collective work agreements, then the strongest fortress of capitalist overlordship, which weighs down upon Germany like a nightmare, would be severely undermined.
> Therein lies the quite special social and political significance of organising workers in the foundries.[87]

But while the larger political significance of organising steelworkers was apparent to trade union and party officials from the 1890s, their attempts to do so were repeatedly frustrated. The leadership of the German Metalworkers' Union blamed the steelworkers themselves. For various reasons, steelworkers seemed unresponsive to trade union appeals and incapable of developing collective solidarities. One line of argument stressed the fact that steelworkers were too closely under the thumbs of their powerful employers. They were more readily dismissed than skilled metalworkers and many of them lived in company housing. A second approach to the problem emphasised the fragmenting effects of the nature of production in the steel industry. A hierarchical ladder of promotion, unrelated to skill qualifications, was thought to encourage workers to view improvement in individual rather than in collective terms. Finally, some observers, like Hue, stressed the debilitating effects of the backward mentality and low expectations of many of the steelworkers who were recent migrants from the German eastern provinces, Sweden or Italy.[88]

The German Metalworkers' Union had few solutions to these problems. When it began to achieve more rapid growth after 1896, it let the question of organising the steelworkers recede into the background of its discussions. But in the early twentieth century, as new recruitment slowed, as the employers' associations became more successful in struggles with labour and as working-class living standards were eroded by inflation, a new discussion of the 'limits of trade unionism' developed which made the problem of organising the steelworkers topical once again. This time, however, the earlier explanations for failure were displaced by a single-minded emphasis upon the low cultural and intellectual levels among the steelworkers that were produced by the extraordinarily long hours of exhausting physical labour.[89]

From the point of view of the German Metalworkers' Union, the first step towards raising the consciousness of steelworkers must be a reduction of working hours and a general improvement of working conditions. Since the steelworkers could not achieve these initial advances by themselves, help must come from the state. In 1907, the union began a detailed investigation of conditions in the German iron and steel industry which was to be placed before the Reichstag as a memorandum for legal reform.[90] Although a federal regulation governing conditions in large iron and steel factories which appeared in 1908 proved completely inadequate, the strategy of petitioning the state for protective measures was not abandoned. As late as 1912, K. Spiegel, writing in the Social Democratic journal, *Die Neue Zeit*, presented a long list of legal changes with regard to the iron and steel industry for which the SPD was attempting to gain a hearing at the Ministry of the Interior.[91]

Steelworkers did not, however, passively await their emancipation at the hands of the SPD, the Free trade unions and the German state. Encouraged, no doubt, by the attention to their problems that the unions once again displayed after 1907 and spurred on by new pressures from their employers in the form of rationalisation of production and the intensification of steel-mill labour, steelworkers began to organise in greater numbers. The increase was not dramatic and it did not produce a major strike wave. But it probably did spread the idea, more widely than the modest numbers of actual paid-up members would indicate, that it might be possible to change the relationship between worker and employer in the steel industry.

The problem was that neither trade unions nor the party had a clear idea of what sort of strategy might bring trade union recognition and success in the steel industry. Obviously, it was thought important to increase the numbers of the organised still further, but this continued to be difficult. The conditions which had earlier hindered organisation persisted. Nor was it true that an increased capacity and willingness to organise necessarily created greater solidarity among steelworkers, as the relationship between the Free and the Christian trade unions in Dortmund and elsewhere indicated. But Dr R. Woldt, an influential SPD observer writing in *Die Neue Zeit* in 1912, argued that the problems the unions confronted in the steel industry were less important than the opportunities. According to Woldt, the Dortmund strike had shown the path the trade unions must follow in heavily mechanised industries such as steel. In the smaller-scale forms of industry, where the workers' skill, not the machine, was central to production, a strike could be effective because employers did not find it easy to replace striking workers with strikebreakers. But in heavily mechanised factories, where machines had largely replaced human skill, fewer categories of workers were indispensable to production. Trade union efforts need not, therefore, be addressed to all the workers in the steel mill but should, he felt, concentrate upon those who were employed in the 'most sensitive' part of the mechanised factory, namely the electric and steam power-producing plants. Without power, production could not continue in the modern steel mill. Bring out on strike the workers engaged in the production of the power that runs the modern steel mill and production would be entirely shut down.[92]

The tactic Woldt recommended was based on the assumption that the workers involved could not easily be replaced. We do not know a great deal about developments in the division of labour within German steel mills during this period. It would seem, however, that Roth's and Brockhaus' image of the uniformly unskilled and interchangeable 'mass worker' is inadequate as a description of all categories of steel-mill labour. Brockhaus seems aware of the difficulties; he actually describes the striking machinists as 'relatively qualified' workers.[93] But this recognition does not cause him to abandon the imagery of the 'mass worker'. In the Dortmund strike, the important fact was that the qualifications of the striking workers were not sufficient enough to give them a strong bargaining position *vis-à-vis* their employers when there were hostile 'Christian' and other workers prepared to take over their jobs. Although the socialist press made much of the incompetence of these strikebreakers, the company was not forced to negotiate with the strikers because production could not continue without their labour. To that extent, the Dortmund strike did not bear out the assumptions which informed Woldt's tactical suggestions.

That workers might consider sabotage in such a situation was not readily admitted by the SPD and the Free trade unions, even though it was a possibility they had helped to create. By construing the events of the 1911 Dortmund strike as manifestations of an autonomous working-class culture, separate from the culture of the labour movement, we run the risk of ignoring the important and often complex ways in which the working-class organisations, 'Christian' as well as socialist, helped, both directly and indirectly, to construct working-class experience and consciousness in Wilhelmine Germany. The conviction that sabotage could only be a spontaneous action presumes a distinction between 'politics' and 'society' which, in this instance at least, appears highly questionable. I am not arguing that we return to writing the history of the German working class as the history of its organisations. But the SPD and the Free trade unions, the Centre Party and the Christian trade unions, as well as the state and the employers, were so important as political, ideological and material forces in working-class life that we cannot ignore the roles they played in shaping working-class consciousness. This, I would stress, is also not a plea for us to return to 'history from the top down' when we have barely begun to write 'history from below', but a suggestion that we abandon both these categories. The value of German working-class history, like the history of other classes and social groups, must in the end be measured by its capacity to illuminate aspects of the nature of German society as a whole. It can do this only when approached as a problem in the reconstruction of certain historical relationships: between the working class and other classes and social groups in German society, between workers and the organisations that sought to represent them and among different sections within the working class. That is not a challenge that either a 'history from below' or 'above' can adequately meet.

Notes

I would like to dedicate this article to the memory of Susanne Depmer, friend and fellow historian. I also wish to express my gratitude for the help and constructive criticism I have received from Michael Schultheiss, Susan Pennybacker, Jonathan Zeitlin, Paul Preston and the members of the Queen Mary College Modern History Seminar at the University of London to whom an earlier version of this essay was presented on 11 February, 1980.

The following abbreviations are used in the notes: *AZD — Arbeiter Zeitung, Sozialdemokratisches Organ für das Rheinisch-Westfälishe Industrie-Gebiet, Publikations-Organ der freien Gewerkschaften, Dortmund; DZt — Dortmunder Zeitung*, Dortmund; *GAD — General-Anzeiger fur Dortmund und die Provinz*

Westfalen, Dortmund; *MAZ – Metallarbeiter-Zeitung, Wochenblatt des Deutschen Metallarbeiter-Verbandes*, Stuttgart; *VW – Vorwärts*, Berlin.

1.   *AZD*, 22 and 27 Mar. 1911. The report carried in the *Arbeiter-Zeitung* on 27 March claimed there were 379 workers on strike. The *Dortmunder Zeitung*, reporting on 25 March, said there were 374 strikers, of whom an estimated 351 were members of the Centralverband der Maschinisten und Heizer sowie Berufsgenossen Deutschlands (Central German Union of Machinists, Stokers and Related Trades).

2.   Eckhard Brockhaus, *Zusammensetzung und Neustrukturierung der Arbeiterklasse vor dem Ersten Weltkrieg. Zur Krise der professionellen Arbeiterbewegung* (München, 1975), p. 144.

3.   *DZt*, 27 Jan. 1912, See, however, the quite different account given in *MAZ*, 10 Feb. 1912.

4.   Erhard Lucas, James Wickham and Karl-Heinz Roth, *Arbeiter-Radikalismus und Die 'andere' Arbeiterbewegung; zur Diskussion der Massenarbeiterthese* (Bochum, 1977), p. 32.

5.   Karl-Heinz Roth, *Die 'andere' Arbeiterbewegung und die Entwicklung der kapitalistischen Repression von 1880 bis zur Gegenwart. Ein Beitrag zum Neuverständnis der Klassengeschichte in Deutschland* (München, 1977), p. 23.

6.   Ibid., p. 24.

7.   Ibid., p. 37.

8.   Ibid., p. 24.

9.   Ibid., p. 24.

10.   Ibid., p. 37.

11.   Ibid., p. 37.

12.   Brockhaus, *Zusammensetzung und Neustrukturierung der Arbeiterklasse*, p. 138.

13.   Ibid., p. 139.

14.   Ibid., p. 136.

15.   Ibid., p. 136.

16.   Lujo Brentano, 'Offener Brief an Herrn Dr. Ludwig Bernhard, Professor an der Universität Berlin', *Frankfurter Zeitung und Handelsblatt*, 28 Apr. 1912 and *Correspondenzblatt der Generalkommission der Gewerkschaften Deutschlands*, 4 May 1912, pp. 400-1. See also *DZt*, 24 Mar. 1911 and Brockhaus, *Zusammensetzung und Neustrukturierung der Arbeiterklasse*, p. 144.

17.   Lujo Brentano, 'Offener Brief an Herrn Dr. Ludwig Bernhard', *Frankfurter Zeitung*, 28 Apr. 1912. See also *Correspondenzblatt der Generalkommission der Gewerkschaften Deutschlands*, 4 May 1912. For biographical details concerning Bernhard and Brentano see *Neue Deutsche Biographie*, Zweiter Band (Berlin, 1955), pp. 119-20 and James J. Sheehan, *The Career of Lujo Brentano: a Study of Liberalism and Social Reform in Imperial Germany* (Chicago and London, 1966).

18.   Lujo Brentano, 'Offener Brief an Herrn Dr. Ludwig Bernhard', *Frankfurter Zeitung*, 28 Apr. 1912.

19.   Ibid. See also *Correspondenzblatt der Generalkommission der Gewerkschaften Deutschlands*, 4 May 1912.

20.   Lujo Brentano, 'Offener Brief an Herrn Dr. Ludwig Bernhard', *Frankfurter Zeitung*, 28 Apr. 1912.

21.   A. Voigt, 'Gibt es Sabotage in Deutschland?' *Zeitschrift für Sozialwissenschaft*, Neue Folge, III Jg. (Leipzig, 1912), p. 652.

22.   Ibid., p. 652.

23.   *AZD*, 28 Mar. 1911. For some earlier comments on the relationship between steelworkers and miners see *VW*, 15 Jan. 1905. A union leader characterised the 1911 'Union' strike as 'a breach which has been made in the heavy

industry of Rhineland-Westphalia. A victory for the machinists is also a victory for other workers' (*AZD*, 27 Mar. 1911).

24.   *AZD*, Beilage, 7 Apr. 1911 and *AZD*, 28 Mar. 1911.

25.   Ronald J. Ross, *Beleaguered Tower: the Dilemma of Political Catholicism in Wilhelmine Germany* (Notre Dame and London, 1976), p. 85. Although the SPD received 33,305 votes in the Dortmund-Hörde Reichstag electoral district in 1903 and 38,849 in 1907, the Catholic Centre Party managed to gain 19,472 votes in 1903 and 22,246 in 1907; see Ralf Lützenkirchen, *Der sozialdemokratische Verein für den Reichstagswahlkreis Dortmund-Hörde. Ein Beitrag zur Parteiengeschichte* (Dortmund, 1970), p. 43.

26.   These figures on membership are derived from a report published in *MAZ*, 25 Mar. 1911. The Christian Metalworkers' Union continued to play an important role in the Ruhr. In 1919, there were 350,000 DMV members in the DMV's 7th District, but no less than 150,000 members of the Christian Metalworkers' Union; see Irmgard Steinisch, 'Die gewerkschaftliche Organisation der rheinischwestfälischen Arbeiterschaft in der eisen- und stahlerzeugenden Industrie 1918 bis 1924' in Hans Mommsen (ed.), *Arbeiterbewegung und Industrielle Wandel. Studien zu gewerkschaftlichen Organisationsproblemen im Reich und an der Ruhr* (Wuppertal, 1980), pp. 121-2, and also Elisabeth Domansky-Davidsohn, 'Der Grossbetrieb als Organisationsproblem des Deutschen Metallarbeiter-Verbandes vor dem Ersten Weltkrieg' in Mommsen, *Arbeiterbewegung und Industrielle Wandel*, pp. 95-116. The unpublished conference paper by Michael Schneider, 'Religion und Arbeiterorganisation: Die Christlichen Gewerkschaften im Wilhelminischen Reich', SSRC Research Seminar Group in Modern German Social History, Fifth Meeting: The Social History of Religion, University of East Anglia, Norwich, 7-8 January 1981, also contains some very useful information. I am grateful to Richard Evans and Ian Farr for furnishing me with a copy of this paper.

27.   See, for example, the comments by Dissman (Barmen) of the DMV in *Protokoll der Verhandlungen des vierten Kongresses der Gewerkschaften Deutschlands. Abgehalten zu Stuttgart im Gewerkschaftshaus vom 16.bis 21. Juni 1902* (Hamburg, 1902), p. 129, and also Schneider, 'Religion und Arbeiterorganisation'.

28.   *Tremonia*, 2 Mar. 1911. The *Arbeiter-Zeitung* responded to such charges by remarking that 'The "Union" strike is as unpolitical as the strike of the zincfoundry workers staged by the "Christians" ' (*AZD*, 27 Mar. 1911).

29.   *Tremonia*, 3 Mar. 1911.

30.   *Tremonia*, 27 Jan. 1912.

31.   See Lützenkirchen, *Der sozialdemokratische Verein für den Reichstagswahlkreis Dortmund-Hörde*, pp. 83-5. In the event, the SPD was able to attract 48,838 votes in the election compared to the Centre Party's 25,708 and the 25,285 votes that were cast for the National Liberals. On the second ballot between Dr Erdmann (SPD) and the Centre Party candidate, Bickhoff, the Fortschrittspartei and the Demokratische Vereinigung advised their supporters to give 'No votes to the Centre', but the National Liberals were told to support the Centre Party. Erdmann managed to increase his vote this time to 55,900, thereby taking a seat in the Reichstag (Lützenkirchen, *Der sozialdemokratische Verein für den Reichstagswahlkreis Dortmund-Hörde*, p. 87). In the following discussion, I have concentrated my attention upon indicating the ways in which the alleged 'sabotage' was dealt with politically and ideologically by the SPD and the Free trade unions. I have also attempted to show how the political and trade union context in which the 1911 strike occurred made sabotage a possibility. This approach seems a more fruitful way to reconstruct the events of the strike, and to recapture their meaning, than trying to determine whether or not Werner, Schröder and the other striking workers had consciously set out to sabotage the 'Union' steel works.

To begin with, the law courts themselves found it extremely difficult to establish such an intent and as we lack the original trial records, we are not able to review the legal evidence in great detail. (Upon inquiring at the offices of the Landgericht in Dortmund on 28 June 1979, I was informed that these documents have not been preserved.) Beyond this, however, it is quite clear that many contemporary observers themselves found it extremely difficult to decide precisely what constituted 'sabotage' when that term was being applied to actions taken in an enterprise as complicated as a steel mill. For further discussion of these issues see the conclusion to this article. See also Dr R. Woldt, 'Die Dieselmaschine-Turbodynamo-Technische Fortschritt und Gewerkschaften im Hüttenwerk — Das System Taylor', *Neue Zeit*, 5 Apr. 1912, pp. 24-6.

32.   *AZD*, 3 Feb. 1912. Originally, some six or seven (reports disagree on the exact number) machinists were charged. The workers argued that they had only meant to go on strike and had no way of knowing, in such a large and complicated factory, what the result of their actions would be. Since it proved difficult to determine which of these striking workers had in fact damaged machines and equipment, the charges against them were dropped and the public prosecutor decided to take to trial only the two machinists, Werner and Schröder, who had allegedly been involved in shutting down the central steam-power plant (Voigt, 'Gibt es Sabotage in Deutschland?', pp. 653-4).

33.   *AZD*, 3 Feb. 1912.

34.   *AZD*, 3 Feb. 1912. See also *Correspondenzblatt der Generalkommission der Gewerkschaften Deutschlands*, 4 May 1912, p. 402: 'In judging this case, one must not forget that accidents occur regularly in heavy industry and just a few weeks before the strike, five workers and then, later, three met with deadly accidents at the "Union", also at a converter. But on those occasions, there was no investigation and Prof. Bernhard did not raise his voice.'

35.   *Tremonia*, 27 Jan. 1912; *Correspondenzblatt der Generalkommission der Gewerkschaften Deutschlands*, 4 May 1912, p. 403.

36.   *MAZ*, 10 Feb. 1912.

37.   Domansky-Davidsohn, 'Der Grossbetrieb als Organisationsproblem', pp. 101-12.

38.   *AZD*, Beilage, 7 Apr. 1911. On 27 March, one of the local union leaders was reported to have said that he 'was pleased that the machinists' union had been able to organise such a large number. Earlier, the lack of understanding among the masses had stood in the way' (*AZD*, 27 Mar. 1911).

39.   *AZD*, 3 Feb. 1912.

40.   Otto Hue, leader of the miners' union, writing in *MAZ*, 25 Mar. 1911. See also K. Spiegel, 'Die Arbeiter in der Schwereisenindustrie', *Die Neue Zeit*, 5 Apr. 1912, p. 21, and *AZD*, 28 Mar. 1911:

The man who has been condemned to work in the foundries and who has not yet lost all sense of his humanity must endure a true martyrdom. Every minute that does not directly serve the production of profit is intentionally made into even more of a torture than the work itself. The toilets have no seats, only long, sharp-edged beams or else they have such sloping seats that the worker can remain there only a few seconds, hanging half in the air. And, on top of that, there is only a faint light or no light at all at night. This is only one of the 'lovely' little pictures from the foundries.

41.   *Die Schwereisenindustrie im deutschen Zollgebiet, ihre Entwicklung und ihre Arbeiter. Nach vorgenommenen Erhebungen im Jahre 1910 bearbeitet und herausgegeben vom Vorstand des deutschen Metallarbeiter-Verbandes* (Stuttgart, 1912), p. 634.

42.   *AZD*, 28 Mar. 1911.

43.   *MAZ*, 10 Feb. 1912.

44.   *Correspondenzblatt der Generalkommission der Gewerkschaften Deutschlands*, 4 May 1912, p. 403.

45.   Klaus Saul, *Staat, Industrie, Arbeiterbewegung im Kaiserreich. Zur Innen- und Sozialpolitik des Wilhelminischen Deutschlands 1903-1914* (Düsseldorf, 1974), pp. 283-394.

46.   Inge Marssolek, 'Sozialdemokratie und Revolution im östlichen Ruhrgebiet. Dortmund unter der Herrschaft des Arbeiter-und Soldatenrates' in Reinhard Rürup (ed.), *Arbeiter- und Soldatenräte im rheinisch-westfälischen Industriegebiet. Studien zur Geschichte der Revolution 1918/1919* (Wuppertal, 1975), p. 240.

47.   Dieter Groh, 'Intensification of Work and Industrial Conflict in Germany, 1896-1914', *Politics and Society*, vol. 8, nos. 3-4 (1978), pp. 375-8.

48.   *Die Schwereisenindustrie*, pp. 484-5.

49.   *AZD*, 22 Mar. 1911. The categories of workers affected were: machinists, stokers, crane, motor and locomotive drivers, boiler attendants, reserve machinists, greasers and repair fitters, when these were temporarily working in the electric plant, and the machinists in the custom foundry.

50.   *AZD*, 22 Mar. 1911. See also *Die Schwereisenindustrie*, p. 516, and *VW*, 25 Mar. 1911.

51.   *AZD*, 22 Mar. 1911.

52.   *Tremonia*, 22 Mar. 1911 and *DZt*, 24 Mar. 1911.

53.   *Tremonia*, 6 Apr. 1911. See also *DZt*, 24 Mar. 1911 and *GAD*, 25 Mar. 1911.

54.   *Tremonia*, 2 Mar. 1911. See also *GAD*, 27 Mar. 1911 and *DZt*, 24 Mar. 1911.

55.   *Tremonia*, 6 Apr. 1911.

56.   Ibid.

57.   *Tremonia*, 27 Apr. 1911.

58.   Ibid.

59.   Ibid.

60.   *Tremonia*, 15 Mar. 1911 and *AZD*, 3 Apr. 1911.

61.   *AZD*, 25 Mar. 1911.

62.   *AZD*, 28 Mar. 1911.

63.   *Tremonia*, 22 Mar. 1911. See also *MAZ*, 8 Apr. 1911 and *VW*, 26 Mar. 1911.

64.   *AZD*, 25 Mar. and 27 Mar. 1911. It was reported in the *General-Anzeiger* that 200 workers were present at a meeting of the local branch of the Christian Metalworkers' Union held on 27 March at which the strike was discussed, but it was not specified how many of those present worked at the 'Union' (*GAD*, 27 Mar. 1911).

65.   *Tremonia*, 2 Apr. 1911. See also *Tremonia*, 22 Mar. 1911.

66.   *AZD*, 28 Mar. 1911.

67.   *AZD*, 27 Mar. 1911.

68.   *DZt*, 24 Mar. 1911:

The management have been able to bring in workers from outside, so that the plant can be kept running, although not at full capacity. Those workers who stay on the job. . .have been granted the 15 per cent pay rise which the workers demanded.

See also *AZD*, 27 Mar. 1911.

69.   *DZt*, 25 Mar. 1911. The management also held back six shifts' pay from the striking workers.

70.   *AZD*, 3 Apr. 1911. See also *VW*, 25 Mar. 1911, in which it was reported that the employers refused to discuss grievances with workers collectively; they would, however, talk to them on an individual basis.

71.   *AZD*, 22 Mar. 1911 and *VW*, 24 Mar. 1911. It was reported that these arrests were made as the result of the accident which claimed Wiscozyl's life.

72.   *AZD*, 31 Mar. 1911.
73.   *AZD*, 28 Mar. 1911.
74.   *AZD*, 27 Mar. 1911.
75.   *AZD*, 27 Mar. 1911.
76.   *AZD*, 28 Mar. 1911.
77.   *AZD*, 31 Mar. 1911.
78.   *AZD*, 28 Mar. 1911.
79.   *Tremonia*, 6 Apr. 1911. See also *AZD*, Beilage, 7 Apr. 1911.
80.   *MAZ*, 8 Apr. 1911: in order not to be considered 'in breach of their contract' (*kontraktbrüchig*), striking workers were required to give notice of their intention to 'leave the job'. As the *AZD* pointed out, however, this was not always possible or tactically wise. In the specific case of the 'Union' strike, 'the union representatives had all wanted to give notice to management. But in the meeting [which preceded the strike] . . .a unanimous "NO! Strike early tomorrow morning!" resounded across the room' (*AZD*, 22 Mar. 1911). According to the *AZD*, it was the activities of the Christian trade unionists that had helped convince the workers that they must strike without giving notice and which also influenced their decision to go into work as usual at 6 a.m. the next morning, but then walk out again at seven: 'It was definitely the obviously treacherous dealings of the Centre Party papers that contributed to the machinists going on strike immediately even against the advice of their union. No one wanted to give them a further opportunity to engage in their shabby activity' (*AZD*, 28 Mar. 1911). The national newspaper of the German Metalworkers' Union also made a point of reporting that, in their discussions before the strike, the Christian trade union leaders had made it known that they would encourage those of their members who were unemployed in other towns to come and work at the 'Union' during the strike: *MAZ*, 8 Apr. 1911. Given the nature of the charges levelled against them, it was understandable that the Christian trade unionists reacted disdainfully to any suggestions that they should have allied with the Free trade unions during the strike: 'It is quite simply out of the question that one day we have to let ourselves be characterised as stooges and accomplices of the bosses but the very next day be expected to pull our "comrades' " chestnuts out of the fire' (*Tremonia*, 22 Mar. 1911).
81.   *Correspondenzblatt der Generalkommission der Gewerkshaften Deutschlands*, 4 May 1912, p. 404.
82.   *AZD*, 27 Mar. 1911. See also *AZD*, 28 Mar. 1911.
83.   *AZD*, 15 Apr. 1911.
84.   The union leader, Franz Scheffel, claimed that Werner was not particularly more militant than any of the other striking workers at the 'Union'; he was not a member of either the wage committee or the strike leadership. However, it is, perhaps, an indication of Werner's previous activities in the plant that he was one of the six strikers whose names were given by the management to the police to be arrested on the first day of the strike (*Correspondenzblatt der Generalkommission der Gewerkschaften Deutschlands*, 4 May 1912, p. 403, and *AZD*, 22 Mar. 1911). Scheffel also suggested that the machinists would have had absolutely no interest in damaging their machinery as they fully expected that the strike would only last a few hours and therefore they would be returning to work on those machines that same day (*Correspondenzblatt*, pp. 402-3). A report of a strike carried in *VW* the next year displayed a rather more ambivalent attitude towards 'sabotage'. During a walk-out of electrical fitters in Cologne, four of the strikers had destroyed work done by other fitters, presumably so as to encourage them to join the strike. The four were charged and originally sentenced to periods in gaol ranging from two weeks to a month. These sentences were later increased to three months. During the same strike, two workers who had not joined the walk-out stole electrical cable worth 180 marks from the company. They were

sent to prison for eight days and two weeks, respectively. *VW* commented that it could not understand the disparity between the two cases: 'two strikebreakers, motivated by dishonourable sentiments, steal and destroy property and yet are treated in the mildest way. . .but strikers, who got carried away by motives which were not sordid. . .are subjected to the severest possible punishment' (*VW*, 13 Apr. 1912).

85.   *Protokoll über die Verhandlungen des Parteitages der Sozialdemokratischen Partei Deutschlands, 1893*, p. 201, cited in Karl Ditt, 'Probleme gewerkschaftlicher Organisierung in der Metall- und Textilindustrie Bielefelds 1890-1914' in Dieter Langewiesche and Klaus Schönhoven (eds.), *Arbeiter in Deutschland. Studien zur Lebensweise der Arbeiterschaft im Zeitalter der Industrialisierung* (Paderborn, 1981), p. 220.

86.   *MAZ*, 25 Mar. 1911.

87.   Ibid.

88.   Domansky-Davidsohn, 'Der Grossbetrieb als Organisationsproblem', pp. 95-116.

89.   *MAZ*, 25 Mar. 1911.

90.   Domansky-Davidsohn, 'Der Grossbetrieb als Organisationsproblem', pp. 102-3 and 104.

91.   K. Spiegel, 'Die Arbeiter in der Schwerindustrie', *Die Neue Zeit*, 5 Apr. 1912, p. 23.

92.   Woldt, 'Die Dieselmaschine-Turbodynamo-Technische Fortschritt und Gewerkschaften', pp. 24-6.

93.   Brockhaus, *Zusammensetzung und Neustrukturierung der Arbeiterklasse*, p. 144.

5 ILLEGITIMACY AND THE WORKING CLASS: ILLEGITIMATE MOTHERS IN BRUNSWICK, 1900-1933

Stefan Bajohr

I

In her study of the history of the legal status of women and mothers in Germany, published in 1907, the moderate feminist Marianne Weber (wife of the famous sociologist Max Weber) declared that capitalism, in so far as it encouraged the formation and growth of large cities, was an indirect cause of increasing illegitimacy rates. Big cities, she said, aided 'the disruption of traditional social communities', 'the formation of new proletarian classes' and the destabilisation of 'marriage and morals'.[1] This traditional view of the relationship between rising illegitimacy rates and urbanisation should not be accepted without reflection.[2] Recent studies of the history of illegitimacy in Central Europe indicate that some rural societies and areas had a considerably higher incidence of illegitimacy than some nineteenth- and twentieth-century cities.[3] The historian Edward Shorter has, in another context, argued against the influence of urbanisation and industrialisation on the illegitimacy rate.[4] But, although their terminologies differ, he none the less agrees with Weber that increasing anonymity, the development of a property-less proletariat and changing value systems[5] were responsible for increased illegitimacy in the nineteenth century. Yet in view of the fact that illegitimacy did not become a general phenomenon when these factors became more widespread, there are difficulties in drawing direct correlations. The statistics refute a simple connection between the development of industrial production and urbanisation on the one hand and a rising illegitimate birth rate on the other. In the 1890s, the decade in which Germany completed the transition from an agricultural to an industrial state,[6] the rate of illegitimacy began to fall,[7] while the numbers of wage labourers increased and urbanisation proceeded apace.[8] This fall, just two decades after marital fertility had begun to decline,[9] continued well into the twentieth century. Illegitimate fertility finally stabilised at a considerably lower level at about the same time as the marital fertility rate, at the beginning of the 1930s.[10] Although there were great regional variations in the rate of illegitimacy before this decline began, and although the decrease commenced at different times and continued at different rates, there was no region in the German Empire that did not follow the overall trend.[11]

In the Duchy of Brunswick, illegitimate fertility, which both before and at the beginning of the decline was above average for the German Empire as a whole,[12] began to decrease at about the turn of the century. By the end of the 1920s it had been halved.[13] In the city of Brunswick as well the rate of illegitimacy declined considerably during the first third of the twentieth century (see Tables 5.1 and 5.2).[14] As research

Table 5.1: Illegitimate Fertility in Brunswick, 1895-1925 (per 1,000 unmarried women)

Year	Ages							Total
	14-19	20-24	25-29	30-34	35-39	40-44	45-49	
1895[a]	15.2	62.4	63.6	37.4	8.8	8.2	1.1	32.9
1900	14.3	50.7	43.5	44.0	18.5	6.2	0.0	28.3
1905	14.7	48.5	36.3	23.1	10.3	7.3	0.0	24.4
1910	14.5	50.1	37.0	26.1	10.8	2.7	0.0	24.6
1925[b]	10.0	34.3	24.5	15.2	3.0	6.4	0.0	24.6

Notes: a. From the census of 2 Dec. 1895 and the birth figures for 1894. b. From the census of 16 Jun. 1925, and the birth figures for 1924, for the figures in the age groups. The 'total' refers to the figures for 1925. The age group results for 1925 are very low as the number of illegitimate births in 1924 was particularly low.

Sources: *Beiträge zur Statistik des Herzogtums Braunschweig*, Heft 19, 1905, pp. 66ff, 84ff; Heft 22, 1908, pp. 122f; Heft 26, 1913, pp 64ff; *Statistik des Deutschen Reichs*, Bd. 401 I (Berlin, 1928), pp. 179ff; StA Wf 14 Neu Zg. 4/46 and 19/58, Nr. 15 II, 15 III, 15 IV, 15 V, 31 I, 31 II.

to date does not allow any definite statements about the connection between industrial society, urbanisation and bastardy,[15] the following is an attempt to formulate hypotheses both about the conditions in which illegitimacy developed and about the social consequences for the mothers by means of a detailed study of their everyday lives in the city of Brunswick during the period when illegitimacy began to decline.

A local history of illegitimate motherhood[16] will not be able to validate more general hypotheses. This is impossible because of the differing conditions obtaining in the various regions before, at the beginning of, and during the decline in illegitimate fertility. However, a study of everyday life can contribute some more general insights into this aspect of the 'production of life',[17] because it enables us to approach

Table 5.2: Illegitimate Fertility in Brunswick, 1890-1933 (per 1,000 single women)

Year	Ages						Total
	15-19	20-24	25-29	30-34	35-39	40-44	
1890	14.2	58.0	65.6	34.5	35.2	27.2	36.8
1895[a]	17.6	62.6	66.6	44.8	14.0	17.7	38.8
1900	16.4	51.1	45.3	53.7	28.4	17.0	33.1
1905	14.7[b]	48.7	38.3	27.2	14.9	18.4	26.8
1910	14.5[b]	50.2	38.6	31.4	15.5	5.1	26.9
1925	–	–	–	–	–	–	28.6
1933[c]	–	–	–	–	–	–	12.0

Notes: a. The number of single women in 12 Feb. 1895 combined with births in 1894. b. Including 14-year-olds. c. Excluding still-births.

Sources: *Beiträge zur Statistik des Herzogtums Braunschweig*, Heft 12, 1895, pp. 48ff; Heft 19, 1905, pp. 66ff, 84ff; Heft 22, 1908, pp. 122ff; Heft 26, 1913, pp. 64ff; *Statistik des Deutschen Reichs*, Bd 401 I (Berlin, 1928), pp. 179ff; Bd 451, 2 (Berlin, 1936), p. 127; *Statistisches Jahrbuch deutscher Städte*, 29 (1934), p. 483; StA Wf 14 Neu Zg. 4/46 and 19/58 Nr. 15 II, 15 III, 15 IV, 15 V, 31 I, 31 II.

and understand the problem of illegitimacy through the experience of the mothers who were directly involved. This 'everyday life' for the majority was predetermined for most of these women. A pre-existing web of relationships constituting the working-class environment formed and shaped their experiences. They were both the subjects and objects of behavioural structures that daily reproduced themselves, were apparently stable, but gradually changed in the long term. These structures were essentially determined by the basically identical manner in which people were involved in them. Participation in the work process, the size and adequacy of income, lack of property and, stemming from this the nature of living quarters, interrelationships, family ties, political preferences, cultural needs and forms of expression, the wishes, fears, hopes and experiences of the individual: all these might vary, but all were subject to a common 'condition of everyday reality'[18] which was bestowed on the individual by the division of labour and the opportunity which it allowed for reproduction. All these aspects of social behaviour changed in the course of confrontation with the reproductive norms dominant in society as a whole, as the burden of work seemed to people to decrease, and the chances for successful child-bearing and child-rearing to increase.[19] In so far as illegitimate motherhood was concerned, these changes revealed themselves statistically in a fall in illegitimate fertility. The following essay hopes to illuminate this process in greater detail.

II

By confession illegitimate mothers in the city of Brunswick belonged mainly to the Lutheran church (between 78 per cent in 1916 and 90.1 per cent in 1904). Roman Catholic illegitimate mothers comprised only between 8.6 per cent (1913) and 20 per cent (1916) of the total.[20] When considered by age, the 20-24-year old women accounted for the largest numbers of the total number of women bearing illegitimate children during this period.[21] This was also true during the last twenty years of the nineteenth century. The age-specific fertility rates also put this group in the lead in the first third of the twentieth century, although the 25-29-year-olds (see Tables 5.1 and 5.2) followed more closely behind than in the simple figures for illegitimate births. There were more births in absolute figures to unmarried women under 20 than to married women in the same age range. Except for the years 1918-21 this age group took second place during the period 1900-24 to the 20-24-year-olds and in front of the 25-29-year-olds.

Despite the fairly high incidence of illegitimate births in the age ranges above 30, their contribution to the total was relatively small. It fluctuated between a low of 6.2 per cent in 1914 and a high of 15 per cent in 1919.[22] Far more than a simple majority of illegitimate mothers were between 20 and 29 years old: at times the 20-24-year-olds accounted for more than 50 per cent.[23] The overwhelming majority of women giving birth to illegitimate infants in the years 1900-30 were single, usually accounting (with the exception of the revolutionary years 1918/19) for over 90 per cent (see Table 5.3).[24] The increase in the proportion of widows giving birth to illegitimate children in the years 1916-21 to over 6 per cent is worth noting. It can probably be explained by the fact that the number of widows in the 20-29-year-old age group increased as a result of the war.

There is no information available on the social origin of illegitimate mothers in Brunswick. However, an examination of the addresses of mothers of illegitimate infants, which is generally possible for those who gave birth at home,[25] reveals that these were concentrated in 31 blocks of streets, while scarcely any or even none at all occurred in others during the period under investigation. This unequal distribution indicates that frequent illegitimate births occurred in a particular

Table 5.3: Illegitimacy in Brunswick 1900-30: Place of Confinement, Legitimations, Name Changes, Adoptions Illegitimate Mothers by Family Status

Year	per 100 Illegitimate Confinements			per 100 Illegitimate Children Born			per 100 Illegitimate Mothers			
	Hospital	Home	Unknown	Legitimised	Received the Surname of the Stepfather	Adopted	Single	Married	Widowed	Divorced
1900	56.2	43.8	–	24.4	5.2	0.6	94.8	–	3.1	2.1
1901	62.1	36.4	1.5	18.8	4.3	0.9	98.0	–	1.4	0.6
1902	62.8	36.6	0.6	20.8	7.7	0.9	95.5	0.9	3.3	0.3
1903	64.0	36.0	–	18.6	8.0	0.9	97.1	–	1.4	1.4
1904	58.8	40.7	0.5	21.8	8.8	1.4	96.6	–	2.0	1.4
1905	58.9	40.2	0.9	23.9	6.3	1.5	97.9	–	2.1	–
1906	58.6	41.1	0.3	19.7	6.9	1.6	94.4	–	4.7	0.9
1907	58.2	41.5	0.3	38.9	11.0	1.2	96.8	–	2.6	0.6
1908	62.6	37.1	0.3	21.1	7.6	1.6	96.7	–	1.9	1.4
1909	64.5	35.0	0.5	29.8	4.3	0.3	96.5	–	2.4	1.1
1910	69.6	29.9	0.5	26.2	6.0	0.8	96.4	–	2.3	1.3
1911	70.5	28.6	0.9	20.2	6.6	1.4	96.5	–	2.0	1.5
1912	73.3	26.2	0.5	21.0	6.5	1.4	95.1	–	2.45	2.45
1913	70.6	28.8	0.6	25.5	6.4	0.8	96.1	–	2.5	1.4
1914	72.5	27.2	0.3	17.6	7.1	0.8	95.7	–	2.5	1.8
1915	73.0	26.7	0.3	21.4	6.5	1.7	96.6	–	1.4	2.0
1916	67.2	32.8	–	15.1	8.2	0.9	93.5	–	6.5	–
1917	71.0	28.1	0.9	12.6	7.9	1.4	92.1	–	6.5	1.4
1918	61.4	38.1	0.5	7.2	10.8	2.6	88.3	–	11.7	–
1919	59.6	40.0	0.4	10.7	12.5	1.4	87.1	–	9.3	3.6
1920	64.15	34.45	1.4	28.4	6.7	1.7	91.0	0.3	7.6	1.1
1921	70.3	27.6	2.1	12.9	7.5	1.1	92.5	–	6.1	1.4
1922	72.8	25.7	1.5	20.7	5.8	3.3	94.6	–	5.1	0.3
1923	59.6	31.4	9.0	16.0	5.9	1.1	94.7	0.5	3.7	1.1
1924	33.3	43.2	23.5	19.8	11.7	1.9	96.9	–	1.9	1.2
1925	51.4	37.4	11.2	13.9	8.1	1.2	96.9	–	2.3	0.8
1926	78.3	20.9	0.8	19.6	7.4	1.7	99.5	–	0.5	–
1927	79.4	18.9	1.7	20.9	6.9	0.6	99.4	–	–	0.6
1928	83.1	14.6	2.3	18.4	7.6	1.5	99.4	0.3	–	0.3
1929	86.1	11.9	2.0	20.1	7.3	1.2	99.4	0.3	0.3	–
1930	87.7	11.3	1.0	21.7	5.4	1.3	98.9	0.5	0.5	–

Source: Baptismal registers, 1900-53.

environment. An analysis of the areas where the illegitimate births took place shows that the social position of the heads of household in those houses where the events occurred, while not of course wholly socially homogeneous, was mainly working-class.[26] Workers accounted for the largest group with 43.6 per cent (1900), 39.8 per cent (1910), 39.5 per cent (1920) and 36.2 per cent (1930).[27] Artisans (including skilled factory workers) followed with 22.3, 18, 19 and 16.1 per cent respectively. Merchants and shopkeepers[28] accounted for only 4.2, 7.2, 6.5 and 6.3 per cent respectively, and white-collar workers and civil servants only 1.8, 4.8, 5 and 9.8 per cent of the heads of households[29] (see Table 5.4). The conclusion indicated by the figures in Table 5.4 is confirmed by a more detailed investigation of the distribution of illegitimate births over the total number of 484 streets and squares in the city of Brunswick. Illegitimate births at home took place in 296 streets; of these only 1-5 births in 170 streets, 6-10 in 51 streets, 11-29 in 44 streets, 30-49 in 21 streets and 50 or more in 10 streets. These figures have little value on their own, as different streets and squares have different numbers of houses, and different houses have different numbers of households contained within them. A closer investigation reveals, however, that, compared with the number of houses and households, in general in those streets in which more than 30 illegitimate births took place, the percentage proportion of illegitimate births per houses and households was also highest.[30]

These streets and squares were mainly inhabited by the working class.[31] If one looks at the distribution of illegitimate births within the working-class districts it can be seen that at the beginning of the twentieth century they were fairly evenly distributed. However, this even distribution changed towards the end of the 1920s in so far as in the newer working-class districts, in which mainly skilled workers and their families lived, illegitimate births became less frequent than in the older, less favourable areas (which − looking at the overall trend − tended to be inhabited by the less well qualified workers).[32] Thus illegitimacy was an event that occurred mainly in working-class areas and, within that, largely in the poorer districts.

A statistical 'ideal type' of illegitimate mother in the city of Brunswick can be distilled from the material; she was Protestant, 20-24 years old, single, lived in a working-class district (and thus probably worked for a living) and had her child at home.

Table 5.4: **The Social Status of Heads of Households of Houses in which Illegitimate Children were Born in Four Sample Years**

Occupation	1900		1910		1920		1930	
	Absolute Figures	Percentage	Absolute Figures	Percentage	Absolute Figures	Percentage	Absolute Figures	Percentage
Gardeners and farm labourers	6	1.1	4	0.9	6	0.9	–	–
Waiters and servants	4	0.7	8	1.8	9	1.4	–	–
Commercial workers	144	26.6	102	22.4	151	22.9	41	23.6
Factory and technical workers	74	13.7	57	12.5	84	12.8	18	10.3
Craftworkers (artisans)	121	22.3	82	18.0	125	19.0	28	16.1
Foremen	–	–	2	0.4	4	0.6	1	0.6
Master craftsmen	14	2.6	15	3.3	16	2.4	3	1.7
Disabled	8	1.5	8	1.8	6	0.9	3	1.7
Pensioners	5	0.9	2	0.4	1	0.1	1	0.6
Private income	–	–	2	0.4	7	1.1	1	0.6
Clerical workers and civil servants	10	1.8	22	4.8	33	5.0	17	9.8
Traders and shopkeepers	23	4.2	33	7.2	43	6.5	11	6.3
Self-employed and professional	9	1.7	13	2.9	15	2.3	3	1.7
Working women	3	0.6	11	2.4	7	1.1	3	1.7
Women with no occupation given:								
Widows	89	16.4	69	15.1	104	15.8	24	13.8
Married women	20	3.7	16	3.5	30	4.6	11	6.3
Unmarried women	12	2.2	10	2.2	17	2.6	9	5.2
Total	542	100.0	456	100.0	658	100.0	174	100.0

Source: Baptismal registers, 1900-53; *Braunschweigische Adressbücher*, 1899, 1901, 1910, 1911, 1920, 1921, 1930, 1931.

III

These women were not behaving in a manner that differed widely from the norms of the surrounding working-class community. There is plenty of evidence to suggest that it was a general practice to enter into pre- or extramarital sexual relationships. This is confirmed by several contemporary writers.[33] Thus sexual relations before, after and outside marriage were not frowned upon.[34] However, in the overwhelming majority of cases these sexual relations did not lead to the birth of an illegitimate child: on the one hand, many of them did not result in conception and, on the other, the birth of an illegitimate child was often prevented by a hasty marriage.[35] Also, spontaneous and intentional abortions held the numbers of illegitimate births in check. Bastardy, although nothing really exceptional, was an exception to the general rule even in this environment. This can be clearly seen from Figure 5.1, on which the total numbers of illegitimate births to Protestant mothers which took place at home are shaded in for one of the various working-class areas.[36]

To the question why such a substantial number of women were ready to face the problems which — even under the most favourable circumstances — bearing an illegitimate child entailed and why they did not seek to terminate their pregnancy once it had occurred, there is a variety of possible answers.[37] In the first instance there was the fear of abortion itself; it could endanger the health or even the life of the woman herself — the illegality surrounding them meant that abortions were performed mainly by the quacks and butchers of the back-street business.[38] It is also possible that the chance of a later marriage and legitimation for the child contributed to this readiness. That this was a realistic hope is shown by the fact that during the period under investigation up to 38.9 per cent of illegitimate children born in any one year were later legitimised (see Table 5.3). The average over the years 1900-30 was 20.5 per cent. It is surprising that an illegitimate child born at home had a greater chance of being declared legitimate later than an illegitimate child born in a maternity ward[39] (see Table 5.5). The men responsible were overwhelmingly working class: skilled or unskilled workers, technical workers or artisans. The self-employed, white-collar workers, civil servants and professional classes were generally less well represented. This indicates that in the working-class environment extramarital sexual relations were often only a preliminary state to marriage, which, provoked by the illegitimate birth, then took place. It is further clear that the illegitimate child's father and mother were generally both from the same background.[40]

Similarly the chances of the mother of an illegitimate child marrying a man who was not the father of the child, but who was prepared to give his surname to that child were higher for those who had their babies at home. In general it was again mainly workers and artisans who were prepared to give their surnames to their wives' bastards. However, the

Figure 5.1: A Working-class District of Brunswick

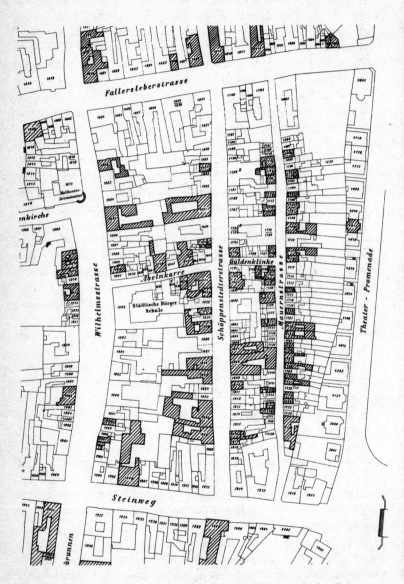

Note: The shaded areas indicate households in which illegitimate children were born at home to Protestant mothers (see p. 149).

Table 5.5: Illegitimacy in Brunswick: Correlation between Place of Confinement, Later Legitimation/Receiving the Name of the Stepfather and the Social Status of the Father/Stepfather

| | | Place of Confinement | | | | | | | | | | | | | |
| | | Public or Private Maternity Clinic | | | | | | | Home Confinement | | | | | | |
		1900	1905	1910	1915	1920	1925	1930	1900	1905	1910	1915	1920	1925	1930
Of the children born in the following years and locations the following percentage	remained fatherless[a]	74.3	71.6	69.0	74.5	77.3	83.5	71.6	64.8	63.2	60.9	58.3	65.3	65.9	76.2
were legitimised or declared legitimate; the father was ...	Worker	9.1	10.7	9.6	7.7	10.1	3.8	7.6	8.5	12.0	8.7	9.4	14.5	2.1	7.1
	Farm worker	2.7	3.0	2.2	1.2	–	0.7	1.8	–	0.8	–	2.1	–	1.0	–
	Skilled worker[b]	7.0	5.1	10.0	5.8	4.8	1.5	8.5	14.1	9.0	11.3	8.3	4.9	8.2	4.8
	Other	2.7	1.5	3.0	4.2	0.4	2.3	3.9	4.9	7.5	11.3	9.4	4.0	12.4	4.8
received the surname of the stepfather who was ...	Worker	2.1	5.6	2.2	3.1	2.2	0.7	3.3	1.4	0.8	2.6	2.1	4.8	4.1	–
	Farm worker	0.5	–	0.7	–	–	1.5	0.6	–	0.8	–	–	–	–	2.3
	Skilled worker[b]	0.5	1.0	1.5	1.9	2.6	0.7	0.6	3.5	1.5	1.7	–	2.4	2.1	–
	Other	–	0.5	0.7	0.8	0.4	4.5	0.6	2.8	2.2	3.5	6.3	3.2	2.1	4.8
	were adopted	1.1	1.0	1.1	0.8	2.2	0.7	1.5	–	2.2	–	4.1	0.8	2.1	–

Notes: a. Includes those who did not receive the surname of their stepfathers. b. Includes craft apprentices.

Source: Baptismal registers, 1900-53.

proportion of self-employed prepared to do this was higher than the proportion of self-employed who later legitimated their own offspring. Measured by the incidence of legitimation and the numbers of men who bestowed their surnames on their wives' illegitimate offspring, the proportion of illegitimate mothers who later married was, on average for the period 1900-30, 27.7 per cent. To assume, however, that this figure accurately reflects the marriage chances of illegitimate mothers would be too hasty. This figure does not include those marriages where the husband was not prepared to give his name to his wife's illegitimate offspring. Furthermore, it does not include those marriages that could have led either to legitimation or the passing on of a surname but did not do so because the illegitimate child died before the marriage took place.[41] Just how great an influence this factor could have had on the statistics can be inferred from the rate of infant mortality, which was even higher for illegitimate infants than for legitimate ones (see Table 5.6). One should not conclude, however, that this higher mortality can be traced back to a greater indifference towards their children on the part of the illegitimate mothers.[42]

One problem with the statistics of infant mortality is that they are not differentiated by class. As has already been indicated, most illegitimate infants were born in a working-class environment. The mortality of infants in this environment — both of legitimate and illegitimate infants — was fundamentally much higher than in the middle or upper classes.[43] This means that the mortality of illegitimate children should first of all be compared with the mortality of working-class children, in order to produce comparable results. If the mortality of illegitimate infants remains higher notwithstanding, then the reason must be sought in the unfavourable economic conditions which faced the single mother. Above all, the need to spend all day working outside the house to earn a living must be mentioned.[44] Under these circumstances the mother was forced to put her child out to care,[45] and generally the illegitimate mother found it impossible to breast-feed her child for a sufficient period.[46]

To return to our starting-point, legitimation and the passing on of a surname[47] served the purpose of creating 'normal' families, i.e. families that conformed to the prevailing social norms. Thus these cases of bastardy represent only a temporary break with social norms. However, the difficulties encountered by families trying to recreate a situation of 'normality' are well documented by the numerous cases where the state authorities tried to hinder those attempts. The following are typical examples.

Table 5.6: Infant Mortality in Brunswick, 1900-30

Year	Live Births		Died in the 1st year of life		Percentage of legit. infant deaths	Percentage of illegit. infant deaths	Over-mortality of illegitimate infants
	Legit.	Illegit.	Legit.	Illegit.			
1900	3,483	527	676	193	19.4	36.6	88.7
1901	3,517	540	654	207	18.6	38.3	105.9
1902	3,378	506	446	126	13.2	24.9	88.6
1903	3,291	507	634	152	19.3	30.0	55.4
1904	3,177	508	530	206	16.7	40.6	143.1
1905	2,931	493	552	149	18.8	30.2	60.6
1906	2,898	487	506	141	17.5	29.0	65.7
1907	2,781	501	379	130	13.6	25.9	90.4
1908	2,788	541	390	142	14.0	36.4	160.0
1909	2,595	543	356	113	13.7	20.8	51.8
1910	2,523	551	311	104	12.3	18.9	53.7
1911	2,413	485	396	126	16.4	26.0	58.5
1912	2,394	536	259	115	10.8	21.5	99.1
1913	2,290	550	290	105	12.7	19.1	50.4
1914	2,379	559	312	115	13.1	20.6	57.3
1915	1,957	525	168	72	8.6	13.7	59.3
1916	1,524	386	167	66	11.0	17.1	55.5
1917	1,249	326	141	55	11.3	16.9	49.6
1918	1,274	361	130	64	10.2	17.7	73.5
1919	2,109	454	191	82	9.1	18.1	98.9
1920	2,564	571	272	114	10.6	20.0	88.7
1921	2,335	525	239	86	10.2	16.4	60.8
1922	2,010	504	222	101	11.0	20.0	81.8
1923	1,796	417	210	84	11.7	20.1	71.8
1924	1,796	371	163	50	9.1	13.5	48.4
1925	1,939	545	179	84	9.2	15.4	67.4
1926	2,029	580	145	71	7.1	12.2	71.8
1927	1,819	513	128	53	7.0	10.3	47.1
1928	1,522	328	149	56	9.8	17.1	74.5
1929	1,626	320	132	46	8.1	14.4	77.8
1930	1,538	324	133	56	8.6	17.3	101.2

Sources: StA Wf 12 A Neu Fb. 13 Nr. 19555; 14 Neu Zg. 4/46 and 19/58 Nr. 15 II, 15 III, 15 IV, 15 V, 31 I, 31 II; *Statistisches Jahrbuch deutscher Städte,* 20 (1914), p. 52; 23 (1928), p. 371; 25 (1930), p. 29; 26 (1931), pp. 16, 555.

The wife of an innkeeper, born on 14 April 1863 in London, was divorced on 14 November 1897 for committing adultery with a waiter. As she required, as a result of the divorce, a special state permit to marry this man,[48] she petitioned the appropriate ministry (*Herzogliches Staatsministerium*) in June 1899. As a result the police made some enquiries about her, taking their information mainly from friends and acquaintances of her divorced husband, so that a very unfavourable picture of the petitioner emerged. The request was not granted, and a further petition at the beginning of 1900 was also refused. In the meantime, however, the woman had become pregnant, a fact which led the police to report that 'from the state of things it can be assumed that she continues to live with and have sexual relations with' the waiter. In this case the illegitimate birth was provoked by the behaviour of the authorities. The couple decided to get married in London.[49]

The printer Rudolf Neumann,[50] born 7 June 1870, and the former cannery worker Auguste Drewes, born 14 October 1877, also had to get married in London. In this instance it was the illegitimate child's father who was divorced for committing adultery with Frau Drewes in 1899. That the affair had started only after Neumann's wife had left him cut no ice with the authorities. It is true they did concede in 1899 that Drewes was a 'respectable, hard-working girl. . .and apart from her sexual misconduct, nothing to her disadvantage has been discovered', but the marriage was forbidden. Two further requests in 1899 and 1900 were refused. In the meantime, however, on 18 February 1900, an illegitimate child was born to the couple, so they decided to get married in London (1901). As a result the public prosecutor attempted to nullify the marriage. However, before the case was heard, the couple, who had now been married for nearly five years, petitioned once more for a dispensation. Finally – as the public prosecutor complained – it was only on the grounds of expediency that the request was granted.[51]

The following instances illustrate how strong the desire to recreate socially recognised family relationships could be in some cases. The barman Ohlendorf, born 1850, who was divorced from his second wife in 1901, after an eight-year separation, for committing adultery with a cleaner, Dorothee Hake, requested a dispensation in order to marry in 1902. His illegitimate child (born in 1899 to Hake) was to be legitimised by this marriage. (Two other illegitimate children born to Dorothee Hake in 1887 and 1893 were not his.) The request was refused as a result of the police report which stated that although Ohlendorf voluntarily paid maintenance to his divorced wife, he had been convicted twice of licensing offences and that formerly he had had the reputation, as manager of an inn, 'of having entered into sexual relations with his female staff and having allowed dissolute persons to frequent the inn'. In the meantime the unmarried mother of three illegitimate children had to earn her living as a charwoman. The children were cared for by their maternal grandmother. The police: 'Morally [the woman] has sunk very low.' Two further attempts by Ohlendorf to obtain permission in 1903 were refused: 'Although it may seem desirable in the interests of the child that the petitioner should be granted the opportunity of legi-timation by marriage to [Hake], in view of... [Ohlendorf's] character and that of ... [Hake] it appears very questionable whether the marriage of these two would be a fitting thing.' Only after Ohlendorf's divorced wife had died in 1905 was the request granted.[52]

The factory painter Heinrich Taube, born 1858, and Wilhelmine Sommer, born 1873, who took in ironing for a living, chose the alter-native of getting married in London like the first two couples mentioned above. Taube, whose first marriage had been dissolved in 1880 because he had committed adultery with his later second wife, and who was divorced for a second time in 1900 for committing adultery with Wil-helmine Sommer, was refused his request for a dispensation to marry. The two children born to him and Sommer (in 1897 and 1899) remained illegitimate until the parents married in England in 1902. Heinrich Taube died in September 1903 and on 20 December 1906 his widow bore another illegitimate child, who this time remained illegitimate.[53]

IV

If the above examples, chosen from a large number of similar cases, seem to prove that even in the working-class behaviour conforming to bourgeois norms of family and reproductive life generally prevailed,[54] the following cases indicate that the working class did not always try to conform. 'Concubinage', where a man and woman lived together with-out attempting to legalise their situation, was not unusual. In these cases requests for permission to marry, i.e. requests to be allowed to end this illegal state of affairs, were generally accompanied by disciplinary meas-ures on the part of the police. The occasion for this was provided by paragraph 19 I of the Brunswick police ordinances,[55] according to which persons 'who, engaging in sexual relations, continue to live together under one roof after a police warning' were to be punished either with a fine or up to six weeks' imprisonment. According to this ordinance the police were also entitled to order the 'enforced separation of persons living together in concubinage'. This law forbidding concubinage was the authorities' answer to a growing trend in the working class in the second half of the nineteenth century to develop their own set of familial living patterns without reference to the prevailing middle- and upper-class attitudes. In its fight to extent bourgeois norms to all sectors the bourgeoisie increasingly turned to legal methods as this law against concubinage indeed demonstrates.

Roland Feller, born 7 April 1865 in Moravia, a worker in the Brunswick jute factory, was divorced in 1900 after 10 years of marriage, for committing adultery with Franziska Heinrich, another jute spinner, born 23 July 1874 in East Prussia.[56] In 1901 he requested a marriage permit. The illegitimate children born in 1896, 1897, 1898, 1899 and 1900 were to be thus legalised.[57] However, as the couple had been warned by the police in 1898 for concubinage, the request was refused. They also travelled to England and married on 21 October 1901 in London, and thus circumvented the obstacles imposed by the state.[58]

For over five years the operative Willi Stange, born 1849 in Berlingerode (Kreis Worbis) and Hermine Fuchs, factory worker (and for a time seamstress and housekeeper), born July 1868 in Brunswick, struggled with the authorities. They also came into conflict with the law against concubinage. 'The two people [Stange and Fuchs] do, it is true, occupy two separate rooms', wrote the police in their first report on the couple in 1900, 'but it cannot be doubted that their relationship has been a sexual one for a number of years and that it continues to be so. In 1894 they were warned by the police for suspected concubinage.' In fact there can be no doubt at all that the relationship involved sex as in 1892, 1894, 1896 and 1898 children were born of this union. A fifth illegitimate child born to Hermine Fuchs in 1887, however, was not fathered by Willi Stange. Further requests in 1901 and 1904 were also refused. In the meantime the mother of these illegitimate children had lost her job. She then moved in with Stange along with the children, as her mother, who had previously looked after the children, had also died in 1902. On 21 June 1905 they were convicted of concubinage – one week's imprisonment each. It was only in April 1906 after one further request that the couple, despite an unaltered state of affairs, were deemed worthy of the 'favour' they had appealed for.[59]

Two other petitioners were more unlucky: they supported their request for the woman to be allowed to marry on the grounds that 'they had been living in the same dwelling for three years'. This alerted the police for the first time to their illegal household. As a result an immediate 'separation of the petitioners who are apparently living in concubinage'[60] was ordered. This instance throws light on the apparent equanimity with which many workers contravened bourgeois norms: growing up in a working-class environment, they did not realise that their behaviour did not conform to the norms of society at large.[61] The following example illustrates the absurdity to which the law against concubinage could lead.

In 1896, 1900 and 1903 the housekeeper Elise Pott, born in 1868 in Salzgitter, bore three illegitimate children. Their father was Johann Meyer, an engine driver, born in 1854 in Schwachhausen. Meyer, who had been divorced from his wife in 1902 as both were found guilty of adultery, requested a lifting of the marriage ban on him in 1904. Elise Pott had looked after his household for him since 1895 and for this she and her two children (the first-born had died in infancy) received their keep. The police report on the request ran as follows: Meyer 'is a slovenly man and held in bad repute and his concubine is of the same low moral standing, for which reason I humbly beseech the ministry not to allow the marriage to take place'. The petition was refused, but repeated several times by Meyer. In November 1906 the police reported:

It may be that the petitioner and the unmarried. . .[Pott] are suffering greatly because they are not allowed to marry. In my opinion this cannot be sufficient reason for granting the dispensation . . .[Meyer] must rather remove the obstacle which stands in the way of his wishes: He must separate from the unmarried [Pott] , so the suspicion of concubinage. . .is removed. If he does this and behaves blamelessly, then I will endorse his request. If he does not I must regard his behaviour as defiance, which would make him unworthy of the favour he seeks.

This order to separate was issued to Meyer with another refusal of his request at the end of December 1906. On 1 March 1907 Meyer and Pott separated. Meyer moved to a nearby street while Pott remained in the flat. In July the police reported 'the time that the couple have been separated has been relatively short; however one must recognise their good will and serious efforts to put aside all suspicion that they are still living together and engaging in extra-marital sexual intercourse', and recommended the granting of their petition, which took place on 9 July 1907.[62]

However, even in the above cases the endeavours of working-class people to create 'normal' marital relationships and families can be discerned. The following case offers a complete contrast. Since October

1901 Frida Kasten, housekeeper, born 1878 in Krotoschin (near Breslau) and Karl Fricke, coachman, had been living together in a flat in a typical working-class area of the old town. Both were without property and lived on Fricke's income. He was widowed and had four legitimate children who were cared for by Frida Kasten. The police took steps against this set-up. On 25 February 1901 they interviewed a neighbour who reported that she had visited Frida Kasten three or four weeks previously. She had noticed that Frida Kasten had moved the beds so that she would be sleeping with Fricke in one room in the same bed. Three days later Fricke and Kasten were interviewed. Both denied sleeping in the same room, insisting that Frida slept with the children in a different room from Fricke. As they were ordered by the police under threat of punishment to separate before 3 March 1904, Kasten took a room in a neighbouring house which contained only a bed, a chair and a table. Fricke paid the rent. Frida Kasten continued her work as housekeeper for Fricke, so that in fact the 'extramarital sexual union' which the police sought to prevent also continued. Even the police recognised this. On 5 March they noted 'it can be assumed with certainty that further sexual intercourse will take place'. On 15 June 1904 Frida Kasten gave birth to their first illegitimate child in Fricke's flat. The police, who had discovered that Fricke's flat was accessible by a back entrance from Kasten's house were searching — in vain — for witnesses that Kasten had used this back entrance to enter the flat unobserved at night. In July and October 1904 as well as in January and April 1905 they had nothing new to report. In July 1905 there was the birth of the second illegitimate child in Fricke's flat to be noted. In December of the same year the police attacked again: they gave Fricke and Kasten an ultimatum that unless their illegal sexual union was dissolved there would be proceedings taken against them. Fricke — who had other objections anyway — insisted that he could not sack Frida Kasten from her job as housekeeper because he needed her to look after his children, and ordered the marriage banns from the public registrar. After the police had taken note of them and taken back their ultimatum Fricke rescinded the banns. A little while later Kasten took a new room, this time eleven houses away, but she remained as housekeeper for Fricke. Police observation started again. There were reports in March, April and July 1906, but there was nothing substantial. Only after police harassment had finally come to an end in July 1907 did Fricke and Kasten voluntarily legalise their union by getting married.[63]

This case, which is not the only one of its kind, shows that defiant nonconformism on the part of working-class people was stringently pursued by the authorities. It is not just one couple and the police that meet here, but two worlds, which, with respect to the prevailing social norms and values, had almost nothing in common. The numerous cases of women who bore several illegitimate children and made no attempt whatsoever to legalise their relationships or find husbands who would pass on their surnames to the children bear witness to the fact that there were present in the working-class environment tendencies which could have led to the dissolution of traditional family structures if they had not — in the long run — been successfully repressed. The analysed material documents various women with up to six co-residing illegitimate children, although the material existence of these women was quite clearly precarious.

This is the case with the unemployed daughter of a locksmith,[64] who bore six illegitimate children in 1900, 1908, 1909, 1911, 1913 and 1915. The frequent changes of abode — the children were born at five different addresses — are an indication of the impermanence which particularly characterised the living conditions of working-class families. Furthermore, this woman received aid from the city (the so-called *Wanderhilfe*)[65] during her last two confinements, a sure index of extreme poverty. The *Wanderhilfe* was supported by a communal fund set up by the city of Brunswick, following the example of Elberfeld, in April 1907, for the 'welfare of impecunious women in childbed'.[66] It had become necessary as

> in the poorer classes of the population there is a lack of the most basic household equipment needed for these purposes [i.e. a home confinement] and the cleanliness of those available leaves much to be desired. In many families the use of bedclothes is apparently unknown.[67]

The name *Wanderhilfe* (lit. 'aid that moves on') was derived from the fact that the articles needed for a home confinement were only lent and therefore moved from house to house. The following articles were loaned: a bucket, two wash basins, a bowl, a small basin, a bag, a sheet, a blanket, three hand towels, four undersheets, one rubber sheet and a bed-jacket. In addition the following were donated: one shirt, 250 grammes of cotton-wool, a tin of soap and two printed mottoes on child care.[68] The first *Wanderhilfe* went out in June 1907. At the end of 1922, the last year for which there are any remaining lists on the use of *Wanderhilfe*, it was 3,984.[69] Women bearing illegitimate children were apparently less well served by this institution than mothers of legitimate children.

Thus the proportion of mothers receiving the *Wanderhilfe* was in all years considerably lower than the proportion of illegitimate children born overall.[70]

V

Two problems, which today might seem rather secondary, but which at the time, judging by the volume of documents dealing with them, had considerable significance, were the not uncommon occurrence of a mother and child bearing two different surnames and the question of whether an unmarried mother should be referred to as 'Miss' (Fräulein) or 'Mrs' (Frau). For the first of these two problems there were many variations on two basic configurations. First, *the child bore the name of the previous husband of a remarried woman.* For example, Karoline Martens, née Schulze, divorced in 1900, bore a child in 1901 whose father was not her previous husband, but a stonemason called Berger. However, as the child was regarded as having been conceived in wedlock, and as the husband did not contest the legitimacy of the child (which seldom happened) it bore the name of Martens. Its mother and Berger married and in 1907 applied to change the child's name on the grounds that it 'would lead to all manner of misunderstandings' if the child continued to be called Martens rather than Berger, 'as school was coming up'.[71] The second possible configuration was that *the child bore the single name of the widowed mother.* Luise Herzog, née Dreyer, born 1870 in Brunswick and widowed in 1899, had three legitimate children (born 1892, 1895 and 1898) and gave birth to an illegitimate child in 1903 that bore the surname Dreyer. From 1904 Luise Herzog lived in at the city nursing home where she helped with the cooking and for this received board and lodgings for herself, her youngest legitimate and her illegitimate children as well as a few marks pocket-money. In 1910 she applied to change the name of the illegitimate child. She said that the reason she had not married the child's father was that, although she had intended to, she had had 'unfortunately to give up the idea due to the dissolute life he led'. He had been 'imprisoned several times for theft etc. If I had married him, the child and I would have been most unfortunate.'[72] Thus differences in surname seemed above all to create difficulties in contact with the bourgeoisie (i.e. teachers, the authorities, etc.). This can be clearly seen from the fact that it was generally when a child started school that a change in name was applied for and this was often given as the reason.[73] This also indicates that a difference in surname which was known of in the child's home environment caused (scarcely) any problems.

The term of address for an unmarried mother had been in dispute for a long time. During the First World War it became evident that the women in question were no longer content to be addressed as 'Miss'. This was not in the main simply because adult unmarried women were now claiming their right to be addressed as such (i.e. as 'Frau'), but rather a further attempt to conceal the illegitimacy of the child that lived with them. It was again a matter of giving at least the appearance of 'normality'. The vast majority of appeals to this effect from all over the German Empire during the First World War came from the so-called 'war-brides' (*Kriegerbräute*). Thus it was mainly women who had only borne an illegitimate child (or at least this is what they said) because the father had fallen in battle before the proposed wedding. Even some women from the working class were successful in their applications to authority for permission to be addressed as 'Mrs' — usually concomitant with taking the surname of the dead man for themselves and the child.[74]

The state institutions in Brunswick were quite obviously not inclined to grant this favour, although other federal states proved themselves far more amenable to such concessions. In Prussia in exceptional cases permission was granted 'to the fiancée to use the title of "Mrs" . . . only on the basis of His Majesty's favour'.[75] Baden, Württemberg and Saxony also allowed unmarried mothers to use the title 'Mrs' on the condition 'that they had been seriously intending to marry one of the participants in the war'.[76] The Bavarian government went so far as to declare that

the title 'Mrs' is neither part of the name nor an addition to it, and that the question of who is entitled to this term of address is not a legal one, but one to be answered on the basis of custom.[77]

In contrast, in Brunswick the question arose as to whether 'the desire of a surviving war-bride to achieve the social status of a married woman. . . represents a sufficient reason to introduce a new practice which contravenes the traditional customs and laws'.[78] It should not be overlooked that

at the present time there are attempts to validate claims that, by allowing every mother of an illegitimate child to use the title of 'Mrs', will result in a fundamental dissolution of the difference between them which rests on the high value we place on marriage, a trend which will of necessity lead to a widespread weakening of the significance of marriage for the common people|...|If this firm line of distinction wavers...there exists the danger that the material significance of the title 'Mrs' will be diminished in the people's mind, and Christian communities rightly fear that the already too widespread lax attitude to the immorality of extra-marital sexual intercourse will be further advanced.[79]

Even after the November Revolution of 1918, when the workers' government of the free state of Brunswick decreed that every woman was free to decide how she was to be addressed, the police — still under bourgeois control — attempted to have the decree retracted. However, they were unsuccessful.[80]

VI

It is particularly hard to find answers to questions about how working-class women reacted when they discovered they were pregnant and had to face the birth of an illegitimate child, and how their families and neighbours behaved. Here we have to enter the field of — more or less well founded — speculation, and must be wary of gross over-generalisation. Finally, what has here been referred to as a 'working-class environment' does not represent a unit in any respect. Rather it is a heterogeneous, disparate set of relationships. Of course the vast majority of people living in this setting were either directly or indirectly subject to the conditions of wage labour, but a common attitude and behaviour towards the prevailing norms of reproduction cannot be deduced from this; the variety of 'the totality of everyday reality with its joys and sorrows, memories and hopes'[81] was not determined solely by material and political or legal criteria.[82]

However, this study indicates that although before the First World War illegitimate motherhood was not of course desirable, it did not generally lead to social discrimination within the woman's own environment. Despite this one must start from the assumption that mothers of illegitimate children, even in a working-class environment, had to face either temporary or more intractable difficulties, which did not have to be faced by mothers of legitimate children; apart from the complications mentioned above, the impermanence of living quarters[83] with the necessity of frequent removals, the problems of staying in the parental home, and the *in effect* discriminatory visits by social and welfare workers[84] should be included.

The situation in the 1920s appears to be different from that obtaining in the first two decades of the twentieth century. With the differentiation of the working class and the increase in white-collar workers with their own social mores,[85] the heterogeneous nature of working-class culture tended to be magnified.[86] The greater job and housing security enjoyed by the skilled working class[87] increased identification with the state and its instruments,[88] and similar developments probably all had an effect on attitudes to the norms of reproduction and the desire to conform to them. Interviews with old people about these problems in the Weimar Republic era serve to indicate this. The following extracts from interviews clearly demonstrate the contradictions between the ideals of freedom, which are particularly apparent in members of the organised working class, and the realisation of these ideals in so far as the individual and/or his or her family is concerned.

One of the men interviewed, in answer to a question about how illegitimate mothers had been regarded in the working-class environment, replied:

> It was all a matter of course. [Answering a further question as to whether these women had experienced any form of discrimination] No, no, in no way. Not in these circles. . .at least not from working-class activists, who belonged to an organisation or felt they somehow belonged to the movement. Of course the — if I can use the word — proletarians who stood around in bars and drank all the time. . .yes, in other circles they sang a completely different tune.[89]

One woman saw it in a less clear-cut manner. At first she replied, 'My God, it could happen to anyone. I used to think to myself: that could happen to you one day.' However, shortly afterwards she went on to describe her fear that it would happen to her: 'Nowadays it's overlooked. Today people would say. . .that's OK, everyone has a moment of weakness. But then it was "Just don't get pregnant!" '[90] A further interviewee (male) believed that he noticed a marked intolerance towards unmarried mothers:

> For example we had a neighbour, Lisa Schulze, who got pregnant. And no one knew whose it was. . . Now, when she went past, there would be three women standing around here, three more there: 'Look at that whore.' 'She was always half-way a whore.'. . . Here [in the working-class environment] no one thought it out of the normal run. She'd let a man in and wasn't married and now she had

a child — 'Look, that's Lisa's bastard' and so on when the child was bigger. It didn't bother us as kids — we just accepted her like anyone else — but then the parents, in particular the mothers — fathers less — they said, 'Don't you play with that child' — 'Why not? Why shouldn't I play with her?' 'You know why, she hasn't got a father. She doesn't know who the father was.' That's how it was more or less. That's how it was.[91]

These descriptions make it clear that illegitimacy was a problem in the working-class environment, both for the potential victims, i.e. unmarried women who engaged in sexual intercourse, and for the by-standers. In the following longer extracts two unmarried working-class mothers speak for themselves. The first, born 1911, was the daughter of a cleaning woman and a skilled plumber who worked as a caretaker. She was brought up in a strictly socialist household, and gave birth to her illegitimate child when she was eighteen years old.

I got to know a young man when I was seventeen, and I believed this was my great love. . .it's natural when a young girl falls in love for the first time and thinks she's met the man for her for life — for me it was all quite clear — I was going to marry him. You think: Now everything's perfect. I believed in it. You always have the example of your parents and of all the couples around you that have got married before your eyes, so you don't think about it. . .My father was always against the idea because he thought he wasn't a proper socialist. He always used that to warn me. And he was too arrogant towards him, which of course made a big impression on me. And then, when I told my parents that I was expecting a child, for them, for my father, then the world was turned upside down. [She was ordered to leave home by her parents and to have the child in its father's home.] I left. . .and a week later returned in tears. . .But you needn't think I was ashamed while I was expecting that child, my eldest son. Never that: my parents tried to make me, but I never for a moment thought of getting rid of it. . . On the contrary. I was happy about it. I was glad. I conceived the child in joy and gave birth to him gladly. And at that time I wasn't quite sure that I wouldn't marry the father. My reason had always told me that it wouldn't be a good marriage, but I was still drawn to the man with my whole being. . . Well, I was living with my parents. . ., those three months I was at home again. . . But don't think I was allowed to set foot outside the door. . . My father and mother didn't want it generally known.

She described then how the neighbours, after the birth of the child, had disapproved of her parents' behaviour and concluded: 'But when the child was born no one was as delighted as my father. From the first day . . .my parents were overjoyed.'[92]

The second unmarried mother, born 1910, gave birth to her child when she was twenty years old. Her father was a sheet-metal worker, her mother worked at home.

> I didn't want to get married any more after she [the illegitimate daughter] had arrived. It's strange what goes on in people's heads. [To the question what had her parents said about the forthcoming illegitimate birth, she replied] My father said nothing, but my mother cursed. 'Such a thing, it's a scandal, a shame upon us.' That's the way people were. My mother was always going on: 'Of course the youngest! Having a child!' She behaved as if I'd picked up the child like an infection in the gutter. And then my boyfriend, as he then was, said: 'Listen, this can't go on. I didn't find Ilse[93] in the gutter. . .'

On the reaction of the neighbours the interviewee reported: 'You were looked at, yes: "Look now, she's got a man, a boyfriend, and he's the cause of her downfall," and "No, that can't be true! A child on the way and not married!" It was dreadful.' The interviewee stated expressly during the further course of the interview that her parents had wanted her to have the child at home; and to the question of whether there had been any danger of her parents turning her out of the house she replied: 'No, no, no. My mother complained and nagged, but they would never have thrown me out. I gave birth to my small daughter; my husband [i.e. her boyfriend, whom she later married] came to see us every day. We were inseparable.'

VII

A tentative answer to the question posed at the beginning of this chapter on the connection between industrialisation, urbanisation and illegitimacy will be given in the following concluding remarks. The tentative nature of these reflections in view of the rudimentary state of research in this area should be emphasised. It has been ascertained that illegitimacy occurred above all in a working-class setting and that it was no unusual phenomenon. As the numerous attempts to recreate 'normal' family relationships demonstrate, illegitimacy in a working-class context was not desirable, but it can also be shown that during roughly the first third of the period under investigation it generally caused little discrimination. The reason for this was that the root cause, i.e. non-marital sexual intercourse, constituted behaviour that was generally accepted. At the end of the 1920s illegitimacy became less frequent and occurred, if the working-class environment is differentiated by streets in which more skilled or unskilled workers lived, more frequently amongst the unskilled working class.[94] Probably during this period greater attention came to be paid to methods of contraception[95] and probably the more highly qualified working class would be more likely to take advantage of the new methods before the unskilled. The contradictions which can be discerned in both interviews with by-standers who described the general reaction to illegitimate mothers and those with unmarried mothers themselves indicate a change in attitude (which had already taken place or was taking place at the time).

This gives rise to the following reflections: illegitimacy represents a necessary concomitant to legitimacy; just as the tracing of a line of descent is based on the man, the absence of it is based on the woman;[96] and this is true not only for legal questions, but also – and this is much more important – for the inheritance of property.[97] In order to regulate the system of inheritance, i.e. the passing on of property to the next generation and the concomitant opportunities, the members of the property-owning classes had to submit themselves to a patrilineal lineage system. Illegitimacy thus entails both exclusion from inheritance rights and excommunication from the social class. But a class which owned nothing had no inheritance rights to forgo. It is in this lack of property that the reasons why the working class felt so little compulsion to conform to the prevailing reproductive norms should be sought.[98] In so far as industrialisation in the nineteenth century increased the mass of propertyless wage workers, and urbanisation crowded them together, these factors both encouraged the spread of illegitimacy.[99] However, later developments in the industrial mode of production and the formation of organised capitalism led to differentiation within the working class. A growing number of skilled workers developed, who experienced in their own lifetimes opportunities for enrichment and advancement which were far greater than those that had been enjoyed by their parents' generation or those still enjoyed by their unskilled colleagues.[100] They were still of course without property (even in the 1920s), still imprinted with working-class culture and at home in the working-class environment; but this itself had changed; social differences within this setting had become more clear-cut than had been the case fifty years previously.

In particular the skilled workers had developed the idea in the course of time that there was a chance of improving their lives within the capitalist system. In this view, a socialist revolution was not the only way out. Bound up with this seems to have been the view which gradually gained credence that it was possible to pass on to one's children more than one's chains:[101] the same social status could be achieved by making it possible for the child to follow an apprenticeship[102] or something similar. Such a change in attitude must have had a considerable influence on the way the prevailing social reproductive norms were regarded, in that at least this group (and later other types of workers as well) came finally to accept these norms.

Marianne Weber's concept of the relationship between industrialisation, urbanisation and illegitimacy needs, then, to be differentiated, in that at different stages in the development of capitalism the effects of these factors on the phenomenon (illegitimacy) were different, and not so direct as she assumed. Thus there was a connection, but it did not always operate in the same way.

Notes

1. M. Weber, *Ehefrau u. Mutter in der Rechtsentwicklung. Eine Einführung* (Tübingen, 1907), pp. 508f.

2. Also R.P. Neuman, 'Industrialization and Sexual Behaviour: Some Aspects of Working Class Life in Imperial Germany' in R.J. Bezucha (ed.), *Modern European Social History* (Lexington, Mass., 1972), pp.270-98; quote p. 283.

3. M. Mitterauer, 'Familienformen u. Illegitimität in ländlichen Gebieten Österreichs', *Archiv für Sozialgeschichte (AfS)*, vol. XIX (1979) pp. 123-88, in particular pp. 123-8; also same author, 'Historische Verbreitung von Illegitimität im europäischen Raum', unpubl. MS., 1980, p. 7; D. Sabean, 'Unehelichkeit: Ein Aspekt sozialer Reproduktion kleinbäuerlicher Produzenten. Neckarhausen um 1800', unpubl. MS., 1980, p. 6.

4. E. Shorter *et al.*, 'The Decline of Non-marital Fertility in Europe, 1880-1940', *Population Studies*, vol. 25 (1971), pp. 375-93, 389ff.

5. E. Shorter, 'Sexual Change and Illegitimacy: the European Experience' in Bezucha, *Modern European Social History*, pp. 231-69, in particular p. 244.

6. See G. Hardach, *Deutschland in der Weltwirtschaft 1870-1970* (Frankfurt/Main, 1977), p. 34.

7. Shorter *et al.*, 'Decline of Non-marital Fertility', p. 392; Shorter, 'Sexual Change', p. 236; G. Mackenroth, *Bevölkerungslehre* (Berlin, 1953), p. 59; F. Prinzing, 'Die uneheliche Fruchtbarkeit in Deutschland', *Zeitschrift für Sozialwissenschaft (ZfS)*, vol. 5 (1902), pp. 37-46.

8. Hardach, *Deutschland*, p. 15.

9. J. Knodel, *The Decline of Fertility in Germany, 1871-1939* (Princeton, NJ, 1974), p. 247.

10. Shorter, 'Sexual Change', p. 236. During the decline in fertility legitimate

fertility sank by 65 per cent and illegitimate fertility by 54 per cent (cf. Knodel, *Decline*, pp. 246ff). Although the developments have certain parallel character-istics (see P. Cutright, 'Illegitimacy: Myths, Causes and Cures', *Family Planning Perspectives*, vol. 3 (1971), pp. 26-48), the two processes, which together form the demographic transition in Germany, are probably attributable to different causes (see also Knodel, *Decline*, p. 79).

11.   Ibid., p. 273.
12.   Ibid., p. 273. From 1886 to 1905 the illegitimacy rate in the Duchy of Brunswick was higher than the overall figure for the German Empire. Cf. *Beiträge zur Statistik des Herzogtums Braunschweig*, Heft 24 (Braunschweig, 1910), p. 9.
13.   Knodel, *Decline*, p. 273.
14.   The quota of illegitimate births varied from 15.1 per cent (1902) to 28.9 per cent (1918, 1926). The average overall for the years 1900-30 is 20.9 per cent (Niedersächsisches Staatsarchiv Wolfenbüttel (StA Wf), 12 A Neu Fb. 13 Nr. 19555; 14 Neu Zg. 4/46 and 19/58, Nr. 15 IV, 15 V, 31 I, 31 II; *Statistischer Vierteljahresbericht der Stadt Braunschweig* (Jan.-Mar. 1931), p. 39).
15.   Neuman, 'Industrialization and Sexual Behaviour', p. 283.
16.   This term is used in preference to the usual term 'unmarried mothers' as this is inadequate: married women can also have illegitimate children, i.e. if they are not married to the father of the child, and paternity is successfully proven in court.
17.   K. Marx and F. Engels, 'Die deutsche Ideologie' in *Marx-Engels-Werke (MEW)*, vol. 3 (Berlin, 1958), pp. 9-530, esp. p. 29.
18.   A. Lüdtke, 'Alltagswirklichkeit, Lebensweise und Bedürfnisartikulation', *Gesellschaft. Beiträge zur Marxschen Theorie*, 11, Hg. H.-G. Backhaus *et al.* (Frankfurt/Main, 1978), pp. 311-50, 318. Also K. Schönhaven, 'Gewerkschafts-wachstum, Mitgliederintegration und bürokratische Organisation in der Zeit vor dem Ersten Weltkrieg' in H. Mommsen (ed.), *Arbeiterbewegung und industrieller Wandel* (Wuppertal, 1980), pp. 16-37, esp. p. 24.
19.   K. Hausen, 'Familie als Gegenstand Historischer Sozialwissenschaft' *GG*, vol. 1 (1975), pp. 171-209, 181. See H. Schelsky, *Soziologie der Sexualität* (Rein-bek, 1955), p. 50, on the way in which norms like these take on an 'absolute character'.
20.   The remainder were divided between other religious communities and the non-religious. (StA Wf. 14 Neu Zg. 4/46 and 19/58 Nr. 15 IV, 15 V, 31 I, 31 II). A more detailed investigation of the relationship between religion and illegitimate motherhood will not be attempted here. (On this subject see A. Lange, *Die unehelichen Geburten in Baden. Eine Untersuchung über ihre Bedingungen und ihre Entwicklung* (Karlsruhe, 1912), p. 71.)
21.   StA Wf. 14 Neu Zg. 4/46 and 19/58 Nr. 15 II, 15 III, 15 IV, 15 V, 31 I, 31 II.
22.   Ibid.
23.   Ibid.
24.   The material on which Tables 5.2, 5.3 and 5.4 are based is taken from the baptismal register of the eleven Lutheran parishes of the city of Brunswick and the military administrative district (hereafter referred to as 'Taufregister'). The illegitimate children born between 1900 and 1930 were sorted out from the num-bers of children baptised between 1900 and 1953. These comprised 9,954 baptisms from 9,901 births. I am indebted to Dorothea Rischau for her help in collecting and evaluating the data and to the Ev.-luth. Stadtkirchenverband Braunschweig for permission to use these sources. The baptismal registers of the military admin-istrative district were made available by the Landeskirchliches Archiv Braunschweig. In contrast to Tables 5.1, 5.2 and 5.5, these tables also include children of mothers not permanently resident in Brunswick, a fact which, with respect to the relation-ship between home and hospital confinements, leads to some misleading results.

In Brunswick, as in other towns, it was noticeable that numerous women came from the countryside or small towns to have their illegitimate children in the hospitals of the larger town in order to avoid the 'shame' at home. On this theme see P. Dittmann, 'Die Bevölkerungsbewegung der deutschen Grossstädte seit der Gründung des deutschen Reiches', diss. Munich, Bamberg, 1912, p. 96; F. Prinzing, 'Uneheliche Geburten', *Handwörterbuch der Staatswissenschaften (HdStW)*, vol. 8 (Jena, 1911), pp. 34-43, esp. p. 35; E. Shorter, 'Illegitimacy, Sexual Revolution and Social Change in Modern Europe', *Journal of Interdisciplinary History*, vol. 2 (1971), pp. 237-72, esp. p. 255.

25. On the relationship between home and hospital confinements see above.

26. Taufregister, 1900-53; *Braunschweigische Adressbücher*, 1899, 1901, 1910, 1911, 1920, 1921, 1930, 1931; 1,830 home confinements were analysed. These were distributed between 100 streets and squares.

27. Skilled and unskilled workers, technical workers in industry, foremen, gardeners, servants, waiters, disabled people.

28. G. Mai, 'Die Sozialstruktur der Württembergischen Soldatenräte 1918/1919', *Internationale wissenschaftliche Korrespondenz zur Geschichte der deutschen Arbeiterbewegung*, vol. 14 (1978), pp. 3-28, who indicates (p. 15) that the term 'shopkeeper' (*Kaufmann*) does not necessarily mean a self-employed person: from the end of the nineteenth century this term was increasingly used to signify other people in commercial employment (assistants, etc.).

29. With respect to social origin (i.e. social environment) the results of the Brunswick data lead to conclusions similar to those found for other large towns by contemporary authors. See for example H. Neumann, 'Die unehelichen Kinder in Berlin und ihr Schutz', *Jahrbücher für Nationalökonomie u. Statistik*, 3. Folge, 7. Bd. (1894), pp. 513-64, esp. p. 518; O. Spann, 'Die geschlechtlich-sittlichen Verhältnisse im Dienstboten- und Arbeiterinnenstande', *ZfS*, vol. 7 (1904), pp. 287-303; same author, 'Die unehelichen Geburten von Frankfurt a.M', ibid., pp. 701-9, here p. 702; Lange, *Uneheliche Geburten*, p. 49; R. Vorster, 'Über die Wertigkeit unehelicher Mütter', *Archiv für Soziale Hygiene u. Demographie (AfSHD)*, N.F. 1 (1925/6), pp. 423-5, here p. 423.

30. The numbers of houses and households in the years 1901, 1915 and 1930 in relation to the number of home confinements in these streets during the years between 1900 and 1930 were used to illustrate this fact.

31. *Braunschweigische Adressbücher*, 1899-1930.

32. Taufregister, 1900-53, and *Braunschweigische Adressbücher*, 1899-1930.

33. M. Hirsch, *Fruchtabtreibung und Präventivverkehr im Zusammenhang mit dem Geburtenrückgang. Eine medizinische, juristische u. sozial-politische Betrachtung* (Würzberg, 1914), p. 24; G. Dehn, *Proletarische Jugend. Lebensgestaltung u. Gedankenwelt der grossstädtischen Proletarierjugend* (Berlin, undated, c.1929), p. 27; E. Oeckinghaus, *Die gesellschaftliche u. rechtliche Stellung der deutschen Frau* (Jena, 1925), p. 159; Vorster, 'Wertigkeit', p. 424; also Neuman, 'Industrialization and Sexual Behaviour', p. 285, comes to the same conclusion on the basis of his analysis of several working-class autobiographies.

34. The questionnaires form part of an 'oral history' project which aims at illuminating the everyday life of working-class families in Brunswick. So far 15 men and 9 women have been questioned, all born between 1890 and 1914. See S. Bajohr, ' "Oral History" — Forschung zum Arbeiteralltag', *Das Argument*, vol. 123 (1980), pp. 667-76.

35. The determining factor here must have been the practice of *coitus interruptus* and the use of contraceptives. In particular the use of *coitus interruptus* was very significant in premarital sex, as the questionnaires indicate. See Hirsch, *Fruchtabtreibung*, p. 97; A. Forel, *Die sexuelle Frage* (6th edn, Munich, 1907), p. 458. The use of contraceptives was more widespread within marriage, mainly because of the cost and need for preparation. Lange, *Uneheliche Geburten*, p. 68;

M. Marcuse, *Der eheliche Präventivverkehr, seine Verbreitung, Verursachung und Methodik* (Stuttgart, 1918). On methods of contraception used by the working class see M. Marcuse, 'Zur Frage der Verbreitung u. Methodik der willkürlichen Geburtenbeschränkung in Berliner Proletarierkreisen', *Sexual-Probleme*, vol. 9, (1913), pp. 752-80; U. Linse, 'Arbeiterschaft und Geburtenentwicklung im Deutschen Kaiserreich von 1871', *AfS*, vol. XII (1972), pp. 205-71, esp. pp. 244ff.

36.   Taufregister, 1900-53; Stadtarchiv Braunschweig (StA BS) H XI Nr. 22/2; Braunschweigische Adressbücher 1925, 1930. The shaded areas indicate an illegitimate home confinement in that house. The real number of these must be higher as only illegitimate children who were eventually baptised in the Protestant church are included. The frequent occurrences of several illegitimate home confinements in one house has not been indicated. I am grateful to Ingo Herde for help with the graphics.

37.   This question refers back to the situation at the time. Today the women's movement rightly questions whether a mother needs a husband at all. B. Bronnen, *Mütter ohne Männer* (Reinbek, 1980).

38.   C. Nedelmann, 'Das Verbrechen der Abtreibung' in L. Jochimsen (ed.), *Para. 218. Dokumentation eines 100jähriges Elends* (Hamburg, 1971), pp. 37-49, here p. 41.

39.   This is probably connected with the closer ties which the child's mother had with her environment and the support she enjoyed here. As mentioned above, a higher percentage of hospital confinements were women from outside the city who received no support from their families. Cf. P. Neumann, *Die unehelichen Kinder in Berlin* (Jena, 1900), p. 14.

40.   The traditional novel plot where the master or his son gets the serving girl pregnant seems to have been quantitatively insignificant. See Spann, 'Verhältnisse', p. 302.

41.   Potential legitimations which only failed to take place because of the death of the father or mother must also be taken into account.

42.   See, for example, R. Kuczynski, 'Die unehelichen Kinder in Berlin', *ZfS*, vol. 3 (1900), pp. 632-41, here p. 633.

43.   I. Hardach-Pinke and G. Hardach, *Deutsche Kindheiten. Autobiographische Zeugnisse 1700-1900* (Kronberg/Ts., 1978), p. 29.

44.   On the living and working conditions of working women see S. Bajohr, *Die Hälfte der Fabrik. Geschichte der Frauenarbeit in Deutschland 1914-1945* (Marburg, 1979), pp. 130 ff, 189 ff.

45.   For information on the mortality and cost to mothers of children left with child-minders see Kuczynski, 'Die unehelichen Kinder', p. 638; Saalmann, 'Ein Beitrag zur Bevölkerungspolitik nach dem Kriege', *Zeitschrift für Bevölkerungspolitik und Säuglingsfürsorge (ZfBS)* vol. 10, no. 1 (Oct. 1918), pp. 232-8, here p. 235; H. Stöcker, 'Zur Reform der konventionellen Geschlechtsmoral', *ZfS*, vol. 10 (1907), pp. 607-76, here p. 611. Only too often the child was moved from one minder to another (See E. Georgi, 'Zur Reform der Unehelichenrechts', *Die Frau*, vol. 36 (1928/9), pp. 621-6, here p. 623). In September 1912 there were 116 child-minders investigated in Brunswick, and no adverse conditions were reported. However, in April 1916 the *Herzogl. Landes-Medizinalkollegium* appeared to regard 'children who were fostered or minded as disproportionately represented in the child mortality statistics' (StA Wf 12 A Neu Fb. 13 Nr. 11835). A law regulating fostering and minding was passed only on 26 June 1919 (StA Wf 12 A Neu Fb. 13 Nr. 8159).

46.   Cf. Neumann, 'Uneheliche Kinder', p. 535.

47.   There is not room here to go into the legal questions and problems of public support, etc. The following few references are representative of a wealth of literature on this topic: Th. Geiger, *Das uneheliche Kind und seine Mutter im Recht des neuen Staates* (Munich, 1920); W. Hanauer, 'Die Fürsorge für uneheliche Kinder u. der Krieg', *ZfBS*, vol. 10 (1918), pp. 201-8; C.J. Klumker, 'Der Gesetzen-

twurf über die Rechtsstellung der Unehelichen', *AfSHD*, N.F. 1. (1925/6), pp. 96-100. See also the *Weimarer Reichsverfassung*, Art. 121; *RABl.* (1925), Amtl. Teil, pp. 459-65. In 1909 a system of professional foster parents (*Berufsvormundschaft*) was introduced. Cf. *Braunschweigische Landeszeitung* Nr. 280, 18 Jun. 1909.

48.   Para. 33, No. 5 of the law on the *Beurkundung des Personenstandes u. Eheschliessung*, 6 Feb. 1875, in *RGBl.* (1875), p. 30; when the BGB came into force the above law was replaced by BGB, para. 1312. This was finally rescinded in 1938.

49.   StA Wf 12 A Neu Fb. 5 Nr. 3304 Bd. 1; StA BS D I 12 Nr. 250.

50.   The names of all participants in this and all following cases have been altered in accordance with the federal German law on the protection of privacy.

51.   StA Wf 12 A Neu Fb. 5 Nr. 3304 Bd. 1, Nr. 3306.

52.   StA Wf 12 A Neu Fb. 5 Nr. 3304 Bd. 2.

53.   StA Wf 12 A Neu Fb. 5 Nr. 3304 Bd. 1.

54.   Cf. F. Engels, *Der Ursprung der Familie, des Privateigentums u. des Staats*, *MEW*, vol. 21 (Berlin, 1962), pp. 25-173, here p. 27.

55.   Gesetz- u. Verordnungs-Sammlung für die Herzogliche Braunschweigischen Lande, vol. 60 (1873), p. 42.

56.   Feller's wife was also convicted of adultery.

57.   The child, born 1900, died after seven short months of life in May 1901.

58.   StA Wf 12 A Neu Fb. 5 Nr. 3304 Bd. 1; StA BS D I 12 Nr. 291.

59.   StA Wf 12 A Neu Fb. 5 Nr. 3306; StA BS D I 12 Nr. 487.

60.   StA Wf 12 A Neu Fb. 5 Nr. 3306.

61.   Also StA Wf 133 Neu Nr. 2064.

62.   StA Wf 12 A Neu Fb. 5 Nr. 3306.

63.   StA Wf 133 Neu Nr. 2147.

64.   The baptismal registers of the parishes of St Pauli, St Michaelis and St Martini.

65.   StA BS D IV 4681, 1: Nachweisung über Inanspruchnahme der Wanderhilfe vom 24.7.1913 und vom 19.4.1915.

66.   StA BS D IV 4681, 1: Schreiben des Stadtmagistrats 27.4.1907 an die Hebammen.

67.   StA BS D IV 4681, 1: Der Kreisbranddirektor am 19.3.1907 an den Stadtmagistrat.

68.   StA BS D IV 4681, 1: On the back of a *Wanderhilfe* receipt.

69.   StA BS D IV 4681, 1: Nachweisung über Inanspruchnahme der Wanderhilfe vom 22.7.1907.

70.   StA Wf 14 Neu Zg. 4/46. 19/58 Nr. 15 IV, 15 V, 31 I, 31 II; and StA BS D IV 4681, 1; Taufregister 1907-53. Here the proportion of illegitimate live births to Protestant women to the number of live births overall was compared to the proportion of Protestant illegitimate children whose mother received the *Wanderhilfe* to the overall number of women receiving the *Wanderhilfe*.

71.   StA Wf 133 Neu Nr. 2047. As Martens' previous husband had died in 1902 permission was granted for the name change. In this particular case the connection with the Social Democratic movement was clearly visible: the solicitor whom the Bergers entrusted with the representation of their case was the later Prime Minister of the Free State of Brunswick, Dr Heinrich Jasper, member of the SPD.

72.   StA Wf 12 A Neu Fb. 13 Nr. 7602; 133 Neu Nr. 2052. The H.St.M. granted permission for the name change on 27 July 1910, although the sister of Luise Herzog's deceased husband raised some objections. See also the cases in StA Wf 133 Neu Nr. 2046 and 2064.

73.   StA Wf 12 A Neu Fb. 13 Nr. 7549: Letter from the H.Pol.Dir.19 Nov 1917 to H.St.M.

74.   There are several relevant entries in StA Wf 12 A Neu Fb. 13 Nr. 7549.

75. StA Wf 12 A Neu Nr. 7549: Letter from the Prussian Justizminister 21 Nov. 1916 to the Staatssekretär in the Reichsjustizamt.

76. Decree of the Grand Duke of Baden, 7 Jul. 1916. Saxony and Württemberg released similar decrees. Cf. StA Wf 12 A Neu Fb. 13 Nr. 7549.

77. StA Wf 12 A Neu Fb. 13 Nr. 7549: the Bavarian Staatsminister des Innern 24 Jul. 1917 to the other Bavarian ministries.

78. StA Wf 12 A Neu Fb. 13 Nr. 7549: H.Pol.Dir. 16 Nov. 1917 to the H.St.M.

79. Ibid.

80. StA Wf 12 A Neu Fb. 13 Nr. 7549: Volkskommissariat für Inneres u. Finanzen 13 Mar. 1919 to the Pol.Dir. – the reply on 10 May 1919 – the recommendation of the Volkskommissar Junke on 15 May 1919.

81. Lüdtke, 'Alltagswirklichkeit', p. 315.

82. G.A. Ritter, 'Einleitung' in G.A. Ritter (ed.), *Arbeiterkultur* (Königstein /Ts., 1979), pp. 1-14, here p. 1.

83. StA BS D I 12. Random sampling on the living quarters of illegitimate mothers indicates that a not inconsiderable proportion of them had to move house as often as five times in one year.

84. G. Bäumer, 'Die Unehelichenschutz und die legitime Familie', *Die Frau*, vol. 36 (1928/9), in contradiction: Georgi, 'Reform', p. 622. See also StA Wf 12 A Neu Fb. 13 Nr. 13924 and 13925.

85. H. Speier, *Die Angestellten vor dem Nationalsozialismus. Ein Beitrag zum Verständnis der deutschen Sozialstruktur 1918-1933* (Göttingen, 1977), pp. 92ff, 161.

86. J. Kuczynski, *Die Geschichte der Lage der Arbeiter unter dem Kapitalismus*, Teil 1, Bd. 4 (Berlin, 1967), p. 302.

87. W. Conze, *Der Strukturwandel der Familie im Industriellen Modernisierungsprozess – Historische Begründung einer aktuellen Frage* (Dortmund, 1979), p. 16.

88. A. Klönne, *Die deutsche Arbeiterbewegung. Geschichte, Ziele, Wirkungen* (Düsseldorf, 1980), p. 220.

89. Ernst W., born 1914, fitter. Father: turner; mother: ironer. Working-class activist. Member of SAJ, SPD, DMV, Reichsbanner.

90. Walli K., born 1913, worked in cleaning and catering in large factories. Father: bricklayer; mother: worker in a canning factory.

91. Robert W., born 1909. Pattern and tool maker. Father:cutter in a tinware factory; mother: assembly line worker. Working-class activist – member of the woodworkers' union, DMV, SPD, Reichsbanner, free-thinker.

92. Two years after the birth of her illegitimate child she married a mechanic who gave the child his surname.

93. The name has been changed.

94. It is noticeable that those areas in which less qualified workers were in the majority at the end of the 1920s and beginning of the 1930s were the ones that voted increasingly for the KPD. Cf. G. Fülberth, 'Die Übereinkunft zwischen SPD u. KPD in Braunschweig nach den Kommunalwahlen vom März 1931', unpubl. MS. See note 36.

95. It can be assumed with certainty that it was not a decrease in the incidence of extramarital sexual intercourse that led to the decrease in illegitimate births. See also Shorter *et al.*, 'Decline of Non-marital Fertility', p. 382.

96. K. Davis, 'Illegitimacy and the Social Structure', *American Journal of Sociology*, vol. 45 (1939), pp. 215-33, here p. 224.

97. Ibid., p. 225.

98. A. Blaschko, 'Prostitution', *HdStW*, Bd. 6 (3rd edn, Jena, 1910), pp. 1227-49, 1229f.

99. The connection postulated here can of course only be assumed to have a certain validity for the development of illegitimacy in large towns and cities. It

cannot account for illegitimacy in villages and small towns in rural areas.

100.   On the signification of the individual's life course to the concrete experience of history see Hausen, 'Familie', p. 184f.; on mobility, D. Crew, 'Modernität u. soziale Mobilität in einer deutschen Industriestadt: Bochum 1880-1901' in H. Kaelble (ed.), *Geschichte der sozialen Mobilität seit der industriellen Revolution* (Königstein/Ts. 1978), pp. 159-85, in particular pp. 166 ff.

101.   K. Marx and F. Engels, *Manifest der Kommunistischen Partei, MEW*, vol. 4 (Berlin, 1959), p. 493.

102.   Shorter *et al.*, 'Decline of Non-marital Fertility', p. 393, however regard it as unlikely 'that higher incomes moved unwed mothers to curb their illegitimate fertility so as to plan better the educational future of their bastards on hand'. See also the criticisms of R.A. Easterlin, 'The Economics and Sociology of Fertility: a Synthesis' in C. Tilly (ed.), *Historical Studies of Changing Fertility* (Princeton, NJ, 1978), pp. 57-133, here p. 125.

6 ORGANISING THE 'LUMPENPROLETARIAT': CLIQUES AND COMMUNISTS IN BERLIN DURING THE WEIMAR REPUBLIC

Eve Rosenhaft

During the Weimar Republic, popular anxieties about the state of society became focused on a field of problems in which youth, political radicalism and a general brutalisation of social and political relations were assumed to be directly linked with one another in peculiarly threatening ways. In this field were to be found both the Communist Party (Kommunistische Partei Deutschlands, KPD), the junior party of the working class, bearer of revolution and political rowdyism, and the cliques (*Cliquen* or *Klicken*), or youth gangs, of the urban centres.[1] This essay examines the actual and formal relationship between the two forms of working-class organisation in Berlin. The points of contact between the two are interesting because they existed on several levels: cliques and Communists met and mingled not only in the rhetoric of the popular press and conservative authorities, but also in the everyday life of sections of the working class. And Communist Party policy was calculated to hasten both these processes. The KPD adopted a style and rhetorical posture which implied that it accepted and even welcomed the role, ascribed to it by its opponents and rivals, of a party of outlaws. It also made periodic efforts to organise and recruit among the cliques. The result was a more than usually self-conscious confrontation between a proletarian culture and the expectations of the party that claimed to represent the proletariat.

The geographical territory on which Communists and cliques met was the old neighbourhoods of working-class Berlin. In the 1920s Germany's capital had some 4 million inhabitants, nearly half of whom lived from industry; 41 per cent of the population at the 1925 census belonged to the manual working class.[2] The largest single employer of male labour was the metal industry, including both electrotechnical and engineering firms, followed by the building trades.[3] With the numerous opportunities for casual labour offered by a metropolitan area in which both manufacturing and distributive operations were prominent (one-quarter of the population depended on trade and transport for its living), Berlin's population included a higher proportion of unskilled and unspecialised labourers than were to be found in the national work-force, about 42 per cent.[4] Berlin's working-class inhabitants were concentrated in the north and east of the city, with significant pockets in the centre. The pre-industrial slums of the old city, Berlin-Mitte, were ringed by districts packed with the tenement houses built to accommodate the workers who had flooded in during the boom years after 1870: Wedding and Prenzlauer Berg to the north, Friedrichshain to the east, Neukölln, Kreuzberg and parts of Schöneberg in the south-east, Moabit and a corner of Charlottenburg in the west. In addition to having heavily or predominantly working-class populations, five of these districts — Wedding, Kreuzberg, Friedrichshain, Mitte and the district in which Moabit lay — housed disproportionate numbers of the least qualified workers.[5] It was in these traditionally proletarian areas that the Berlin KPD had maintained its strongholds since 1919; the most solid of these were Wedding, Neukölln, Friedrichshain, Mitte and parts of Kreuzberg. Here, too, most notoriously in Neukölln, Kreuzberg and Wedding, flourished the cliques. The Communists' attitude to this shared milieu was a contradictory one. Once the cliques have been characterised, the examination of the KPD's response to them and the aspects of working-class life they represented makes it possible to draw out some of the contradictions and their implications for the practice of the Communist movement.

I

As it was used in the late 1920s and early 1930s, the expression 'clique' ordinarily referred to a category of unofficial hiking clubs, 'the wild hiking cliques'. They were made up of working-class adolescents, usually unskilled or unemployed. The image of the cliques comprehended elements of style and cultural consumption as well as behaviour, but it was their capacity for anti-social action that made them interesting and frightening to the public. They drew their sinister cast from a section of their members who had turned to a life of vagrancy or crime and from a still larger number who, without being involved habitually in economic crimes, nevertheless cultivated aggressiveness and physical violence as a function of their organisational life. During 1930 a former clique member estimated that there were 600 cliques in Berlin, 'of which perhaps ten per cent are criminal cliques, while 20 per cent are borderline, between criminal and [merely] hiking cliques. The other 70 per cent are hiking cliques.'[6] In the view of one professional youth worker, 'the very existence of a clique exercises an unhealthy influence on the youth of an area'; at worst 'they represent the first step on the road to organised crime.'[7]

We cannot be certain where the cliques came from. It is as difficult to identify a coherent reality behind their overwhelmingly negative image as it is to describe the phenomenon of the cliques without reference to it. The spontaneous and unofficial nature of their organisation meant both that they were *a priori* suspect in the eyes of the authorities and that their internal workings are not well documented; it also fixes them in a very much wider range of more conventional, relatively 'harmless' smoking, savings and social clubs, organised by young people in their own neighbourhoods, with which the cliques certainly merged at many points.[8] The history of the cliques is the history of the stages by which sections of this unofficial youth movement came to be associated in the public mind with a certain style and the resulting image became a focus for anxieties about the potential, both criminal and political, of working-class youth. The antecedents of this development lie in the events of the first two decades of the twentieth century: the identification of youth as a social issue and the growth of self-conscious and relatively autonomous 'official' youth movements from about the turn of the century, followed by the radical disruption of social norms and expectations during the years of war and revolution. At the height of their notoriety the cliques represented both a degenerate parody of the former and a terrible nemesis of the latter.

It has become a commonplace of the historiography of modern Germany that the years around 1900 witnessed a new concern with youth and its problems on the part of the bourgeoisie, the 'discovery of the adolescent'.[9] That this phenomenon is still most commonly approached by way of discussions of the activities and attitudes of young people themselves is very largely a consequence of the successes of the *Wandervogel* (or Wander-bird).[10] Perhaps the most remarkable example in modern history of a coherent movement both initiated and led by young people, the *Wandervogel* was essentially middle-class in character and composition. It originated among students and progressive teachers at a Berlin secondary school between 1896 and 1900, and by 1913 had become a national movement with a bureaucracy of its own and an extensive literary output. The small groups of secondary-school students which made up the movement were regarded by its theorists as providing the ideal milieu for the development of the spirit and faculties of the adolescent striving towards maturity and social leadership. Outward and visible sign of this striving was the practice of wandering or hiking in the countryside, a familiar form of recreation to which the earliest groups gave a new and special character by wearing romantic clothing and accompanying themselves on guitars and mandolins. *Wandervogel* became a catchword for the whole of the German youth movement, and provided an impulse for the creation, before the First World War, of groups like the government-sponsored and militaristic Young Germany League and the German section of the Boy Scout movement.

The numerical and cultural significance of the *Wandervogel* has prompted historians to concentrate on relations within the educated middle classes when discussing the problematisation of youth at the turn of the century. In this context, the 'problem of youth' was defined as the problems that the bourgeois adolescent suffered. But the identification of the middle-class adolescent coincided with new approaches to working-class youth as well, and in these young people appear as a source of problems for society rather than their victims. During the first years of the century campaigns were initiated to create new regulations and institutions for the control of the young and their protection from undesirable influences of all kinds. In Prussia, restrictions on working hours were accompanied by measures to limit the sale of alcoholic drinks to minors.[11] Concern for the moral health of young people was also expressed in a wave of intensive lobbying and literary polemic against *Schundliteratur*, the penny-dreadfuls and adventure serials bought by schoolchildren in their hundreds, which were blamed not only for the 'systematic stultification' of youth, but also for 'a series of crimes, many of the most serious kind'.[12]

In a period when the youthful work-force had increased rapidly while its working conditions deteriorated, and where there was an active and growing Social Democratic movement, the principal fear of German officialdom was the political radicalisation of the young. When this fear was realised, with the launching of the Social Democratic youth movement in 1905, the government responded with both overtly repressive and nominally welfare-oriented measures. The Imperial Law of Association of 1908 prohibited the political activity or organisation of youths under 18, while a ministerial decree of 1911 declared active care for the social needs of youth 'a national duty of the first order', its aim 'the formation of a cheerful, physically productive, morally sound youth filled with public spirit and piety, love of home and fatherland'. At the same time the Prussian government made its first substantial grant of funds to the newly consolidated, non-socialist private foundations for youth welfare.[13]

All of these developments continued under the Republic, receiving a new impetus from the conditions of war and revolution. In the critical years 1914-19 it was unequivocally the circumstances of proletarian youth that were at issue. As the boom in munitions production for the war effort coincided with the absence of much of the adult male population at the front, there emerged the spectre of an unsupervised economy entirely peopled by youths. The streets of Berlin, it was said, were made unsafe by scores of teenaged lorry-drivers and cabbies.[14] Too many young people had too much money to burn, and the fear that they would spend it on drink and debauchery led to the introduction of compulsory savings plans for minors by the military authorities. The possibilities of maintaining such plans in peacetime, along with more conventional measures like curfews and restrictions on alcohol and tobacco consumption, were widely discussed, though ultimately rejected.[15] And where 'artificially' stimulated appetites came up against the shortages that Germany's cities suffered during the last two years of the war, observers began to complain of an increase in the incidence of juvenile crime.[16] Germany's collapse in 1918, finally, threatened the structure of authority in this as in other spheres. The Versailles Treaty, by bringing the tradition of the conscript army to an end, removed one of the most effective means of socialisation and control of lower-class youth. The revolution and the Spartacist uprisings of 1919, in which the threat of Bolshevism was not only raised but institutionalised in the formation of a German Communist Party, fulfilled every conservative anxiety about radicalisation and social degeneracy. By the end of that year, even the Social Democratic daily newspaper, *Vorwärts*, could treat the interrelationship of debased consumer culture, inadequate moral sense and radical politics as a given:

> Many an irresponsible youth who recently took part in [the Spartacist uprising] drew his enthusiasm for violence from the murky dregs of bloody penny-dreadfuls. Not the *Communist Manifesto*, but the nameless *Schundliteratur* prepared the ground for this sprouting of political fantasies.[17]

The Social Democrats who presided over the creation of the new Republic also assumed responsibility for transforming the 'social imperialist' police state of the Bismarckian Empire into a genuine social state in which the interests of the working class would be protected and its conditions of life improved. But their own ambivalence and the continuing strength of social conservatism in parliament and the country were such that the institutions that arose out of this initiative were distorted in conception and practice by a compromise between the purposes of social service and of control. The first five years of the Republic saw the creation and consolidation at the national level of a machinery of youth welfare and juvenile justice through which young people were accorded a special legal and institutional status, while the parties and pressure-groups of the political right continued to press for such measures as censorship and the creation of alternatives to military service.[18]

II

This was the context in which the 'dark side' of the youth movement became visible. Although the pre-war years had seen reports of thefts by gangs of youths, the word 'clique' itself, used to denote a criminal gang, appears to have found its way into the jargon of the Berlin under-world only after 1918.[19] The earliest use of it in the sources on which the present study is based comes from 1923; only in early 1929 does it begin to be used routinely by clique members, police, social scientists and press alike. The same sources concur in reading the development of the cliques back into phenomena of the war and early post-war years. The hiking aspect of the movement, in particular, is reminiscent of the *Wandervogel*, and one reporter maintained that their less respectable counterparts, popularly dubbed 'Wander-boors' (*Wanderflegel*), had already appeared on the Berlin scene by 1916.[20] Their tumultuous appearance at suburban railway stations, conspicuously kitted out with beer and *Schnaps* bottles, nurtured anxieties about the effects of a war which left lower-class youth overpaid and undersupervised, and contributed to the image of a catastrophic brutalisation of urban youth. The amnesty decrees of 1918, prescribing exceptionally mild treatment for juveniles convicted of certain non-economic crimes, were criticised on the grounds that, among other things, they were sure to encourage the criminality of organised youth gangs.[21]

By 1923 what *Vorwärts* called 'that hiking movement whose ranks are filled with the dual morality of today's culture, whose members were exposed to the influence of the low instincts fostered in wartime'[22] was an explicit object of concern to the official youth movements of both left and right. Now known as 'Wander-boors', 'Wander-crows' (*Wanderkrähen*), or simply 'the wild ones', they not only gave hikers in general a bad name by refusing to use the hostels and permitted camp-sites, drinking and littering the forests, but also behaved in an offensive and sometimes threatening manner to others whom they met during their outings.[23] On 25 August 1923 about 30 youths marched to the

Silesian Station in Friedrichshain, 'singing and playing the mandolin'. When a policeman told them to get off of the pavement and into the road, they reportedly fell upon him and beat him with knuckle-dusters until two more groups of officers were summoned and used their revolvers to drive the youths off.[24] This is one of the earliest reports in which a particular element of the visual image of the cliques appears: the youths were carrying a yellow flag with a black hand stencilled on it.

Like the war years, the inflation year 1923 was marked by heightened social and economic distress, bringing with it a plague of crimes against property and a new wave of concern for the moral health of city youth. As prices outstripped wages and the urban population suffered from shortages of vital commodities, Berlin's mayor sketched the situation of the young:

> Children are often urged or forced by their parents to beg or even steal — hawking, rubbish-picking. . .by children — decline in honesty — increase in greed — currency speculation frequent among children — increasing alcoholism among youths — loss of parental authority — increasing degeneration of morals.[25]

The conclusion of all this was not far to seek. Referring to the most notorious of Europe's criminal subcultures, the columnist of the liberal daily newspaper *Berliner Tageblatt* warned:

> They say that the Apaches of Paris. . .were descended from the youth that went to the bad during the war of 1871. Considering the length and privations of the last war and the state of war that prevails even in peacetime, we could get a species of Apaches in Berlin that would make the Parisian ones pale by comparison.[26]

The same newspaper columns that complained of the 'Wander-boors' now regularly carried reports of the criminal activities of juvenile gangs. Unlike the anonymous bands of Wilhelmine Berlin, but like the cliques as described a few years later, some of the gangs of 1923 and 1924 reportedly had names: Association of Bloodhounds of Reinickendorf, May-Column, Noble-Guild of Moabit.[27]

After an apparent lull in gang activity in the mid-twenties, the years 1927 and 1928 were identified by many observers, most notably by sources close to the police and public administration, as the hey-day of the cliques.[28] The question that presents itself here is whether this new perception reflects changes within the unofficial youth movement itself or shifts in police and administrative practice that made the cliques visible. The impact of the recession that set in in the autumn of 1925 was such that the answer probably lies in a combination of the two. In the 'purging crisis' that followed the collapse of the inflationary boom of 1923, hundreds of German businesses were liquidated. Between February 1925 and the end of the following year the number of registered unemployed in Berlin doubled three times. Of the more than 112,000 working men in the city who were registered as out of work in the summer of 1926, nearly 15,000 were under 21, a figure which represented something over 15 per cent of working-class males aged 14 to 21. This first shudder of stabilisation presented itself, at the time and in retrospect, as a crisis for the young in particular, for juveniles never again formed such a large contingent of Berlin's unemployed.[29]

Where social analysts recognised 'the first signs of the formation of a stratum of chronically unemployed',[30] moreover, they were looking not only at the catastrophic unemployment of 1925-6, but also at the shape of the labour market that survived the crisis.[31] The German economy was carried into its brief phase of prosperity on a wave of industrial rationalisation whose earliest and most active proponents included Berlin's largest employers, engineering and electrotechnical manufacturing. The effect of this process was both to compound the contraction that had already taken place between 1923 and 1925 and to make the employment situation of young workers in industry less stable. Mechanisation reduced the demand for skilled labour to a minimum that could be supplied by experienced workers, and at the same time eliminated large numbers of unskilled ancillary tasks. The number of apprenticeships available to ambitious youths shrank, and while trained, half-trained and unskilled young people could now compete for the semi-skilled jobs created by the machines on an equal basis (and often with greater chances of success than older workers), they became equally subject to the intensified fluctuations in size of work-force of plants newly responsive to changes in demand.

For many of the young people themselves, then, the recession meant poverty and the enforced leisure of catastrophic unemployment, to be succeeded by a career in which low-paid work alternated with idleness. In response to this situation there arose a set of new institutions, official and unofficial, that provided the means of surveillance as well as social service. During the winter of 1926-7 it was reported that a number of taverns had opened up in the vicinity of one of the central labour exchanges, which specialised in offering credit to young vagrants and runaways from the reform-school system. Identity- and work-papers or valuables were required as security. By thus drawing young people into a cycle of unemployment, indebtedness and crime, these taverns were held to have contributed to the regeneration of the cliques.[32] At about the same time, the Berlin youth bureaux began to establish day centres for unemployed youths. By late 1927 the cliques had been identified by the youth workers as a particularly disruptive element within the centres,[33] and when the day centres were threatened by cuts in public expenditure during 1931, this very function was cited in their defence; they were described as

> the only official institution which has so far succeeded in getting close to members of the cliques, to which, indeed, we owe any deeper understanding of [their] shadowy nature... the only tried and proven method of influencing cliques and above all would-be clique members.[34]

In these years, too, the press played a part in reflecting and shaping changes. During 1927 the incidence of brawling and stabbings among young people was reported to have increased, and newspaper readers began to learn of youths assaulting passers-by 'for fun', or without apparent motive.[35] The year 1928 brought the first reports in which all the elements of the clique image appear and the first generally reported trial of members of a clique.[36] In early 1929, when a second such trial took place — this time involving members of what looked like a federation of cliques — the groups were already being described as 'criminal societies', in explicit analogy to the organised 'rings' of the Berlin underworld; these were very much in the news as a result of a spectacular brawl the preceding Christmas.[37] There are indications that the police thought they had got the cliques under control after 1928,[38] but the depression that set in at the end of 1929, throwing more than 600,000 Berliners out of work in three years and ushering in the Republic's last and most fatal period of distress and disruption, aroused fresh anxieties about juvenile delinquency. In 1931 the correspondent of the left-liberal weekly, *Die Weltbühne*, summing up a new wave of publicity in the gutter press, characterised the cliques as 'a phantom, impossible to grasp or to unmask', lurking in the background of all criminal prosecutions of juveniles in Berlin.[39]

III

All we know of the reality of the cliques marks them as a product of the culture of the lower-paid working class.[40] Estimates of the actual numbers involved in the cliques varied widely; figures of from 100 to 600 individual groups, with memberships of between 10 and 100 were proposed during the 1930s. Although numbers as high as 30,000 were mentioned, a cautious guess would suggest that something under 10,000 youths were involved at any one time. This represents roughly 7 per cent of Berlin's male working-class population between 14 and 25 years of age, still only a fraction of the total numbers of unskilled or unemployed youths who were known to supply most of the cliques' recruits. In their structure, though, the cliques were none the less typical of a particular and familiar working-class milieu, one in which home life played a limited and precarious part. If new values of domesticity had begun to penetrate the working class during these years, the minimum precondition for their realisation was the family's ability to escape the overcrowded conditions that were still the norm in the old working-class neighbourhoods. For workers with neither regular incomes nor contacts in the trade union and co-operative organisations that sponsored many of the new, suburban housing projects, the street remained the principal locus of sociability and socialisation, the peer group their chief vehicle.[41] The character and activities of the cliques reflected, often in exaggerated form, the circumstances and values of that section of the working class whose best expectation was a life of physical labour for uncertain return.

Aggressive masculinity was an important element in that character. The sexual composition of the cliques varied; there existed a handful of girls' cliques, as well as a few mixed ones. But a certain male exclusiveness formed part of the image of the most dreaded gangs. The former clique member cited above reported that the female groups had been formed in reaction to efforts to purge the cliques of girls. He interpreted this as primarily a hygienic measure: many members suffered from venereal diseases, a circumstance that reflected the emphasis on the erotic which was one of the most worrying aspects of clique life. Even the all-male groups were ordinarily accompanied on their adventures by one or two 'clique-darlings', whose responsibilities reportedly included 'looking after the sexual needs' of the boys. One 16-year-old outlined the activities of his group in these words:

> We go through the streets and look for girls to take along on our hikes. I am in the hiking clique Storm-proof. . . At Easter I go with four other clique-boys to Kloster Chorin [a tourist spot about 35 miles from Berlin]. I want to quit the clique, because they whore around too much with girls.[42]

The programmatic rejection of female company was expressed in such clique names as Girl-Shy and Girl-Haters.

The names which, as has already been suggested, were intrinsic to the public image of the cliques, also offer an insight into their cultural roots. Many of them were taken from the world of the penny-dreadfuls with which, it was said, their club-rooms were crammed. From the same source came many of the nicknames by which the members knew each other and the models for their grotesque rituals and collective adventures. At the same time, the particular names that the groups selected for themselves reflect their own self-image and aspects of their activity. Alpine-Glow and Heath-Flower, for example, refer directly to the romance of the *Wandervogel* movement which the cliques imitated and caricatured. The principal aim and central experience of life in the 'classic' clique was the weekly camping trip.

The extent to which the *Wandervogel* element in clique life represented an adaptation of cultural forms that were familiar to all classes in German society is suggested by the value that members placed on having the costumes, emblems and club flags that fitted the traditional image of a hiker or scout. But the form was one that was suited to many contents and contexts; it had its own utility for proletarian children. For young workers with limited free time, hiking provided physical recreation and escape from cramped housing conditions; in Berlin, with its extensive parks, lakes and outlying villages accessible by public transport, the flight to the country was a traditional leisure activity of the lower classes.[43] For unemployed youths the cohesiveness and mobility fostered by the experience of camping could provide the basis for a new moral and material way of life. Further aims of the cliques, as perceived by the authorities, included mutual support, a common front against the representatives of the youth bureau, the reform-school system and the police, or, in the case of truly vagrant gangs, co-operation in the daily search for food and shelter.

No single group necessarily pursued all of these aims at any given time; rather, the cliques provided a context in which problems and challenges could be dealt with collectively as they arose. When and how they arose was largely out of the hands of the clique members themselves, although a working-class boy might well have known what to expect by the time he was 16 or 17. This is one reason why it is practically impossible to categorise the cliques; the attempt of the former clique member to distinguish amongst essentially harmless, border-line and criminal groups is as naïve as the conclusion of criminologists and youth workers that the cliques, however they started out, had an innate tendency to degenerate into the hooligan clubs familiar to the courts. What seems most likely is that the functions of the clique changed as the circumstances of its members changed. Although one source speaks of a high rate of membership fluctuation within the cliques, there are examples of groups nominally existing for three to five years with some stability of membership.[44] This was a long time in the conditions of the Weimar Republic, and the members of a clique might go through several cycles of work and unemployment. The peculiar lability of their social situation was compounded by the fact that if they were known to have engaged in pilferage or other offences, young labourers were more likely to be both dismissed and reported to the police than apprentices and skilled workers guilty of the same crimes.[45] Finally, it was largely a matter of luck whether any group of youths spending a good deal of time in the open air could avoid coming into conflict with the police.

One aspect of clique life that increased the chances of such conflict was the high value that clique members placed on toughness in word and deed. This was related to the aggressive masculinity characteristic of workers whose livelihood traditionally depended on the exercise of physical strength. It was reflected in some of the clique names: Farmers' Fear, Red-Apaches, Bloody Bone, Sing-Sing, Death-Defiers. The gang was led by a youth known as the 'clique-bull', often its founder. In order to maintain his position he had constantly to prove his ability to keep the group together, to hold his own in a fight, and to work out successful schemes for realising the aims of the clique and defending the interests of its members. The authority of the 'bull' was such that his arrest could mean the dissolution of the group. Toughness was also an important qualification for rank-and-file membership; some cliques reportedly required that new members undertake some act of petty theft or vandalism as a test of aptitude and good faith. 'The regulations of the cliques are usually of a lapidary brevity: The member must always pay for his round. . ., he must defend an attacked or insulted comrade under all circumstances, he must never "rat".'[46]

The corollary to absolute solidarity within the clique was an aggressive posture towards outsiders. On outings they would attack or ambush official hiking and scouting groups, seizing their badges or pennants as trophies. Individual hikers, too, were sometimes assaulted. Outsiders spoke of a 'continuous state of war' between the cliques, observing that the landlord who played host to two rival gangs on the same evening could expect to have his tavern demolished in the ensuing battle. Press reports suggest a somewhat more complicated picture.[47] If there was a state of war between them, it was one tempered by tactical alliances and diplomatic manoeuvres, in which violence was either a ritualised form of self-representation and mutual entertainment or the ultimate sanction for some actual insult or offence against the code of mutual solidarity. When used against outsiders on a sufficiently large scale to be reported in the newspapers, physical violence most often appears as a means of enforcing the right of the clique to some form of entertainment — where fighting itself or the aggressively maintained freedom to intrude on other people's amusements could be construed as entertainment. The most common targets seem to have been landlords who refused to serve ill-dressed or disorderly youths and interfering police officers. In either case, the lines were clearly drawn: two fighting gangs might turn on the officer trying to separate them or — as occurred in the 'North-Ring' case of 1928 — an alliance of cliques might organise a punitive expedition against a tavern where some of their members had been refused service.

The characteristic offences of the cliques in periods of relative prosperity were thus disturbing the peace, damage to property, assault, robbery and petty larceny, occasionally the theft of a car or a motorcycle for a joy-ride. Even during the depression, when many of them must have been tempted to engage in serious crimes, few achieved the notoriety of Egg-Slime, a Schöneberg clique whose members undertook some 16 motorised robberies during 1931 and 1932, ending with an attack on a wages transport that cost the life of a guard.[48] In spite of popular fears, the cliques also remained largely independent of the structures of organised crime in Berlin, although many of their members clearly aspired to and some succeeded in gaining entrée into the influential circles of the underworld.[49]

The case of Tartar's Blood, which was widely reported in 1928, contains all the elements of the typical clique style. In February of that year 18 members of this gang, unemployed youths from Neukölln, attacked a group from the Academic Athletic Club of Berlin in one of the city's parks. They searched them and carried off their club badges as well as all their money and provisions. When the police caught up with them, the members of the clique were found to be carrying knuckledusters, knives and other dangerous instruments — and their banner: red, with a white border and rising golden sun, inscribed *W.C. Tartarenblut*. According to the report in *Vorwärts*, the youths were dressed 'in Tyrolean style', with knee-socks, black 'Fascist jackets', open shirts and feathered hats. At the end of a short trial the following December several members of Tartar's Blood received commuted prison sentences. In January 1929 members of the clique were again convicted and again released for their part in the North-Ring affair. Finally, in 1929, the 'bull' himself was sentenced to serve a prison term for brawling, and the clique broke up.[50]

As long as the clique maintained the hiking tradition — and, again, their capacity to do so was a matter as much of economics as of inclination — their geographical horizons extended beyond the city and into the suburbs. At the same time they were always closely identified with their home districts and neighbourhoods. Attachment to the immediate residential area is, of course, a characteristic of young children, and many of the cliques probably had their origins in friendships formed on the block or in school.[51] A series of thefts at a Neukölln primary school in 1931 led to the discovery 'that a group of friends in the Pannierstrasse has formed a street-clique, which gets up to no good during their free time. Pupils from all the neighbouring schools belong to the clique, even those of differing [confessional] orientation.'[52] This says at least as much about the expectations of the educational authorities as about the actual origins of adolescent gangs. The question of whether Germany was witnessing the development of child gangs comparable to the *besprisornyi* of famine-stricken Russia was widely mooted during the depression,[53] and while expert opinion remained dubious, it was only too easy to read the clique phenomenon into the associations formed among children. But the structure and demands of the school system were as much a part of the everyday life out of which the cliques developed as the tenements and courtyards of working-class Berlin. The child's allegiance to the neighbourhood was not weakened by the existence of local schools, although in the Neukölln case the ties of friendship and locality were explicitly seen to cross institutional boundaries. At the same time children living in a notoriously depressed area were assumed to be especially susceptible to the temptation to unsocial behaviour. And in practice the exercise of sanctions against what looked like the beginnings of criminality (in the case of this relatively liberal school, the transfer of the ringleaders to another school with a note on their records) might actually promote the transformation from 'group of friends' into 'clique' by setting in motion a process of criminalisation in which the individual child's self-image as well as his life chances were affected.[54]

The element of territoriality in the life and attitudes of the cliques was reinforced by their choice of meeting-places. That choice generally fell within the range of options offered by the traditional forms of working-class entertainment, which were small-scale, relatively cheap and easily accessible within the local neighbourhood. The most common meeting-place for a clique, as for any other local association, was the tavern. Gang members met regularly in the same one, either in the bar or, if they had enough money or were on good terms with the landlord, in the clubroom at the rear. If they could not afford to spend much time in the tavern, if there was no landlord willing to harbour them, or if they preferred other forms of amusement, a nearby park, dance-hall or *Rummelplatz* might provide an alternative hang-out. Thus we read not only about hiking cliques and street cliques, but occasionally about *Rummel-*, dance- or park-cliques. Among these unofficial institutions, the *Rummelplätze* in particular were popularly associated with the genesis and nurturing of juvenile delinquency. These were a kind of small travelling carnival, offering freak-shows, wrestling matches, erotic displays, shooting-ranges and other amusements, which were set up on areas of waste land in the city. Even before the First World War, the *Rummel* was an acknowledged and deplored fixture of the old working-class districts of Berlin.[55] In its association with the cliques we may identify again a link between the youth gangs and that section of the working class which was relatively 'backward' in terms of the new styles of life and forms of consumption available to better qualified or more secure workers.

'A few cliques', one observer reported in 1930, 'dominate and terror-ise whole streets and districts.'[56] This may serve to underline both the territoriality of the cliques and their aggressiveness, but it takes us a step further, since it implies a closer and more self-conscious link between the clique and the neighbourhood than mere proximity. Like the struc-ture of the clique itself, both the sense of locality and the capacity and readiness to practise physical violence within it were more than simply aspects of style or inherited values. As ways of organising and exercising power, they could be applied instrumentally to the pursuit of material aims as the need arose. At the most crudely economic level, the clique that supported itself from 'street crime' depended on violence or its threat both in carrying out its attacks and in defending its 'hunting-ground' against rival gangs. The early 1920s provide an example of this sort of conflict developing between a gang of youths (the May Column) that persisted in harassing local landlords and shopkeepers, and the underworld ring which was operating a protection racket in the same area — with unpleasant consequences for the youths.[57] In a less unambig-uously exploitative relationship, a familiar neighbourhood could provide cover and support for the gang living by its wits. A clique in the north-east of the city, which called itself at first Death-Defiers and later Gypsy Love, was able to keep its hiding place a secret, avoiding arrest and supporting itself by begging and stealing for a considerable length of time, because its members knew the area and were aided by local residents.[58]

In principle, the cliques were also available for the enforcement of other people's material interests or of collective values particular to the neighbourhood. The forms of enforcement that organised gangs of toughs had to offer became more important as the waves of economic dislocation that characterised the Weimar years both intensified the struggle for material survival and diminished the possibilities for the economic or financial mediation of power relations within neighbourhoods.[59] The degree to which the cliques were actually engaged in local networks of power and control must remain an open question, but it needs to be raised, for it is directly relevant to the efforts that were made to involve them in the contest for public and supra-local influence — that is, to politicise them.

IV

By the 1930s, the assumption that at least some of the cliques had identifiable political sympathies was as common as the general rhetorical association between political radicalism and the rising crime rate. The Berlin police characterised the Neukölln cliques as 'Communist oriented', and *Vorwärts* showed considerable interest in the question of whether the lads of Tartar's Blood were Communists in disguise or simply had left-radical leanings.[60] The best informed of contemporary writers estimated in 1930 that while approximately 71 per cent of non-criminal cliques were apolitical, 21 per cent had left-wing and 7 per cent right-wing sympathies — where left-wing ordinarily meant Communist, right-wing radical nationalist or racist.[61]

The coalescence of criminal and party youth groups was made a matter of general concern by the combined spectacle of widespread politicisation of youth and the rise in the incidence of political violence during the twenties and early thirties. By the end of the First World War, the idealistically apolitical impulse of the *Wandervogel* had dissipated. Many of its older members became professional social workers, and the bourgeois youth movement collapsed into a welter of organisations more or less militarist and nationalist in character.[62] At the same time, the political parties and associations of the Weimar Republic began to make specific appeals to young people. To the Social Democratic youth were added the Bismarck Youth of the conservative German

National People's Party, the youth arm of the right-wing veterans' organisation Stahlhelm, the Communist Youth, the National Socialists' Hitler Youth, and others. The most radical parties of right and left, Communists and Nazis, even set out openly to organise schoolchildren.[63] Young people were also among the most avid recruits to the paramilitary organisations that the parties created during the course of the Weimar Republic, chief among which were the mainly Social Democratic Reichsbanner, Stahlhelm, the Red Front-Fighters' League (Roter Front-kämpferbund, RFB) of the Communists and the Nazi Stormtroops (Sturmabteilung, SA).[64] These developed out of the insurrectionary troops and vigilante organisations formed between 1918 and 1923, when Germany was in a state of simmering civil war. In the period of relative stability that followed, they became the bearers of a substantially new form of political gang-fighting. During the late twenties, every major political campaign was punctuated by mutual disruptions of meetings or demonstrations and street-corner brawls. The onset of the depression was accompanied by a surge in activity of and popular support for the radical parties, chief beneficiary of which was the Nazi Party; in the general elections of September 1930, the National Socialists won over 6 million votes, their Reichstag delegation increasing from a handful of seats to being the second strongest in the house. This gave fresh impetus to a spiralling 'battle for the streets' in proletarian neighbourhoods; as the SA attempted to establish itself in the strongholds of the Communists, knives and guns were brought into the conflict as well as fists. Between May 1930 and November 1931, 29 people died in Berlin as a result of what had become largely a three-way fight between Nazis, Communists and police.[65] The pattern of arrests and convictions in Berlin during these years suggested that 'the outrages with which the newspapers of every political colouring are filled' were the peculiar province of young men, especially 18- to 21-year-olds.[66]

Given this development, it was natural that observers should seek links between radical politics and the traditional bearers of youthful violence, drawing parallels between 'awakening' and 'delinquent youth'.[67] For the combatant parties themselves, whose credibility depended on their displaying an active and effective response to the threat of violence that each claimed the other posed, the advantages of mobilising the energies of the cliques in their own cause must have been apparent. Such instrumental considerations played an important part in the attitude of the KPD. The interest of the political left in the unofficial youth movement had a fairly long history. Before the war the Social Democratic press had warned its readers about the dangers of the wild youth clubs whose members allowed themselves to be lured into a life of senseless consumption — 'swilling and "loving" ' — urging them not simply to avoid such excesses but to confront and combat the clubs on their own ground.[68] *Vorwärts* showed a similar attitude of distanced sympathy combined with reforming zeal in discussing the 'Wander-boors' a decade later, and in 1931 Adolf Lau published an article in its columns, countering the claims in the bourgeois press that the cliques as such were identical with criminal gangs. He argued that the cliques, whatever their faults, fulfilled important functions in promoting cohesion and co-operation among working-class young people and outlined the role that Social Democrats had played in trying to educate and organise them.[69] All the evidence suggests that in Social Democratic activities the functions of education and moral leadership were deliberately and effectively distinguished from those of political agitation and practical advocacy. During the late 1920s and early 1930s the SPD press displayed an anxiety about the politicisation of young people very much in keeping with the temper of bourgeois 'public opinion'.[70] The Communists showed themselves on the whole less eager and less able to keep their distance. Their attitude was never articulated in programmatic terms, but took the more active form of direct approaches to the cliques.

Those approaches formed a very minor aspect of the agitation of the KPD during the Weimar Republic. They are interesting, however, because they illustrate in a particularly vivid way some important contradictions in the party's understanding of its constituency. The cliques represented a proletarian reality with which the Communist movement engaged most vigorously in practice, but which it was unable to comprehend within the understanding of the working class that legitimated its existence.

At one level, the cliques and the Communists could hardly have kept apart. With a party membership that fluctuated between a low of 11,000 (in 1927) and a high of over 30,000 (in 1923), and several thousand more organised into its auxiliary formations like the RFB, the KPD was a highly visible and active presence on the streets of Berlin.[71] It claimed as its strongholds the very neighbourhoods in which the cliques were at home, and the milieu of the cliques was reflected in its social composition. By comparison with the population at large and with the SPD, the KPD's membership normally included high proportions of manual and unskilled workers, of men, of younger (though not of the youngest) people, and of the unemployed. These groups were still more clearly over-represented in the party's militant auxiliaries, and with the swelling of the KPD's ranks in the course of the depression (the Berlin membership nearly doubled between 1929 and 1932) the bias towards the young and unemployed became overwhelming.[72]

The interplay of social conditions and political interests in the constitution of the cliques also gave them an affinity with the Communist Party. The cliques existed as such in the realm of everyday life outside the workplace; they appear to us as a product not only of relative poverty, but of the quality of housing that poverty implied, the neighbourhoods in which such housing was to be found and the expectations that the authorities and the press expressed about the behaviour of young people living in those neighbourhoods. The same general structural conditions applied to Communist residents of the same areas. Among the most important of these was the presence of the state and its direct intervention in daily life. This was more obvious in the neighbourhood than at the workplace. Moreover, the attentions of the police or of a system of public welfare which was complicated, under-financed and increasingly punitive in its administration were most likely to be experienced as intrusive or constraining by the least affluent workers. In the late 1920s it was the new state agencies that helped to make the cliques visible and to define them as a fit object of both service and control; in turn, the cliques were portrayed as organising in opposition to the police and the reform-school system. This represents the 'objectively' political component of the cliques, and it is entirely congruent with the practical concerns of the KPD. The KPD was an avowedly insurrectionary party, whose *raison d'être* consisted in providing a revolutionary alternative to Social Democracy. As such, it adopted a policy of opposition to the Weimar state, not excepting those welfare measures for which the Social Democrats took responsibility and which, in Prussia and Berlin, Social Democratic officials often administered. An important aspect of Communist activity was neighbourhood-based agitation around such institutions as the police, the welfare bureaux and labour exchanges and the schools, involving both direct action – demonstrations or, in the case of the police, the advocacy of physical resistance – and repeated demands for such radical reforms of the system as workers' control.[73]

In terms both of who they were and what they represented, then, the cliques were characteristic of the KPD's own constituency in the big cities, embodying in distilled form the section of the working class whose immediate grievances were most clearly and vigorously articulated by the Communist Party. But the Communists did not recognise them as such. In spite of their flexibility in practice, the idea of class struggle that the Communists represented had no room in it for specific interests shared by members of the working class but determined by relationships outside the workplace, the sphere of direct confrontation between labour and capital. This reflected an understanding of the working class and its relationship to the party that was problematic in both theory and practice: in keeping with its leading role in the International founded by Lenin, the KPD defined itself not simply as the vanguard of the working class and leader in the class struggle, but as the embodiment of the class-conscious proletariat. As an axiom, this self-definition implied a denial of the possibility of any legitimate working-class politics outside the party. As a programmatic statement, it directed the Communists to organise the workers within the factories, since these were seen as both the foci of class conflict and the principal power bases in the capitalist system. The 'proper' constituency of the KPD, then, was made up of those workers who experienced their collective interest and their collective strength at the point of production. In fact, Social Democracy and the Free trade unions retained the allegiance of the great majority of organised workers; after 1924 the Communists found it very difficult to operate within the factories and were often compelled to seek recruits outside the ranks of the organised and employed working class. In its efforts to mobilise various sections of the population, the KPD showed considerable sensitivity to the concerns of specific interest groups; its unemployed agitation and its participation in campaigns against the abortion law are cases in point. But when the movement approached the worker outside the workplace, or the child of workers who had never known a workplace, it always did so with some suspicion.[74]

V

The pattern of official Communist approaches to the cliques indicates that when the party leadership thought about the gangs it saw them as possible allies rather than as members of its own constituency. Those approaches were undertaken during the most openly radical phases of party activity. They coincided with deliberate efforts of the Communists to distance themselves from Social Democracy and to extend their influence to sections of the lower and working classes which they construed as being outside the 'revolutionary vanguard' embodied by the party. Moreover, the appeal to the cliques was sounded at times when the party recognised a danger that young people would be drawn into right-wing movements, and it always accompanied the call for physical resistance to 'Fascism' in its current avatar, through which the workers were to be steeled and schooled for the insurrection.

The earliest of those occasions was in the spring of 1923. The national crisis precipitated by the French occupation of the Ruhr and runaway inflation led the KPD to organise widespread mass protests, to issue loud and frequent warnings about the dangers of an Italian-style Fascist movement engulfing Germany, and finally to begin preparations for a workers' revolution.[75] In this situation, members of the Communist Youth in Berlin reportedly conceived the idea of organising their own umbrella organisation for the cliques which were so much in the news.[76] The organisation was called the Red Hiking Ring (Roter Wanderring, RWR), and it issued a paper under the title *Der Rote Wanderer (The Red Hiker)*. The first number of the paper carried an appeal headed: 'Degenerate youth! Guttersnipes! Pimps! Bums! Thieves! Plunderers!' Its authors did not offer a judgement on the accuracy of these epithets, beyond expressing contempt for the bourgeois press that applied them to the cliques and its 'gibbering about the alleged "moral degeneration" of youth'. They emphasised that *Vorwärts* had joined in the outcry against the hiking clubs. Now 'the only recreation available to the young proletarian who slaves all week' was under threat from inflated transport costs, hostile publicity and attacks of the 'Fascists' (members of the Bismarck Youth and Jungsturm in particular),[77] and adherents of the 'Free Guild'[78] had resolved to form a common front. It was reported that a delegate assembly had been held in Berlin in April, at which 700 clique members and the representatives of 74 different clubs had agreed on a programme of mutual aid. The only points in the programme that betray the fact that the RWR was more than a cartel of ordinary recreational clubs are the provisions for free legal aid, 'collective defence against our enemies', support for revolutionary organisations and the establishment of a common housing list. According to *Der Rote Wanderer*, a group of clubs objecting to the radical posture of the Ring split off at the first meeting to form a 'Free Hiking Ring'. If the very scant evidence can be believed, it was in the 'national congress' of this organisation that Social Democratic youth leaders took part during the same year.[79]

Although the RWR was a sufficiently serious undertaking to merit the establishment of an office and hostels of its own, the moment and occasion of its founding were not directly acknowledged in the main KPD press until many years later.[80] During the late summer of 1923, however, the party's political daily paper, *Die Rote Fahne*, reported several occasions on which 'comrades' from the RWR stood by Communist and Socialist Youth members in confrontations with police and Bismarck Youth. Sections of the Ring also appear as active — alongside other, not easily identified local social and political clubs — in the 'proletarian youth cartels' formed all over Berlin in the last phase of the KPD's proto-revolutionary agitation.[81]

According to one police report, members of the RWR were still being arrested for brawling in the spring of 1924.[82] But the Ring did not survive long. The collapse of the Communists' revolutionary effort at the end of 1923 and the three-month ban on the party that followed may have weakened the political impulse. It was also reported that the more hard-bitten clique members were alienated by the reforming zeal of the Communists. Others, however, remained faithful to the movement. Some joined the Communist Youth, and when the Red Youth Front (Rote Jungfront, RJ), the youth arm of the RFB, was founded at the end of 1924 clique members showed particular enthusiasm. Although activists in both of these organisations were aware that clique life could involve excesses of behaviour that ought as far as possible to be suppressed, it was generally acknowledged that current and former clique members had made important contributions to party life.

Even during the mid- to late twenties, when the Communists made no particular effort to win them over, sympathetic cliques continued to operate on the fringes of the party. With the Nazi movement growing in Berlin from 1926 on, these groups were ever more likely to be drawn into the political fight, as politics took on the character of a ubiquitous public entertainment. The members of the Neukölln clique Eagle's Claw, for example, swore up and down that their club was entirely unpolitical. One evening, they tried to get into a National Socialist meeting but were turned away because they could not pay the admission charge. A short time later they were arrested in a crowd which had attacked a group of SA men.[83] This incident occurred in May 1928. A year later the RFB and RJ were officially banned, after illegal May Day demonstrations had ended in serious and prolonged battles between police and residents of Wedding and Neukölln.[84] Observers noted that 'a large section' of the Berlin membership of the RJ, loosed from its political moorings, floated back into the cliques.

The year 1929 also marked the beginning of a new epoch in the tactics of the Communist Party; the turn to an 'ultra-left' policy required the development of new forms of mass agitation. In their attempt to gather in the 'labouring masses', and particularly to win the young and unemployed to their cause, the Communists devoted themselves more vigorously and more self-consciously than ever before to agitation in the neighbourhoods. An important aspect of this agitation was the propagation of a movement for self-defence against the terror of the SA, the 'militant fight against Fascism', and among its preconditions were the construction of legal and covert successor organisations for the banned paramilitary formations and the recruitment of young activists to the local self-defence squads.[85] At the end of 1930, in the wake of the National Socialists' sensational gains in the Reichstag elections, the leadership of the RJ, already reconstituted as an underground organisation, instructed its Berlin and Hamburg sections 'to work out a plan for agitation among the cliques and to compile their experiences in this field in a report to the leadership, so it can be considered for use by the whole organisation'.[86]

This second initiative in the recruitment of 'asocial elements', although more obviously part of a national policy, was carried on with less colourful propaganda than the campaign of 1923. Now the emphasis was on co-optation of the cliques rather than public representation of their particular interests as such. From 1929, the party was deeply involved in a campaign against the reform-school system, in which noisy and sometimes violent protests by reformatory inmates were combined with extensive public agitation.[87] But outside this context there was only one widely circulated item of literary propaganda which might have been directed towards the winning over of actual or potential clique members: Walter Schönstedt's *Kämpfende Jugend*. This volume was issued in 1932 in the 'Red One-Mark Novel' series of the Communist publishing house. The advertisements for it that were printed in other party publications aimed at a youthful audience recommended as 'humorous and interesting' its 'depiction of how Tomcat and Spider and their wild hiking clique become members of the Communist Youth'.[88] The author was a RJ leader in Kreuzberg, and his portrait of a Kreuzberg clique emphasised the aspects of its mentality that were most relevant to the hopes and expectations of the party. As Schönstedt pictures them, the boys of Noble Sow are temperamentally sympathetic to the Communists, openly admiring the party's leading personalities, but contemptuous of official jargon and the regimentation implicit in party discipline. 'Punch-ups, a little Thälmann [Ernst Thälmann, KPD Chairman], and as for the rest, they don't care. . . Like caged beasts of prey, with the wildness still in their bones'. At the same time, the value of just such elements in current struggles is unmistakable:

> But when word went out: The Nazis are coming through the Nostizstrasse, then the lads were better than many of the organised ones. 'Getting ready to make another speech, Theo? [asks the clique member Spider] Don't bother, man. You know, if anything happens, we'll be there, we know what we've got to do. Just smash 'em, smash 'em, till the roof falls in!'[89]

The Central Committee member who reviewed *Kämpfende Jugend* for the literary journal of the Communist Society of Proletarian-Revolutionary Writers, *Die Linkskurve*, recommended that each Communist Youth local should organise public discussions of the book, involving 'not only their own members, but the youth of the cliques'.[90]

As in 1923, the official press and propaganda organs of the party itself treated this agitation gingerly, if at all. When a 17-year-old bricklayer's apprentice was shot dead by Nazis in Schöneberg in March 1931, *Vorwärts* reported it as the murder of a member of a 'Communist hiking-club'.[91] In successive reports of *Die Rote Fahne*, the victim was transmogrified from an 'unorganised worker who belonged to a hiking-club' and whose friends had now vowed to join the anti-fascist movement, to a 'valiant young proletarian. . .on the way to [joining] the Communist Youth', who 'organised the comrades in his hiking-club into the [Communist] Red Aid', to 'member of a hiking-club, red "shop-steward" and organiser of the militant fight against fascism' in his vocational school.[92] These reports reveal a tension between the wish to provide an example to those outside the party, like the cliques, of how one of their own might make (or be forced into) common cause with the Communists, and the need to reassert the axiom that there was no real proletarian politics outside the organised working-class movement and no anti-fascist politics outside the Communist movement. This ambivalence had other consequences, which will be discussed below; here it may suffice to account for the fact that there were no public declarations about recruitment from the cliques to match the KPD's repeated claims of converts from rival parties.

The evidence available from other sources, principally police records, of the activity of the Communist self-defence formations in Berlin, is fragmentary but illuminating: Erich Irmer, another bricklayer's apprentice, arrested at the age of 16 as a participant in the Eagle's Claw incident, joined one of the early successor organisations of the RJ in 1929; at the end of 1931 he was treasurer of a Communist cell and squad-leader in another anti-fascist formation. In 1926 Alfred Jäger, 15 years old, joined Tartar's Blood; he was twice arrested, for illegal camping and assault on Stahlhelm members, and moved on to a Communist formation and a series of political offences when the clique broke up three years later. During the investigation that followed two shoot-outs between Communists and National Socialists in Friedrichshain in December 1931, the police learned that one local RJ leader was a former member of Apache Blood, while another belonged to a clique which called itself the Ever-Broke Savings Club. The names of two more groups, Wood-Birds and Sea-Pirates, were mentioned in the course of the enquiry.[93] There were other cases in which young people took part in clique and political activities concurrently or, as the outline of developments above suggests, moved from Communist organisations into the cliques. The charter members of Egg-Slime, for example, had belonged to the Communist Youth; one of them had been expelled for his clique activities. The clique nevertheless continued to hold its meetings in a Communist tavern, and its members remained politically active, to the extent of provoking fights with Nazis, while pursuing their criminal career.[94] More generally, the political organisations that lived shoulder to shoulder with the cliques in the working-class districts could not avoid sharing with them in the life of the neighbourhood. And at this level it is clear that the Communists were not the only group for which the cliques represented a potential recruiting ground. After the shooting of a Hitler Youth member on the Lausitzer Platz (Kreuzberg), the police initially sought an explanation for the incident in a conflict between members of the clique Gay Blood and other local youths. Although no direct connection could be established, it became obvious as the investigation continued that the boundaries between political and non-political formations were very fluid. Shortly before the killing the newsletter of the Kreuzberg RJ had characterised a local SA leader in these words: 'This character, who is also known by the name of "Scholli", has already made off with the treasuries of the hiking-club Gay Blood and the social club Hand-in-Hand.'[95]

VI

In addition to its periodic recruiting efforts, there were other, less direct but more public ways in which the Communist movement declared its affinity with the cliques. Right-wing publicists vilified the KPD with such formulae as 'the identity of Communism with the fifth [i.e. criminal] estate'.[96] Even the Social Democrats regularly accused the Communists of having brought an unheard-of coarseness and brutality into political life, on the streets and in the parliamentary chambers, well before the Nazis began to present a threat to public order.[97] And in its radical phases the KPD did its best to live up to these accusations. Not only did it openly espouse the causes of delinquent youth through the campaign against the reform schools and its agitation against the police; the Berlin leadership of the KPD also adopted the role of bearer of a culture of proletarian toughness calculated to contrast with the 'respectability' of the Social Democrats. When the Interior Minister remarked in the wake of the May Day riots of 1929 that the Social Democratic police authorities stood accused of behaving like Jagow, the anti-socialist police chief in pre-war Berlin, a member of the KPD delegation in the Reichstag he was addressing interjected, 'Aber Jagow war noch ein Kerl!' — 'Jagow was a *man*!'[98] If the cliques can be said to have inhabited what was publicly regarded as outlaw territory, in cultural and social terms, then the party that struck such poses, that was known to be relatively tolerant of ex-convicts in its own ranks,[99] and whose chief political newspaper named spies and traitors to the movement and urged readers to 'teach them a lesson',[100] declared itself an outlaw party by inviting itself on to that territory.

A party less constricted in its vision by received notions of class and of politics might have been expected to develop an analysis of the cliques that reflected this anarchic retreat from the traditional categories of acceptable behaviour. Logically, there were two lines of argument open to the Communists: on the one hand, they could acknowledge that the cliques and all they represented were marginal to the working class or that they were a symptom of the actual pathology of the proletariat under capitalism, but that the party nevertheless took an instrumental and/or charitable interest in them. On the other, they might adopt an approach analogous to those of more recent revolutionary movements involved in organising 'lumpenproletarian' populations, arguing that the fact that individuals or groups were categorised as criminal was the result not of intrinsic qualities that disqualified them from participation in the revolutionary movement, but of belonging to a single and universally (if not uniformly) oppressed proletariat, all of whose members were potentially subject to the same pressures and processes of categorisation.[101] In terms of the KPD's preoccupations, this would have meant accepting that the cliques were no less representative of the working class for not being at work. In fact, KPD comments on the cliques and on such related questions as crime, youth and the family hover between these two approaches.

The very idea that the party should actively engage with such issues at all was hotly contested in the early years of the Communist movement. A politics of everyday life concerned with seeking out the peculiarly proletarian elements in social and cultural practice and injecting them with socialist content, which was proposed as a way to shield working-class youth against the influences of the bourgeois media and institutions, was rejected by many as a distraction from the class struggle and a temptation to Social Democratic complacency. Even when the idea of this kind of 'cultural struggle' had been accepted, it took second place in the Communist understanding of politics to the self-evident tasks of industrial action, public agitation and parliamentary activity, and training for the armed insurrection.[102] Where we do find the elements of a Communist analysis of culture, it is probably significant that the two bursts of deliberate agitation among the cliques coincide roughly with phases in that analysis when leading representatives of the movement displayed a readiness to re-evaluate the aspects of proletarian daily life conventionally defined as degenerate. In the 1930s, *Kämpfende Jugend* formed a visible link between the clique agitation and a literary movement whose exponents showed a new concern with the analysis of mass cultural consumption. Members of the Society of Proletarian-Revolutionary Writers investigated the popularity of penny-dreadfuls and pornographic magazines, no longer simply to deplore but to consider the possibilities of a socialist analogue, a proletarian novel with mass appeal.[103] In the early twenties similar, though more unambiguously hostile discussions of popular literature and film had coincided with the articulation by Edwin Hoernle, a leading figure in the party, of a challenge to the idea that the family as such was identical with the bourgeois domestic unit. The problems of the working-class family, he argued, were those not of disintegration but of being forced into a mould that was inappropriate in the first place; agitation and education should start from the grim reality of proletarian life rather than from attempts to create artificial institutional alternatives to it.[104]

In the course of the campaign against the reform-school system in 1930-1 there emerged the beginnings of a critique of the concept of delinquency that might have implied a readiness to accept the cliques as a normal phenomenon and a legitimate recruiting ground for the parties of the working class. The cliques were generally held to be characterised by a condition of *Verwahrlosung*, or waywardness. Evidence of this condition was one of the principal grounds on which children were referred to reform schools or placed in care. But the word itself was particularly ambiguous, for in its active form *verwahrlosen* could mean to neglect, to suffer from neglect, or simply to go to the bad. In its use, active delinquency was automatically identified with lack of supervision, individual depravation with an inadequate family life.[105] For much of its history, the Communist movement, when it considered the question of delinquency, used this term uncritically; its representatives accepted that the proletarian child was subject to *Verwahrlosung* as a consequence of the destructive effect that wage-labour had on the family, or concerned themselves at most with the danger that political radicalism could be interpreted by the authorities as evidence of *Verwahrlosung*.[106] In 1931, however, a spokesman for the reform-school agitation, writing in the party's social policy journal, characterised the term as 'one of the usual elastic concepts of bourgeois society' which could be mobilised against 'any proletarian youth who comes into conflict with the state apparatus', who 'rebels morally or criminally against the capitalist social order'.[107] But this was a minority voice. The more popular organs of the party continued to present the simpler, more compelling and by no means unrealistic argument that many reformatory inmates were indeed sick, but only because capitalism had made family life impossible for them.[108] Communist critics continued to argue as though true proletarians could not be criminals.[109] And the handful of statements about the cliques that the Communist movement produced during its second phase of agitation reflect neither a general shift in theoretical perceptions of delinquency nor a unified view of the nature of the cliques themselves as a class phenomenon. It is characteristic of the Communists' cautious approach to this agitation that none of those statements even offers a direct comment on why the party should have been interested in them.

One of the statements appears in *Kämpfende Jugend*. It has already been pointed out that the usefulness of gang violence to the Communist self-defence movement is one of the central themes of the novel. By way of a general characterisation of the cliques, the protagonist, a Communist Youth leader, acknowledges that the activities of Noble Sow represent a form of collective resistance against the depredations of the capitalist system. The fact that they are not content to be passive victims is counted in their favour. But the Communist warns that they are in danger of sliding into the lumpenproletariat if they persist in pursuing their personal rebellion in isolation from the organised workers' movement.[110]

For Schönstedt's reviewer in *Die Linkskurve*, there was both rather more and rather less in it than that. In half-conscious acknowledgement that the cliques were not so external to the party's actual constituency as normative declarations about the 'class-conscious proletariat' implied, he described the politicisation of Noble Sow as a natural event, 'the confluence of two streams from the reservoir of the street'. But he also displayed some confusion about what did or should distinguish the two streams, Communist Youth and cliques. In his view, the most important thing the clique had to offer was a kind of instinctual solidarity, 'the feeling that each cares for the other', a personal concern too often lacking in the party organisations. He nevertheless criticised the author for portraying the gang in more vivid and lively terms than the Communist cell, speculating that the hardships of life which gave Schönstedt his insight into the clique had left him 'no opportunity for the thorough... study of historical materialism'.[111]

Still more remarkable for its obstinate telescoping of ideal and reality was an article devoted to the cliques that Gertrud Ring published in the cultural supplement of *Die Rote Fahne* in April 1931. The piece was clearly written in response to publicity about the cliques in the non-Communist press, but it does not engage explicitly with any existing analysis of them; it is purely descriptive in style. It ends with the characterisation of the cliques as an 'instinctual self-defence against the pressures weighing upon proletarian youth', a sketch of the history of the RWR, and the assurance that many cliques were once again disbanding as their members became 'fighters on the anti-fascist front'. But in the depiction of their structure and activities that precedes these assertions, the cliques already appear as models of Bolshevik discipline and democratic centralism: The 'bull'

> is elected at a meeting on democratic principles for an unlimited period. Everyone owes him absolute obedience, every clique keeps the strictest discipline. If anyone puts a foot wrong, he is thrown out, and not with kid gloves, either... New members are apprentices and have to go through a strict probationary period...

To be sure, the cliques are boisterous, even violent on occasion; their class-conscious mischief extends to 'embittered struggle' against Stahlhelm, Nazis, scouts and all bourgeois youth organisations. But they always clean up after themselves when they go camping, 'unlike the vulgar petty bourgeois [*Spiesser*], who decorate the párk with...sandwich wrappers'.[112]

Appearing as it did in the party's chief political organ, Ring's article is the nearest thing we have to an official statement on the cliques. Its distortions are characteristic of the incapacity of the party's political leadership to come to terms with forms of agitation that did not accord with its self-image as the leader in the struggle between labour and capital. In its clique agitation, the Communist movement sought and gained support from a proletarian group whose defining characteristic was its refusal to conform to normal expectations about the revolutionary working class. The practical confrontation with reality apparently allowed fresh analyses to develop of the way class relations shaped proletarian life, but these either remained inchoate or were confined to the ghetto of the party's special-interest mass organisations, like the one that issued the Communist social policy journal.[113]

VII

The confusion of voices with which the Communist movement spoke matched the ambiguity of its intentions towards those whom it set out to win. The process of politicisation might mean simply mobilising social resources, resentments and forms of struggle present in the culture for application in the current fight — the instrumental function so obvious in the case of the cliques. It might also, and in the German socialist tradition did, represent an emancipatory process itself, in which, as attitudes and practices were reshaped, the socialist man was formed who would proceed to build socialism. The two aims are not mutually exclusive, but the character of Bolshevist Communism as a movement which strove to transform every action into an immediate concrete struggle for power was bound to bring out the tension between them. The tension was explicit in the debates over the value of 'cultural struggle'. In the clique agitation, it appears as the contradiction between the view that the cliques *qua* cliques had something to offer the Communist movement and the apparently self-evident proposition that becoming 'fighters on the anti-fascist front' meant dissolution of the gang. The same ambiguity emerges in answer to the question of what politicisation meant to the politicised. It is impossible to be sure how many clique members joined the Communists as a means of escape from the wretchedness and constrictions of daily life, seeking to broaden their horizons and realise alternatives, and how many saw in the party's apparatus and material resources an opportunity to consolidate and legitimate their position in the existing local power structure or, less cynically, the means of more easily pursuing aims which they shared with the Communists.

One consequence of this mutual ambivalence can be seen in the problems that arose when young Communists behaved like clique members. The active formations of the Communist Youth engaged in fighting the Nazis in Berlin were characterised by a style and mentality strikingly similar to those of the cliques. Within the Communist organisations, these similarities were modified at certain points by the elements of a deep-rooted political culture. At others they remained a source of conflict between the Communist leadership and the rank and file.[114]

The least problematic aspect of the defence formations, from the point of view of the leadership, was the fact that, like the cliques, they were explicitly territorial. The party-political context of their activities coloured the definition of territory, just as it determined the character of the outsider. Since the electoral successes of Social Democracy in the Wilhelmine era certain sections of Berlin were popularly regarded as 'Red' territory. The idea that all Berlin's working-class districts were properly the preserve of the 'Reds', propagated by the KPD in its turn, was adopted by the Nazis as the organising principle for their campaigns in Berlin. The SA men were portrayed by their own leaders as invaders in the neighbourhood, determined to break the Marxist hegemony by installing themselves in one area after another. Moreover, the Communist defence movement was organised by street and neighbourhood. Within this context, however, the statements of the Communists reveal a very acute sense of the limits of their own districts and their responsibilities within them. They congregated for party and leisure activities alike in the tavern or *Rummelplatz*, park or other open space – places that were generally recognised in the neighbourhood as their own hang-outs. Among the most common forms of group activity was the *Durchzug*, a policing action within the neighbourhood: known and suspected Nazis were stopped and searched, usually to the accompaniment of verbal and physical abuse; their badges and insignia (along with any weapons that might be found) were then 'confiscated' by the Communists, who hoarded them as prized trophies.

In the realm of verbal and material imagery, the political formations shared with the cliques an attachment to the visible affects of group membership, partly symbolic and partly utilitarian: badges, uniforms, weapons. On this issue the Communist leadership was constantly torn between tolerating the mania for self-presentation and display as a form of behaviour natural and attractive to young people and condemning it as dangerous to the interests of an organisation in which the capacity to operate inconspicuously and in secret was highly valued. Instead of the anonymous ciphers recommended by the leadership as an aspect of such conspiratorial activity, the Communists often used nicknames. Names like Tarzan, Sinalko (the brand-name of a soft drink), Gypsy and so on are reminiscent of the cliques, and some had even been won by the young activists during their clique days. They did not necessarily guarantee anonymity; their principal function was to underline the specialness of the individual while identifying him with the group.

The forms of internal discipline and the structure of authority within the defence formations also show parallels with what we know of the cliques. The fate of Otto Regenthaler illustrates the problematic coexistence of organisational and communal codes:

Since I hadn't taken part in the Communist demonstration at the New Year [1931], on my father's orders, some RFB members came to our courtyard in the early hours of the morning, blew on a signal trumpet and shouted: This is where the coward [Regenthaler] lives! Come on down, we'll punch your face in! The very next day I went to the RFB leader and got the shouters expelled. From then on I felt as though I was always running the gauntlet. Because of the constant abuse I cut myself off completely from the Communists and devoted myself. . .exclusively to my girlfriend.

The cohesiveness and collective self-confidence that made this kind of internal terror possible depended to a large extent on the force of individual personalities. In the section of Kreuzberg where the unfortunate Regenthaler lived, the figure to reckon with was Otto Singer, 19, the unemployed son of a construction worker. As organiser for the local Communist Youth he was known to be tough: 'Because of his extremely radical attitude he was respected but also feared by his comrades. He never suffered hangers-on in his group.' The leader of a Neukölln group, Hermann Lessing, was a similar type. A neighbour reported that he was notorious in the area for his activism and violence: 'If you don't go along with what he says, you're eliminated and can't work in the organisation any more.' The importance of strong personal leadership is also illustrated by examples of failure. When the leader of a self-defence group in Berlin-Mitte was arrested, the group began to disintegrate; it continued to lose members until he returned from prison and set it on its feet again.

In the plethora of competing organisations, it was characteristic of these leaders that they were able to maintain their own power bases and even to challenge the authority of the party leadership through the formation of new groups. Hermann Lessing was the founder of the Neukölln Fighting Column, which he had led into the Communist movement, and he was sufficiently confident of the support of his members to defy the local party secretary when she tried to enforce the leadership's objections to his violence. Alfred Richter, leader of a street squad in Wedding, was expelled from the Communist Party in 1929; he went on to take over the leadership of the (not otherwise identified) Wedding Youth Defence, and in 1932 he was taken back into his local party cell against the wishes of the KPD's Berlin office. And with the case of Otto Singer we find ourselves once again in the world of the street youth: after he had been expelled from the party several times he resigned himself and founded his own group — 'But only ace lads [*knorke Jungen*] would be eligible for this.'

The party's attitude to the indiscipline that personal power made possible can be gauged by the repeated expulsions of local 'bulls'. On the general problem of toughness as an organisational style, the views of the leadership were ambivalent. A report of 1928 implies that bullying, particularly of younger members, 'so-called rowdiness', was a well known practice within the Berlin Communist Youth. The leadership did not see such practices as contributing to group cohesion and confidence; on the contrary, the extraordinarily high rate of membership turnover in Wedding was blamed on internal rowdyism. The report concluded, however, that although the bullies themselves 'are often not around when it comes to day-to-day [party] work, and often even disrupt it. . . they are absolutely revolutionary elements, which we need and must educate'.[115]

The character of the social bond within the group also deserves comment. From time to time doubts were expressed within the Communist movement about the mechanistic way in which organisational principles were applied in efforts to forge a disciplined solidarity, and this was the concern that lay behind the reviewer's approval of the 'proletarian comradeship' displayed by the clique in *Kämpfende Jugend*. This form of comradeship, however, was inconsistent with a larger political expediency, for it depended on emotional and material reciprocity continually tested and confirmed in immediate experience. The cohesion of the defence formations was often of this kind, resting on a web of sentimental bonds among the members and between them and the neighbourhood which could be overstretched and even torn apart by the demands of party discipline. One young Communist fighter had to spend several months in gaol following a shooting; in a badly spelled letter from his cell he wrote, mixing the languages of politics and disappointed comradeship:

Dear Comrade Erich the hearings coming up if I get off I can do without the organisation working with you, since you'll never make it to a Red United Front and I'd never have thought you'd leave me in the lurch. . .

Two aspects of group life brought the tensions between leadership and rank and file to a point of open conflict. The first, and less politically dangerous of these, was the male exclusiveness of the defence groups. Communist policy-makers had always regarded women in politics with a certain ambivalence. The whole problem of putting into practice the kind of free and equal relations between the sexes that the KPD's inherited principles prescribed — 'the sexual question' — was an embarrassing one for many Communists and a constant source of inconclusive debate. Where one commentator saw demoralising 'dirty fantasies' arising from the hole-and-corner sexuality that too many Communist youths shared with the cliques and other working-class adolescents, another found 'genuinely proletarian jokes'.[116] When it came to strictly organisational relations, women were nowhere more discriminated against than in that section of the movement that emphasised the military virtues. But by 1930 at the latest the official line prescribed that the role of women in all areas of party life, including the organising of physical defence, was identical with that of men. Very early on, however, the leadership encountered explicit resistance to any form of co-operation on the part of its male rank and file. Significantly, among the Berlin defence formations the toughest and most active of the sections, Berlin-Mitte and Neukölln, were the most tenacious in their opposition;[117] the fact that the party secretary in Neukölln was a woman certainly did not ease the tension between Hermann Lessing and the local leadership.

Still more problematic was the violence of certain groups itself. In the form of the deliberate persistence in the practice of 'individual terror' — isolated, gang-style acts of violence — against the SA, this represented one of the most explosive moments of conflict within the party as a whole. The definitive statement by the party's Political Bureau of its rejection of 'individual terror', issued in November 1931 and accompanied by a concerted campaign against all 'terroristic' and 'adventurist' tendencies within the Communist movement, touched off angry debates and even fights within the defence formations and the Communist Youth in Berlin. The party's leaders were openly accused of having abandoned their revolutionary ideals and betrayed their followers; for the maintenance of the party's tenuous legality, they had traded the right of the young Communists to an effective defence against the deadly attacks of the Nazis.[118]

To these recriminations the leadership responded that tendencies to 'individual terror' reflected a mood of 'desperation' and 'revenge', 'motives that characterise the uprooted, insecure petty bourgeoisie run mad. . .alien to the socialist working class'.[119] In a similar vein, members who resisted organising women were labelled 'red-painted petty bourgeois [*Spiessbürger*]'.[120] Neither of these characterisations is an accurate reflection of the social position of the Communist activists. Nor, of course, were they intended as such; they purport to provide a measure of the extent to which those activists had lived up to — or failed to live up to — an ideal of behaviour appropriate to the working class and, still more, to the tasks of its emancipation. But it is significant that the party had no words to describe those who were neither perfectly disciplined Communists nor members of an alien class, no way of acknowledging that one might be a worker and yet behave in undesirable ways. There was a genuine confusion that arose within the Communist movement whenever a distinction had to be drawn between what was proletarian and what the proletarian ought to be, what the party had to deal with in terms of an actual working-class culture and what it meant to make of it; and this confusion was not irrelevant to the party's own capacity to carry out the political tasks it set itself.

By virtue as much of common socialisation as of mutual recruitment, the cliques and the defence formations in Berlin shared a social code and an organisational culture in which the gang style of organisation was closely associated with toughness, masculinity, a solidarity based on mutual aid and affection, a strong tie with the local neighbourhood and violent competition with or resistance to outsiders. The respective elements of the code were mutually reinforcing and the whole was shaped and sustained by the conditions of life in the working-class neighbourhoods of Berlin in the 1920s. In its 'raw' form, as some Communist diagnoses recognised, this was essentially a defensive culture; the style of the cliques and the kinds of consumption they represented reflected the models and materials made available by bourgeois society, and their functions ranged between the enrichment of leisure time and the guarantee of bare survival. They offered no alternative to the existing system of economic and power relations and no escape for their members. Within this culture, though, there were openings to forms of activity that had the potential to attack and change the system; these consisted in the objectively political conflicts that the cliques were involved in by virtue of belonging to that culture and in the ways in which aspects of social behaviour were explicitly politicised in twentieth-century Germany. The visibility of the cliques was a function of the presence and expectations of certain state agencies on the one hand and of a long-standing association between social indiscipline, violent crime and political radicalism in public discourses about youth on the other. This was the 'ideological territory' on which the cliques and the Communists met, their affinity compounded by the fact, peculiar to the Weimar Republic, that the state itself was directly associated with a single party and the KPD's chief rival, the SPD, and by the KPD's practice of actively adopting the interests and concerns of the cliques as its own. When clique members began to see the police and other adversaries as part of a system that had to be fought politically, it was not unlikely that they would choose the Communist movement as the framework for their fight.

The aim of the party, in its turn, must have been to hasten the moment when this perception would become inevitable, through agitation and education to transform the defensive culture into an offensive movement. In fact, the Communists showed less awareness of the specific congruence of interests between themselves and the cliques than of the instrumental value of one aspect of clique activities, namely their violence. Whether they were viewed as a proletarian group with particular but legitimate interests or as a ready-made fighting force, though, effectively mobilising the cliques meant fracturing the unity of the culture they represented. For while the cliques met real needs and nurtured allegiances generated in their common milieu, the political movement as such — a bureaucratic apparatus engaged in action and argument and subject to demands and pressures at every level of politics — had special needs and demanded a new kind of allegiance. In order to sustain a new synthesis, the party had to be able to provide concrete alternatives to the material conditions to which the clique culture was a response, or to offer in some other form the kinds of defence that the clique provided, or at least to make credible the promise that alternatives could be created. To do less than this was to demand extraordinary sacrifices of the party's recruits, the most obvious of which, in the situation of the party in Berlin in the twenties and thirties, were the near certainty of arrest and imprisonment and the danger of political violence.

The party's capacity to realise an alternative society through independent political action, that is to bring about the revolution which was its *raison d'être* and which, in the final crisis of the Republic, the KPD presented as the only way to avoid the impending Fascist dictatorship, was limited by forces beyond its control. It would be a mistake (and one entirely characteristic of the KPD leadership) to imagine that a more coherent class analysis alone would have made it possible to overcome those obstacles. But if it was even to assess the prospects for change accurately and present them convincingly to actual and potential followers, the party had first to understand the reality it was aiming to change, to confront the nature of its own constituency as well as the general political situation. And this it could not do with any consistency. The party's self-image was dominated by a view of class struggle that implied that it should not be dealing with the cliques in the first place. This view had no place in it for the analysis of proletarian cultures as they reflected the construction of collective interests outside the workplace. It also tended to block initiatives for the active creation of a 'movement culture' which would provide the necessary alternative for working-class youth before the revolution and would be distinct in quality from both the Social Democratic cultural organisations and the defensive culture of the neighbourhood. There is no question that the elements of a new and inventive approach to the politics of everyday life were present in the theoretical utterances of some spokesmen for the movement, and even more obvious in the actual practice of the KPD. But as long as the party's leaders continued to argue as though the progressive, politicised culture it expected its members, more or less spontaneously, to represent was the only real culture of the working class, they ran the risk both of blinding themselves to the points of vulnerability in class and movement alike, and of alienating their own followers, who knew better.

Notes

This chapter has been presented in different forms on several occasions. I am grateful to the members of the SSRC Research Seminar Group in Modern German Social History, the European History Research Seminar at the University of East Anglia, the King's College Social History Seminar, Cambridge, and to my fellow contributors to the present volume for their comments and suggestions. Special thanks are due to Richard Evans, David Crew, Nigel Swain, Paul Ginsborg, David Feldman and Nick Bullock for shared ideas and enthusiasm.

   The presentation below rests to a large extent on the reports of several Berlin daily newspapers, which are abbreviated in the notes as follows: *BT (Berliner Tageblatt)*, *DAZ (Deutsche Allgemeine Zeitung)*, *RF (Die Rote Fahne)*, *VW (Vorwärts)*, *VZ (Vossische Zeitung)*; (M) denotes morning, (E) evening and (P) postal editions, where applicable. The following abbreviations are also used for frequently cited sources: *ZGStW (Zeitschrift für die gesamten Strafrechtswissenschaften)*, *StJB (Statistisches Jahrbuch der Stadt Berlin)*. Finally, where archival material has been used, the names of the archives are abbreviated: GehStA (Geheimes Staatsarchiv Preussischer Kulturbesitz, Berlin-Dahlem), LABln (Landesarchiv Berlin), StA Br (Staatsarchiv Bremen).

   1.   Analogous organisations in Hamburg and the metropolitan areas of Western Germany and the Rhineland are described in H. Kelb, 'Meine Kindheit' in W. Emmerich (ed.), *Proletarische Lebensläufe* (2 vols., Rowohlt Taschenbuch Verlag, Hamburg, 1976), vol. 2, p. 236; D. Peukert, *Die Edelweisspiraten* (Bund-Verlag, Cologne, 1980).
   2.   *StJB* (1927), pp. 8f.
   3.   Cf. G. Böss, *Berlin von heute* (Verlag von Gsellius, Berlin, 1929), pp. 10f.
   4.   *StJB* (1928), p. 24; *Statistik des deutschen Reiches*, vol. 462, section 3, p. 9.
   5.   Neukölln recorded a relatively small unskilled population in 1925, but this may reflect the fact that the administrative and census district Neukölln comprised both the older workers' settlements and large tracts of suburban land on which new and more expensive workers' dwellings were being constructed during the twenties: *StJB* (1928), pp. 18ff; *Berlin und seine Bauten* (Wilhelm Ernst, Berlin, 1970), part 4, vol. A.

6.   O. Voss and H. Schön, 'Die Cliquen jugendlicher Verwahrloster als sozial-pädagogisches Problem' in *Sozialpädagogische Schriftenreihe, I: Erfahrungen der Jugendlichen* (Alfred Prott Verlag, Potsdam, 1930), pp. 69-89 and 155-60, here p. 85. (O. Voss was director of a home for unemployed youths, H. Schön a former clique member and youth worker.)

7.   J. Ehrhardt, 'Cliquenwesen und Jugendverwahrlosung', *Zentralblatt für Jugendrecht und Jugendwohlfahrt*, vol. 21 (1930), pp. 416f.

8.   Cf. G. Dehn, *Proletarische Jugend* (Furche Verlag, Berlin, [1929]), p. 45. The following account of the cliques owes much to recent sociological approaches to working-class and youth cultures, to the way political and social concerns crystallise around questions of style and behaviour and to the way particular, notionally deviant groups are 'constructed' by the public media: S. Cohen, *Folk Devils and Moral Panics* (MacGibbon and Kee, London, 1972); S. Hall and T. Jefferson (eds.), *Resistance through Rituals* (Hutchinson, London, 1976); P. Willis, 'Shop-floor Culture, Masculinity and the Wage Form' in J. Clark *et al.* (eds.), *Working Class Culture* (Hutchinson, London, 1979), pp. 185-98.

9.   On Germany, *inter alia*: S. Fishman, 'Suicide, Sex and the Discovery of the German Adolescent', *History of Education Quarterly*, vol. 10 (1970), pp. 170-88; J.R. Gillis, 'Conformity and Rebellion: Contrasting Styles of English and German Youth, 1900-1933', *History of Education Quarterly*, vol. 13 (1973), pp. 249-60, and J.R. Gillis, *Youth in History* (Academic Press, New York, 1974).

10.   On the *Wandervogel* and the German youth movement, cf. *inter alia*: H. Becker, *German Youth. Bond or Free* (Routledge and Kegan Paul, London, 1946); K.O. Paetel, *Jugend in der Entscheidung 1913-1933-1945*, 2nd edn (Voggenreiter Verlag, Bad Godesberg, 1963); W.Z. Laqueur, *Young Germany* (Routledge and Kegan Paul, London, 1962); U. Aufmuth, *Die deutsche Wandervogelbewegung unter soziologischem Aspekt* (Vandenhoeck & Ruprecht, Göttingen, 1979).

11.   A. Hall, 'Youth in Rebellion: The Beginnings of the Socialist Youth Movement 1904-1914' in R.J. Evans (ed.), *Society and Politics in Wilhelmine Germany* (Croom Helm, London, 1980), pp. 241-66, here p. 245; *Preussisches Archiv* (1902), pp. 331ff.

12.   K. Peschke, 'Die Schundliteratur', *ZGStW*, vol. 21 (1911), p. 671. On the campaign against *Schundliteratur*: R. Schenda, *Die Lesestoffe der kleinen Leute* (Verlag C.H. Beck, Munich, 1976), pp. 78-104.

13.   Hall, 'Youth in Rebellion', pp. 241ff; G. Roger, *Die pädagogische Bedeutung der proletarischen Jugendbewegung Deutschlands* (Verlag Roter Stern, Frankfurt a.M., 1971), pp. 1-36; R. Ahlheim *et al.*, *Gefesselte Jugend. Fürsorgeerziehung im Kapitalismus* (Suhrkamp Verlag, Frankfurt a.M., 1976), pp. 50f.

14.   G. Dehn, *Grosstadtjugend* (Carl Heymanns Verlag, Berlin, 1919), p. 76.

15.   *VW*, 19 Mar. 1916 (M); E. Schwandt, 'Der Lohnsparzwang Jugendlicher', *Soziale Praxis*, vol. 27, no. 7 (15 Nov. 1917), pp. 97-9; W. Bloch, 'Kriegstagung der deutschen Jugendgerichtshilfen in Berlin', *Soziale Praxis*, vol. 27, no. 32 (10 May 1917), p. 645. This measure had been adopted locally in previous periods of economic boom; during the war its imposition led to collective resistance by young workers in some areas, like Brunswick: F. Boll, 'Spontaneität der Basis und politische Funktion des Streiks 1914-1918. Das Beispiel Braunschweig', *Archiv für Sozialgeschichte*, vol. 17 (1977), p. 358. There is no evidence of such resistance in Berlin. Cf. also L. Preller, *Sozialpolitik in der Weimarer Republik*, reprint (Athenäum/Droste Taschenbücher, Kronberg/Düsseldorf, 1978), p. 41.

16.   Prof. von Liszt, 'Der Krieg und die Kriminalität der Jugendlichen', *ZGStW*, vol. 27 (1916), pp. 496-516; A. Hellwig, *Der Krieg und die Kriminalität der Jugendlichen* (Buchhandling des Waisenhauses, Halle, 1916); K. Wittig, *Der Einfluss des Krieges und der Revolution auf die Kriminalität der Jugendlichen und ihre Behandlung im Jugendgefängnis durch Willensübungen* (H. Beyer und Söhne, Langensalza, 1921), pp. 5-37. Cf. Preller, *Sozialpolitik*, pp. 10f.

17. Cited by Wittig, *Der Einfluss des Krieges*, p. 41.

18. The National Youth Welfare Act, passed in 1922 and put into effect in 1924, gave a statutory basis to the establishment of youth bureaux in all municipalities and comparable administrative units, as well as consolidating and codifying earlier provisions for the protection, education and rehabilitation of children and youths. The National Juvenile Courts Act of 1923, nominally aimed at replacing the principle of punishment of juvenile offenders with that of education, established a new apparatus of special courts, procedures and penal institutions for young people; as in the case of the Youth Welfare Act, the new law represented a consolidation under the aegis of the national government of developments already in train in certain parts of Germany before the war: *Reichsgesetzblatt* (1922), I, p. 133; (1923), I, p. 135. Cf. Anlheim *et al., Gefesselte Jugend*, p. 51; Dr Blaum, 'Die Träger der Jugendwohlfahrtspflege', *Soziale Praxis*, vol. 29, no. 24 (10 Mar. 1920), pp. 548-50; C.J. Klumker, 'Jugendamt', *Handwörterbuch der Staatswissenschaften*, 4th edn (8 vols., G. Fischer Verlag, Jena, 1923-9), vol. 5, pp. 515-25. On the political compromises associated with Weimar's welfare provision, see Preller, *Sozialpolitik, passim*. On censorship, see the Reichstag debates about the Act for the Protection of Youth against Trashy and Pornographic Literature (*Schund- und Schmutzschriften*) of 1926 and the Bill for Protection of Young People at Places of Amusement of 1927, and the documents themselves: *Verhandlungen des Reichstags*, vols. 391 and 393 and vol. 401, no. 972 (draft Bill of 1927); *Reichsgesetzblatt* (1926), I, p. 505. On plans for alternatives to military service for young people, which became feasible in the context of state responses to the depression, see Preller, *Sozialpolitik*, p. 452.

19. *Trübners deutsches Wörterbuch* (4 vols., Walter de Gruyter, Berlin 1939-40), vol. 2, p. 8. Cf. E. Wulffen, *Gauner- und Verbrechertypen* (Langenscheidt, Berlin-Gr. Lichterfelde, 1910), pp. 22, 24; Hellwig, 'Der Krieg und die Kriminalität', p. 99; and the remarks of C. Bondy about comparable gangs, pre- and post-war, in other cities, especially Vienna: C. Bondy, 'Die jugendliche Verbrecherbande als psychologisches Problem', *Die Erziehung*, vol. 1, no. 3 (1925), pp. 146-59.

20. Voss and Schön, 'Die Cliquen', p. 83. Cf. C. Fournier, 'Ringverein der Jugend', *Die Weltbühne*, vol. 27 (1931), part I, pp. 89-95, especially p. 90.

21. *Preussisches Archiv* (1918), p. 1587; Wittig, *Der Einfluss des Krieges*, p. 44.

22. 'Nun geht das Wandern wieder an', *VW*, 5 Apr. 1924 (M).

23. H. Lögger, 'Wandervögel und Wanderflegel', *Jugend-Vorwärts* (supplement to *VW*), 3 Mar. 1923 (M); 'Die "Wilden" ', *VW*, 20 Jul. 1923 (E); 'Wanderflegel', *VW*, 20 Sept. 1924 (E).

24. 'Jugendliches Gesindel', *DAZ*, 27 Aug. 1923 (E).

25. G. Böss, *Die Not in Berlin. Tatsachen und Zahlen* (Zentralverlag, Berlin, 1923), p. 24. Cf. E. von Liszt, 'Die Kriminalität der Jugendlichen in Berlin. . . 1.1.1925 − 31.12.1925', *ZGStW*, vol. 47 (1927), pp. 459f; *eadem*, 'Die Kriminalität der Jugendlichen in Berlin in den Jahren 1928, 1929 and 1930', *ZGStW*, vol. 52 (1932), pp. 250f.

26. E. Wulf, 'Arbeitslosigkeit und Verwahrlosung der Jugend', *BT*, 2 Nov. 1923 (E).

27. See reports in *DAZ*, 19 Apr. 1923 (P), 4 Jun. 1923 (E), 14 Jul. 1923 (E), 2 Nov. 1923 (E); *BT*, 2 Nov. 1923 (E); *VW*, 29 Oct. 1923 (E), 15 Apr. 1924 (M), 30 Sept. 1924 (M), 4 Oct. 1924 (E), 26 Nov. 1924 (M).

28. E.g. Ehrhardt, 'Cliquenwesen', p. 413 and *idem*, 'Die Lage der gefährdeten und verwahrlosten Grosstadtjugend in Deutschland nach dem Krieg', *Revue internationale de l'enfant*, vol. 8 (1929), p. 811; 'I.A.II[2]', Berlin, den 28. November 1930' (police report), GehStA, file 219, vol. 15, sheet 162.

29. Preller, *Sozialpolitik*, p. 336; *StJB* (1927), p. 129; (1928), p. 125; numbers of working-class youths calculated on the basis of 1925 and 1933 censuses: *StJB* (1928), pp. 6, 24; (1934), p. 9; (1936), p. 15. Unfortunately, the 21- to 25-

year-olds, who made up the numerically most significant group among young workers, are not represented as a separate group in the unemployment figures for 1926. Cf. E. Herrnstadt, *Die Lage der arbeitslosen Jugend in Deutschland* (Preussisches Ministerium für Volkswohlfahrt, Berlin, 1926), p. 5.

30.   T. Geiger, *Die soziale Schichtung des deutschen Volkes* (Ferdinand Enke Verlag, Stuttgart, 1932), p. 96.

31.   On the following characterisation of rationalisation and its effects, see H.H. Hartwich, *Arbeitsmarkt, Verbände und Staat 1918-1933* (Walter de Gruyter, Berlin, 1967), pp. 75ff; E.C. Schöck, *Arbeitslosigkeit und Rationalisierung* (Campus Verlag, Frankfurt a.M./New York, 1977), pp. 153ff; U. Stolle, *Arbeiterpolitik im Betrieb* (Campus Verlag, Frankfurt a.M./New York, 1980) pp. 187ff.

32.   Voss and Schön, 'Die Cliquen', pp. 75f.

33.   Ibid., p. 73; A. Lamm, *Betrogene Jugend. Aus einem Erwerbslosenheim* (Bruno Cassirer, Berlin, 1932), pp. 81f; *Bericht über die Tätigkeit des Landesjugendamts Berlin vom 1.4.1925 bis 31.3.1927* (Landesjudgendamt, Berlin, 1928), p. 131; von Liszt, 'Kriminalität. . .1925', p. 33.

34.   C. Pol, 'Cliquen-Jungen über 18' (reader's letter), *VZ*, 24 May 1931 (P); cf. J. Ehrhardt, 'Jugendliche Verbrecher', *VZ*, 22 May 1932 (P).

35.   E.g. reports in *VW*, 30 Jan. 1927 (M), 5 Mar. 1927 (M) and (E), 8 Jun. 1927 (M), 2 Jul. 1927 (E), 30 Jul. 1927 (E), 3 Sept. 1927 (E), 12 Sept. 1927 (E), 26 Sept. 1927 (M), 10 Oct. 1927 (E), 7 Nov. 1927 (M), 24 Nov. 1927 (M); *DAZ*, 30 Jul. 1927 (E), 24 Sept. 1927 (E), 3 Dec. 1927 (E).

36.   See below, pp. 186-7, on the Tartar's Blood case.

37.   'Immertreu des Nordens', *VW*, 24 Jan. 1929 (M); 'Rachezug des "Nordrings" ', *VW*, 24 Jan. 1929 (E); ' "Nordring"-Piraten vor Gericht', *VW*, 30 Jan. 1929 (M); 'Verbrechervereine zerstören ein Ausflugslokal', *DAZ*, 31 Jan. 1929 (E); 'Verbrechervereine vor Gericht', *BT*, 30 Jan. 1929 (M). The 'Ringvereine' of the Berlin underworld, organised as savings clubs or friendly societies, acted as protective organisations and employment agencies for criminals of all kinds; they also controlled significant sections of the entertainment, service and vice operations in central Berlin. At Christmas 1928, members of one of these groups got into a long and bloody battle with visiting members of the Hamburg Carpenters' Guild. See H.H. Liang, *The Berlin Police in the Weimar Republic* (University of California Press, Berkeley, 1969), pp. 145ff; F. von Schmidt, *Vorgeführt erscheint* (Verlag Deutsche Volksbücher, Stuttgart, 1955), p. 396; E. Engelbrecht, *In den Spuren des Verbrechertums* (Peter J. Oestergaard, Berlin-Schöneberg, [1931]), pp. 83ff; H. Berl, *Der Kampf gegen das rote Berlin, oder Berlin eine Unterwelts-Residenz* (Kairos-Verlag, Karlsruhe, 1932), pp. 42ff; H.R.B., 'Wie ist die Berliner Unterwelt organisiert?', *VZ*, 5 Jan. 1929 (P); F. Ruhla [Werner Dopp], *Wir sind doch kein Gesangverein, sagten die Ganoven, und so war es auch* (Rosenheimer Verlag, Rosenheim, 1971). Documents on the 1928 brawl are filed in LABln, series 58, file 2220.

38.   'I.A.II^2, Berlin, den 28. November 1930' (see n. 28).

39.   Fournier, 'Ringverein', p. 89. The gutter press was not accessible for the present study, but there are echoes of the new publicity in the more respectable *Vorwärts:* *VW*, 3 Jan. 1931 (E), 18 Jan. 1931 (M), 28 Jan. 1931 (E), 26 Feb. 1931 (M), 22 Mar. 1931 (M), 25 Apr. 1931 (E), 13 May 1931 (M), 19 May 1931 (M), 18 Jun. 1931 (M).

In the first months after the National Socialist seizure of power, the new authorities prided themselves on having stamped out youth gangs. During the following years, however, there were repeated reports of new gangs being formed. Finally, elements of the characteristic clique style appear in the forms of youth resistance to the Nazi system that developed before and during the Second World War: J. Ehrhardt, 'Die Kriminalität der Jugendlichen in den Jahren 1932 und 1933', *ZGStW*, vol. 54 (1935), pp. 683f; Becker, *German Youth*, pp. 205ff; D. Horn,

'Youth Resistance in the Third Reich: a Social Portrait', *Journal of Social History*, vol. 7 (1973), pp. 26-50; Peukert, *Edelweisspiraten, passim.*

40. Except where otherwise noted, the following account is based on Voss and Schön, 'Die Cliquen'; Fournier, 'Ringverein'; Ehrhardt, 'Cliquenwesen'; *idem*, 'Jugendliche Verbrecher'; Berl, *Kampf*, pp. 63ff; E. Haffner, *Jugend auf der Landstrasse Berlin* (Bruno Cassirer, Berlin [1932]); R. Dinse, *Das Freizeitleben der Grosstadtjugend* (R. Müller, Berlin, [1932]), pp. 108ff; the press reports cited in nn. 37 and 39.

41. On changing life-styles within the working class, see J. Wickham, 'Working-class Movement and Working-class Life' (paper delivered to the fourth meeting of the SSRC Research Seminar Group in Modern German Social History, University of East Anglia, July 1980); on overcrowding and differential access to new housing in Berlin during the Weimar Republic, see, *inter alia*, W. Hegemann, *Das steinerne Berlin*, 3rd edn (F. Vieweg Sohn, Brunswick, 1979), pp. 332ff; N.O.A. Bullock, 'Social Policy and the Housing Market in Germany 1918-1930', unpublished conference paper, Cambridge, 1979; for contemporary reports by working-class children of their experience of space within the household and observations of the importance of the street as a locus of socialisation: Dinse, *Freizeitleben*, pp. 14ff; O. Rühle, *Zur Psychologie des proletarischen Kindes* (Fischer Taschenbuch Verlag, Frankfurt a.M., 1975), pp. 100ff; for socio-historical approaches to the relationship between housing, family structure and socialisation and the role of street life and peer groups as socialising agents: L. Niethammer and F. Brüggemeier, 'Wie wohnten Arbeiter im Kaiserreich?', *Archiv für Sozialgeschichte*, vol. 16 (1976), pp. 61-134; J. Schlumbohm, ' "Traditional" Collectivity and "Modern" Individuality: Some Questions and Suggestions for the Historical Study of Socialization', *Social History*, vol. 5 (1980), pp. 71-103.

42. Dinse, *Freizeitleben*, p. 109.

43. Cf. A. Lange, *Das wilhelminische Berlin* (Dietz Verlag, East Berlin, 1967), pp. 551ff; for a description of lower-class Berlin at play in the parks, J. Huret, *En Allemagne: Berlin* (Bibliotheque Charpentier, Paris, 1910), pp. 52ff. On differential experiences of leisure among working-class youths, see Dinse, *Freizeitleben*, pp. 3ff.

44. Voss and Schön, 'Die Cliquen', p. 85. Cf. the club Hand-in-Hand, which was active in the Kreuzberg district in 1927 and 1931: below, p. 198 and 'Jugendliche Strolche', *VW*, 24 Nov. 1927 (M), and the case of the Tartar's Blood member Alfred Jäger, below, p. 197.

45. This emerges from the results of a questionnaire sent to Berlin industrialists in 1917: Bloch, 'Kriegstagung der deutschen Jugendgerichtshilfen'. What was policy during a period of relative labour shortage may be expected to have been applied at least as rigorously under conditions of over-supply of labour.

46. Ehrhardt, 'Cliquenwesen', p. 415.

47. Cf. the reports cited above, nn. 35, 37, 39.

48. Judgement in the Egg-Slime case: LABln 58/31, appendix. Cf. von Schmidt, *Vorgeführt erscheint*, pp. 343ff; Ehrhardt, 'Kriminalität', p. 685.

49. Cf. Ruhla, *Wir sind doch kein Gesangverein*, p. 59.

50. *VW*, 6 Feb. 1928 (E), 30 Jan. 1929 (M); *BT*, 7 Feb. 1928 (E); *Tägliche Rundschau*, 6 Feb. 1928 (E); *DAZ*, 6 Feb. 1928; *VZ*, 7 Dec. 1928 (M); statement of Alfred Jäger, 18 Oct. 1931, LABln 58/29, I, 34f.

51. Cf. Voss and Schön, 'Die Cliquen', p. 82.

52. Minutes of teachers' conferences at the 41./42. Volksschule, Neukölln, on 9 and 23 March 1931, LABln 214/525, vol. 32, pp. 12-15.

53. Cf. Ehrhardt, 'Jugendliche Verbrecher'; Berl, *Kampf*, p. 145.

54. The function of schooling in shaping the attitudes and expectations of lower- and working-class children is the subject of a massive body of psychological and sociological literature. For a contemporary perception of the relationship

between the pressures and demands of the educational system and truancy, vagrancy and criminality on the part of the child, see Rühle, *Zur Psychologie*, pp. 110ff.

55. On the *Rummelplatz* and its effects: H. Ostwald, *Sittengeschichte Berlins* (Barsch Verlag, Berlin, n.d.), pp. 395f; Dinse, *Freizeitleben*, pp. 79ff; Ehrhardt, 'Die Lage', p. 811; 'Berliner Nachrichten: Rummel', *VW*, 25 Feb. 1914 (M).

56. Ehrhardt, 'Cliquenwesen', p. 414.

57. Ruhla, *Wir sind doch kein Gesangverein*, pp. 61ff.

58. Voss and Schön, 'Die Cliquen, p. 75; cf. ibid., p. 71.

59. For an example of this, see E. Rosenhaft, 'Working-class Life and Working-class Politics: Communists, Nazis and the Battle for the Streets, Berlin 1928-1932' in R. Bessel and E.J. Feuchtwanger (eds.), *Social Change and Political Development in Weimar Germany* (Croom Helm, London, 1981), pp. 207-39, especially pp. 229ff.

60. 'I.A.II^2, Berlin, den 28. November 1930' (see n. 28); cf. 'P.P. Abt. IA, Tgb. Nr. 1154 IA 3/1928' (police report), LAB1n 58/116, 28. For *Vorwärts* reports, see n. 50.

61. Voss and Schön, 'Die Cliquen', p. 85.

62. See W. Kindt, *Die deutsche Jugendbewegung 1920 bis 1933. Die bündische Zeit* (Eugen Diederichs Verlag, Düsseldorf/Cologne, 1975); Paetel, *Jugend*, pp. 65ff; Laqueur, *Young Germany*, parts III and IV.

63. Nearly a million young people were registered members of political youth groups in the mid-1920s, excluding Communist and National Socialist formations: Paetel, *Jugend*, p. 63. See also ibid., pp. 86ff; P. Stachura, *Nazi Youth in the Weimar Republic* (Clio Books, Santa Barbara/Oxford, 1975), Ch. I and *passim*; Roger, *Die pädagogische Bedeutung*.

64. On these groups, see most recently J.M. Diehl, *Paramilitary Politics in Weimar Germany* (University of Indiana Press, Bloomington, 1977).

65. A. Grzesinski, *Inside Germany* (E.P. Dutton, New York, 1939), p. 132; cf. P. Merkl, *The Making of a Stormtrooper* (Princeton University Press, Princeton, 1980), Chs. II, IV; E. Rosenhaft, 'Gewalt in der Politik; Zum Problem des "Sozialen Militarismus" ' in K.J. Müller and E. Opitz (eds.), *Militär und Militarismus in der Weimarer Republik* (Droste Verlag, Düsseldorf, 1978), pp. 237-59.

66. Von Liszt, 'Kriminalität . . . 1928, 1929 und 1930', p. 259.

67. G.T., ' "Helden" der Strasse', *BT*, 17 Jul. 1930 (E).

68. 'Jugendbewegung: Die Gefahr der Versumpfung', *VW*, 8 Nov. 1913 (M).

69. A. Lau, 'Jugendliche Verbrecherbanden', *VW*, 9 Jul. 1931 (E).

70. C. Rülcker, 'Arbeiterkultur und Kulturpolitik im Blickwinkel des "Vorwärts" ', *Archiv für Sozialgeschichte*, vol. 14 (1974), pp. 128ff.

71. Membership figures in H. Weber, *Die Wandlung des deutschen Kommunismus* (2 vols., Europäische Verlagsanstalt, Frankfurt a.M., 1969), vol. 1, pp. 369f.

72. Ibid.; W. Kaasch, 'Die soziale Struktur der Kommunistischen Partei Deutschlands', *Kommunistische Internationale*, vol. 9 (1928), pp. 1050ff; K.G.P. Schuster, *Der Rote Frontkämpferbund 1924-1929* (Droste Verlag, Düsseldorf, 1975), pp. 239ff; O. Pjatnitzki, *Brennende Fragen* (Carl Hoym Nachfolger, Hamburg/Berlin, 1931), p. 32; A. Creutzburg, *Die Organisationsarbeit der KPD* (Carl Hoym Nachfolger, Hamburg/Berlin, 1931), pp. 15, 17, 49f.

73. There is not space here to illustrate this characterisation of KPD agitation in detail; the author has explored some aspects of it in E. Rosenhaft, 'Between "Individual Terror" and "Mass Terror": the German Communists and "Paramilitary" Violence 1929-1933', (PhD dissertation, Cambridge, 1979, to be published by Cambridge University Press, 1982), Ch. II; *eadem*, 'Working-class Life and Working-class Politics', pp. 209ff, 220ff. For examples of KPD activity that fall within this range, see R. Huber-Koller, 'Die kommunistische Erwerbslosen-

bewegung in der Endphase der Weimarer Republik', *Gesellschaft. Beiträge zur Marxschen Theorie 10* (Suhrkamp Verlag, Frankfurt a.M., 1977), pp. 89-140; S. Kontos, *Die Partei kämpft wie ein Mann. Frauenpolitik der KPD in der Weimarer Republik* (Stroemfeld/Roter Stern, Basel/Frankfurt a.M., 1979); *Das proletarische Kind. Zur Schulpolitik und Pädagogik der KPD in der Weimarer Republik* (Das europäische Buch, Berlin, 1974). Both Kontos and Huber-Koller comment on the contradiction between the party's flexibility and relative sensitivity in practice and the limitations on its capacity to articulate the specific interests of the respective groups among which it agitated.

74.   Cf. the Programme of the Communist International adopted at the Sixth Comintern Congress, September 1928:

> The Party is the vanguard of the working class, composed of the best, most conscious, most active and bravest among them. It embodies the essential experiences of the entire proletarian struggle . . . representing day by day the permanent, general interests of the entire class, the party personifies the unity of proletarian principles, proletarian will, and revolutionary proletarian action . . . it achieves this position by the class consciousness of the proletarian vanguard, by its devotion to the revolution . . . and by the correctness of its political leadership, which is constantly verified and clarified by the experiences of the masses themselves.

(J. Degras (ed.), *The Communist International 1919-1943. Documents* (3 vols., Oxford University Press, London, 1960), vol. 2, p. 520) On the practical consequences of this self-image, especially the imperative to organise in the factories: H. Neumann, *Was ist Bolschewisierung?*(Carl Hoym Nachfolger, Hamburg, 1925); O. Pjatnizki, *Die Bolschewisierung der kommunistischen Parteien der kapitalistischen Länder durch Überwindung der sozialdemokratischen Traditionen* (Carl Hoym Nachfolger, Hamburg/Berlin, 1932). Cf. also the critique of the Communist understanding of working-class politics in O. Negt and A. Kluge, *Öffentlichkeit und Erfahrung* (Suhrkamp Verlag, Frankfurt a.M., 1977), pp. 384ff, 390ff.

75.   On this period, see W. Angress, *Stillborn Revolution: The Communist Bid for Power in Germany 1921-1923* (2 vols., Princeton University Press, Princeton, 1963).

76.   On the RWR and relations between cliques and Communists 1923-9, except where otherwise noted: Voss and Schön, 'Die Cliquen', pp. 84f and appendix, pp. 155ff, where excerpts from *Der Rote Wanderer* are reprinted. Cf. the sensationalised version of Berl, *Kampf*, pp. 70f.

77.   The Jungsturm was a small right-wing formation founded in 1897: Schuster, *Der Rote Frontkämpferbund*, p. 128.

78.   It is not entirely clear whether this is simply a jocular appelation for vagrants and vagabonds or whether, as Lau's article (n. 69) implies, there was actually a cartel of hiking clubs by this name.

79.   Cf. Lau, 'Jugendliche Verbrecherbanden'.

80.   G. Ring, ' "Südpostpiraten" und der "lange Stamm". Die "wilden Klikken" ', *RF*, 3 Apr. 1931.

81.   *RF*, 4 Aug. 1923, 10 Aug. 1923, 15 Sept. 1923, 22 Sept. 1923. Cf *VZ*, 14 Sept. 1923 (E), which refers only to 'left-radical *Wandervögel*'.

82.   'P.P. Abt. IA, Tgb. Nr. 521 IA 7.27, 22.4.1927' and Statement of 13 May 1927, LAB1n 58/302, III, 108 and 175.

83.   Documents in the Eagle's Claw case: LAB1n 58/116.

84.   On the events of May 1929, see Rosenhaft, 'Working-class Life and Working-class Politics', pp. 223ff.

85.   On the KPD in this period, see S. Bahne, *Die KPD und das Ende von*

Weimar (Campus Verlag, Frankfurt a.M./New York, 1976); E. Doehler, 'Zur Rolle des wehrhaften antifaschistischen Kampfes in der Politik der KPD', 1, *Militärgeschichte*, vol. 17 (1978), pp. 534-41; F. Claudin, *The Communist Movement. From Comintern to Cominform* (Penguin Books, Harmondsworth, 1975), pp. 152-66.

86. 'Rotes Oktoberaufgebot', Landeskriminalpolizeiamt (LKPA) Berlin, Mitteilungen Nr. 23 (1 Dec. 1930), StA Br 4,65/VI.1000.44.d.

87. Cf. Ahlheim *et al., Gefesselte Jugend*, Ch. VI.

88. In this case, the pamphlet *Fürsorgehöllen*, issued by the Central Committee of the Kommunistischer Jugendverband Deutschlands (Verlag der Jugendinternationale, Berlin [1932]).

89. W. Schönstedt, *Kämpfende Jugend*, reprint (Oberbaum-Verlag, Berlin, 1972), pp. 25, 14. On Schönstedt's career, see the autobiographical notes, ibid., p. 129, and police report, LAB1n 58/138, 16. On the novel's character as a 'proletarian mass-novel' directed at groups outside the Party: H. Möbius, 'Der Rote Eine-Mark-Roman', *Archiv für Sozialgeschichte*, vol. 14 (1974), pp. 157-212, especially pp. 209f.

90. L. Anton [L. Kaufman, 'Ein Buch der Jugend', reprinted in A. Klein, *Im Auftrag ihrer Klasse* (Aufbau-Verlag, East Berlin/Weimar, 1972), pp. 766-72, here p. 772.

91. *VW*, 12 Mar. 1931 (M), 17 Apr. 1931 (E).

92. *RF*, 12 Mar. 1931, 13 Mar. 1931, 15 Mar. 1931, 21 Mar. 1931.

93. All names of Communist fighters have been changed. Statements of and reports on E. Irmer and A. Jäger, 1931: LAB1n 58/29, I, 34f and appendix, III, 21, IV, 126, V, 185ff; Statements in the Friedrichshain case: LAB1n 58/2624, I, 129 and 135, II, 27.

94. Judgement, statements and reports in the Egg-Slime case: LAB1n 58/31, II, 79 and appendix.

95. Reports and statements: LAB1n 58/2595, I, 15 and 17; 'Bemerkenswerte Parolen und Agitationsmethoden der KPD und ihrer Hilf- und Nebenorganisationen' (compilation of Berlin police, June 1931), StA Br 4, 65/IV.13.i.

96. Berl, *Kampf*, p. 100.

97. E.G. *VW*, 29 Mar. 1923 (E), 9 May 1923 (E), 11 May 1924 (M), 3 Jan. 1929 (E).

98. *Verhandlungen des Reichstags*, vol. 425, p. 2217.

99. See, for example, the statement of one member that he joined 'because in this movement you're not looked down on for having a police record, as long as you're a useful person otherwise': LAB1n 58/37, XII, 21ff, and Social Democratic complaints that the Communists were nominating ex-convicts for public office, *VW*, 6 Mar. 1931 (M).

100. *RF*, 10 Jul. 1928, for example.

101. Cf. the discussion of the question of crime as a 'potential basis for a viable class strategy' in S. Hall *et al., Policing the Crisis* (Macmillan, London, 1978), pp. 361-97.

102. For examples of the debate within the Communist Youth Movement: 'Eine Aufgabe unserer Massenbildungsarbeit' and 'Zur Frage der Arbeit in den Kulturorganisationen', *Jugend-International*, vol. 5, no. 2 (Oct. 1923), pp. 48ff; 'Klarheit über die Kulturorganisation', *Jugend-International*, vol. 6, no. 2 (Oct. 1924), p. 50. The legitimacy of establishing a 'red cultural front line' was acknowledged by the party Congress of 1927, as a function of the recognition that revolution was no longer imminent and that the party had to establish itself on a mass basis, but the idea of 'cultural work' tended to be restricted to the pursuit of broadly 'cultural' interests – sports, social events, literature, theatre – within particular organisations or institutions, rather than encouraging the analysis of

ways of life. See W. Sorin, 'Belebung der politischen Arbeit – oder Kulturarbeit' in *Der 5. Weltkongress der Kommunistischen Jugendinternationale. Diskussions-Sonderheft der 'Jugend-Internationale'* (Verlag der Jugendinternationale, Berlin, 1928), pp. 428ff; cf. R. Burns, 'Theory and Organisation of Revolutionary Working-class Literature in the Weimar Republic' in K. Bullivant (ed.), *Culture and Society in the Weimar Republic* (Manchester University Press, Manchester, 1977), pp. 122-49.

103.   F. Erpenbeck, 'Das literarische Söldnerheer', *Die Linkskurve*, vol. 3, no. 8 (Aug. 1931), pp. 19-22; *idem*, 'Leihbibliothek am Wedding', *Die Linkskurve*, vol. 2, no. 7 (Jul. 1930), pp. 14f; K, Kläber, 'Der proletarische Massenroman', *Die Linkskurve*, vol. 2, no. 5 (May 1930), pp. 22-5. Cf. Möbius, 'Der Rote Eine-Mark-Roman'; Klein, *Im Auftrag*, pp. 339ff.

104.   E. Hoernle, 'Erziehung zum Klassenkampf', *Das proletarische Kind*, vol. 2, no. 5 (May 1922), reprinted in *Das proletarische Kind. Zur Schulpolitik*, pp. 50ff. Cf. 'Gegen Kinoschund und Schundliteratur', *Die Junge Garde*, no. 17/18 (20 Mar. 1920), pp. 134f; B. Balász, 'Der Detektive-Roman', *RF*, 12 May 1922.

105.   On *Verwahrlosung*, cf. Ahlheim *et al.*, *Gefesselte Jugend*, Ch. II; M. Heinemann, 'Normprobleme in der Fürsorgeerziehung' in M. Heinemann (ed.), *Sozialisation und Bildungswesen in der Weimarer Republik* (Ernst Klett Verlag, Stuttgart, 1976), pp. 131-56.

106.   See, e.g., 'Thesen zur Schaffung der kommunistischen Kindergruppen', *Das proletarische Kind*, vol. 1, no. 1 (Feb. 1921), reprinted in *Das proletarische Kind. Zur Schulpolitik*, p. 249; 'Jugend von heute', *Die Junge Garde*, 12 Apr. 1919; 'Hinter den Kulissen der Fürsorgeanstalten', *Die Junge Garde*, Sondernummer 6 (Dec. 1922), p. 67; F. Fränkel, 'Zum Bewahrungsgesetz', *Proletarische Sozialpolitik*, vo. 1 (1928), pp. 153-6. Both Otto Rühle and Siegfried Bernfeld, two leading exponents of Marxist psychoanalysis with close links to the Communist movement, regarded gangs of wayward youths – Bernfeld named the cliques – as a sociopathic phenomenon: Rühle, *Zur Psychologie*, pp. 112f; S. Bernfeld, *Antiautoritäre Erziehung und Psychoanalyse* (3 vols., Ullstein Verlag, Frankfurt a.M., 1974), vol. 2, pp. 332f.

107.   E. Schellenberg, 'Fürsorgeerziehung und Proletariat', *Proletarische Sozialpolitik*, vol. 4 (1931), pp. 21f.

108.   E.g. *Fürsorgehöllen*, p. 4. Cf. also the presentation of Soviet solutions to the problem: ibid., p. 15; A. Rudolf, 'Der Weg ins Leben', *Die Linkskurve*, vol. 3, no. 11 (Nov. 1931), pp. 13-15.

109.   This is particularly clear in Communist responses to the interest shown by leading artists and writers on the underworld during the 1920s. See for example, ' "Vom alten und neuen Berlin": ein neues Zille-Buch', *RF*, 18 Sept. 1927, on the drawings of Heinrich Zille: 'the everyday life of semi-proletarian and lumpenproletarian groups and even a little bit of the Berlin proletariat'; or 'Die Dreigroschenoper', *RF*, 4 Sept. 1928, on Brecht: 'If you don't know how to portray the revolutionary movement of the working class, then you fool around with the aimless and unformed rebellious moods of the lumpenproletariat'; O. Biha, 'Herr Döblin verunglückt in einer "Linkskurve" ', *Die Linkskurve*, vol. 2, no. 6 (Jun. 1930), p. 24, on *Berlin Alexanderplatz*: 'Döblin has dressed up the battered ego of a complicated petty bourgeois in proletarian style . . . and maintains resolutely that that's a dyed-in-the-wool proletarian.'

110.   Schönstedt, *Kämpfende Jugend*, p. 95.

111.   Anton, 'Ein Buch der Jugend', p. 770f.

112.   Ring, ' "Südostpiraten" und der "lange Stamm" '.

113.   *Proletarische Sozialpolitik* was issued by the Collective of Revolutionary

Social-Policy Organisations (Arbeitsgemeinschaft Revolutionärer Sozialpolitischer Organisationen, ARSO), founded in 1928, which included the International Workers' Aid, Red Aid, International League of War Invalids, children's, youth and educational organisations and other groups concerned with health, welfare and sexual questions. See Ahlheim *et al., Gefesselte Jugend*, pp. 277ff; F. Bender, 'Proletarische Sozialpolitik', *Proletarische Sozialpolitik*, vol. 1, no. 7 (Dec. 1928), pp. 193-6. On the place of these and other 'mass organisations' (including the defence formations), nominally independent of the party, within the Communist movement, see K. Finker, 'Revolutionäre Massenorganisationen in der Zeit der Weimarer Republik', *Geschichtsunterricht und Staatsbürgerkunde*, vol. 6 (1964), pp. 919-34; Bahne, *KPD*, pp. 19ff.

114. The following characterisation of the defence formations is based on the author's research on the Communists' 'militant fight against Fascism' in Berlin 1929-33. For sources and details, except where otherwise noted, see Rosenhaft, 'Between "Individual Terror" and "Mass Terror" ', Ch. VI.

115. E. Auer, 'Ein Beitrag zum Kapitel Fluktuation', in *Der 5. Weltkongress*, pp. 426ff.

116. I. Klapholz, 'Warum Fluktuation?' and E. Auer, 'Die Arbeitsmethoden dürfen nicht freideutsch erweitert werden . . .', *Jugend-Internationale*, vol. 9, no. 11 (Aug. 1928), pp. 578ff. On the 'sexual question' in the Communist movement, as reflected in the party's mass novels, cf. M. Rohrwasser, *Saubere Mädel – Starke Genossen* (Verlag Roter Stern, Frankfurt a.M., 1975).

117. L. Ullrich, 'Die proletarischen Frauen gehören in die Wehrorganisation des Proletariats', *Internationale*, vol. 12 (1929), pp. 558ff; 'Richtlinien für die Arbeit der Frauen- und Mädchenstaffeln des Kampfbunds gegen den Faschismus', StA Br 4,65/II.H.4.a.32; 'Bericht der Kartelleitung zur Kartellkonferenz, 2./3.11.1929', LKPA Berlin, Mitteilungen Nr. 22 (15 Dec. 1929), StA Br 4,65/II. H.4.a.30.

118. See Rosenhaft, 'Between "Individual Terror" and "Mass Terror" ', Ch. III; *eaden*, 'Die KPD und das Terrorismusproblem in der "Dritten Periode" (1929-1933)' in W.J. Mommsen and G. Hirschfeld (ed.), *Sozialprotest, Gewalt, Terror* (Klett-Cotta, Stuttgart, 1981); text of the resolution *RF*, 13 Nov. 1931, reprinted in *Geschichte der deutschen Arbeiterbewegung* (8 vols., Dietz Verlag, East Berlin, 1966), vol. 4.

119. 'Für revolutionären Massenkampf gegen individuellen Terror', *RF*, 13 Nov. 1931. The criticism of an un-socialist sentimentality, manifested by the thirst for revenge, is still levelled at Walter Schönstedt by the East German critic A. Klein, *Im Auftrag*, pp. 541f.

120. 'Richtlinien für die Arbeit' (see n. 117).

7 IDENTIFYING MILITANCY: THE ASSESSMENT OF WORKING-CLASS ATTITUDES TOWARDS STATE AND SOCIETY*

Dick Geary

How can we discover what workers really thought about life outside the framework of the formal institutions (trade unions and political parties) which have normally been the object of historical research? In looking not just at the organised labour *movement*, nor just at leisure — very much in vogue with a certain kind of social history at the moment and yet one which may tell us little about other aspects of working-class aspiration — the articles in this volume suggest how difficult it is to pigeon-hole the attitudes of labour into the strait-jackets of the terminology of 'respectability' or 'roughness', 'revolution' or 'integration'. Working-class activities which embrace extramarital sexual relations, drinking habits, criminality and the world of youth gangs certainly give us a much wider view of daily reality in late-nineteenth and early-twentieth-century Germany than the study of formal institutions and may help to elucidate the tensions between both the leadership and the rank and file or organised labour on the one hand, and within the more general working class on the other. The question remains, however, what are the most accurate indices of working-class radicalism or reformism?

I

Marx once wrote of the proletariat in capitalist society: 'its aims and its historical activity are ordained for it in a tangible and irrevocable way, by its own situation as well as by the whole organisation of present-day

---

* An earlier version of this article was presented to the second meeting of the SSRC research seminar group on Modern German Social History at the University of East Anglia in January 1979. As such it attempted and still attempts to put forward an argument about the supposed indices of working-class 'radicalism' or 'reformism' which is independent of the preceding articles and with which some of my fellow contributors may be out of sympathy. In this sense I have not attempted to provide a systematic summary of the other contributions in this volume, nor have I tried to discover therein a new 'orthodoxy' or 'consensus'.

civil society';[1] and in both the *Poverty of Philosophy*[2] and the *Communist Manifesto*[3] he went on to clothe this skeleton with the flesh of an argument which basically ran as follows: first, conflicts of interest arise and are seen to arise between individual workers and individual employers. Workers in a single factory then come to recognise the identity of their interests and subsequently how those interests correspond to the interests of other workers in other factories locally, then nationally. In consequence a national organisation of the industrial proletariat comes into existence. At the same time the historical enemy also achieves an awareness of common interest and organises itself. A situation has been created in which workers and employers now confront one another as classes. It is here that Marx's argument suddenly makes a crucial leap: 'but every class struggle is a political struggle'.

In many respects this description of the evolution of class conflict in the economic sphere applies to virtually all societies that have undergone a process of industrialisation. The central problem, therefore, concerns the transition from economic to political struggle; and it is possible to see in this the major lacuna in the work of Marx.[4] Before the end of the last century Engels was forced to reflect upon the curious way in which the English labour movement had succeeded in combining industrial militancy with an apparent acceptance of the prevailing political order; in explanation of which tragic occurrence he resorted to a theory of labour aristocracy and the benefits that accrued from the possession of Empire.[5] Not surprisingly, therefore, many of the leading Marxists since his day have been preoccupied with the problem of 'revolutionary consciousness' and its origins. Hence Gramsci's concern, undergoing fashionable revival and, one might add, emasculation today,[6] with the mechanics of ideological as well as physical hegemony and Lenin's theory, largely borrowed from Kautsky, of 'consciousness from without'.[7] This latter theory states in essentials that working-class consciousness is bound to remain at a purely 'economistic' and 'trade unionist' level without the intervention of the revolutionary intelligentsia or party, who import scientific revolutionary political understanding into its ranks. This Leninist theory is still with us, of course, in John Foster's controversial study of industrial militancy and political radicalism in mid-nineteenth-century Oldham, which attributes a vital role to a radical local intelligentsia;[8] and above all it dominates orthodox Russian and East German historiography, which explains the failure of socialist revolution in non-Russian Europe and in Germany in particular to the absence of a 'party of the new type' and hence to failures of organisation and leadership.

It is not my intention here to deny that the leadership of German Social Democracy betrayed its working-class rank and file in the revolutionary upheavals of 1918/19. Nor do I wish to deny the possibility that the existence of a tightly organised and well disciplined party, purged of reformist elements, is essential for the actual seizure of political power by revolutionaries, as happened in Russia in October 1917. What I dispute is the contention that the difference between revolutionary success and failure can be explained effectively simply by reference to this Leninist model; and more importantly that it was the existence of a Leninist party that transformed working-class *consciousness*. It is not clear to me that revolutionary success in Russia and failure in Germany necessarily indicate that the Russian proletariat was in some way 'more revolutionary' than its German counterpart, although such has been the assumption of a great deal of comparative historical analysis.[9]

Obviously the triumph of revolutionary groups in Russia might be explained in such a way. The point, however, is that it does not have to be so explained. For example, failure to complete the socialist revolution in Germany at the end of the First World War could be explained in terms of the much greater strength of counter-revolutionary forces, a strength derived in part from the utterly different social structures of the two countries: the Russia of 1917 did not possess a numerous and powerful industrial bourgeoisie which could be relied upon either to form the social basis for liberal democracy or fund counter-revolution.[10] Thus there existed a polarised social structure in which a parasitic landed elite confronted not only an alienated urban proletariat but a revolutionary (albeit non-socialist) peasantry and a radical intellegentsia. Such was hardly the case in Germany, where a numerous and powerful middle class, with support from a landowning peasantry and significant sections of the artisanate and white-collar salariat, constituted a powerful opposition to radical urban workers. The degree of working-class isolation is indicated, for example, by the ability of the counter-revolutionary Freikorps to recruit no fewer than 400,000 men in a very short space of time in the wake of the November Revolution.[11] Even had the German working class been uniformly revolutionary in this period, therefore — and this is something which I do not claim — the prospects of victory would still have been dimmer than in neighbouring Russia.

More central to my critique of the Leninist model, however, is the possibility of explaining the radicalisation of Russia's urban workers without reference to the Bolshevik party at all. To repeat, I am not saying that the existence of the Bolshevik party was not necessary for the actual seizure of power; but it can be shown that the radicalisation of some Russian workers in 1917 followed directly from an objective situation which of necessity tied the rectification of massive economic grievances to the ending of the war, and thereby to the overthrow first of the Tsarist and then of the Provisional Government. Thus the process of radicalisation that took place in Moscow and Petrograd in 1917 can be explained without reference to Lenin's arrival at the Finland station and the bringing down of the word from on high. This interpretation receives some support from the fact that the factory committees moved to the left before Lenin's return and subscribed to an activism that might better be described as anarchist than Bolshevik;[12] and further because the July rising of 1917 happened almost in spite of the Bolsheviks, because, as Lenin himself admitted, 'the masses were more Bolshevik than the Bolsheviks', and because some of the placards carried by the Menshevik insurgents bore slogans which were more akin to the demands of the Bolsheviks than to those of their own party.[13] That this should have been the case, that it was not necessary to be a Bolshevik or have been educated by the leadership of the Bolshevik party in order to engage in revolutionary politics, is hardly surprising, given the continued governmental support for the Russian war effort, the most obvious source of urban deprivation. Furthermore, the lack of contact between the Bolshevik leadership and ordinary workers is explicable in terms of the long exile or imprisonment to which many, such as Lenin, had been condemned; and to the social gulf which separated the bourgeois intellectual leadership of *both* the Bolshevik and the Menshevik parties from their proletarian rank and file, a gulf witnessed by innumerable tensions in the earlier history of Russian Social Democracy.[14]

The above is intended to suggest that any explanations of radical working-class consciousness in terms of ideological and organisational factors is open to question; and further that the appearance of Russian workers on the barricades in 1917 does not necessarily say as much about their general 'level of consciousness' as might be imagined. Indeed, I would argue that this was one of the reasons why the relationship between the Bolshevik party and the urban working class of Russia became more problematic in the subsequent years. The role of ideology is equally dubious when another supposed bastion of working-class radicalism before 1914 comes under investigation, namely the French anarcho-syndicalist movement. It is true that French workers in the *syndicats* went on strike more regularly than their German counterparts in this period, that strikes were often accompanied by violence and that industrial sabotage was not unknown. Furthermore, the national confederation of the *syndicats*, the CGT, adopted a specific commitment to the revolutionary general strike at several of its conferences before the outbreak of the First World War.[15] It is far from clear, however, that the cause of the apparent militancy of the rank and file of the *syndicats* is to be found in any general acceptance of anarcho-syndicalist theory in those ranks. In this context the response of the union leader Griffuelhes to the question 'Have you read Georges Sorel?' — 'No, I only read Alexandre Dumas'[16] is quite revealing, though less so than the fact that the patterns of strike behaviour of anarcho-syndicalist union members in no way differed from that of non-anarchist unionists in France.[17] In fact the militant style of the French *syndicats* is amenable to a far from ideological, albeit far more prosaic explanation: the organisational weakness of the French working class. As late as 1914 over 90 per cent of the French labour force remained outside the ranks of economic or political organisations. What organisations did exist were financially insecure, as many unionists did not pay their membership dues, and numerically tiny: at the turn of the century the average *syndicat* recruited something in the order of two hundred persons! In such circumstances unions hardly possessed the requisite industrial muscle to bring employers to their knees simply through the withdrawal of their members' labour. As a result French workers were obliged to turn more direct and sometimes more spectacular forms of protest than the peaceful strike. Indeed, they even retained a charming predilection for threatening their employers with hanging well into the twentieth century.[18] This same weakness also helps to explain a further phenomenon which is central to Shorter and Tilly's account of strike activity in France,[19] namely the way in which French strike waves tended to peak at times of *political* crisis. Precisely because the economic impact of strikes was limited by the numerical and financial weakness of the *syndicats*, French strikers directed their attention beyond the industrial arena to the local community and to the state. To a certain extent strikes became demonstrations, the prime function of which was to influence both the government of the day and public opinion at large to bring pressure to bear on the side of the working class in the struggle against an uncompromising *patronat*. This was likely to be especially true when certain political changes suggested that government would be sympathetic to the claims of labour, as with Millerand's entry into the French Cabinet in 1900 and at the time of the election of the Popular Front in 1936. On both occasions there was a marked increase in strike action. Whether this justifies the claim that these strikes were 'political', as Shorter and Tilly wish to argue, is a different matter:[20] for it is possible that their principal motivation remained the rectification of economic grievances, rather than political change as such. Once again, therefore, a certain form of militant behaviour on the part of the European working class does not *necessarily* indicate the possession of 'revolutionary consciousness' by those involved in such behaviour.

This suggests that even where the industrial working class has become involved in radical *action* one does not need to postulate the existence of a world-historical revolutionary consciousness which found a home perhaps only in the writings of a Lukács. It is possible for workers to become committed to the overthrow of governments, as many did in Russia in 1917 and some did in Germany in 1918,[21] without any necessary belief on their part that they are about to introduce the socialist millennium. The use of the terms 'radical', 'revolutionary' and 'militant' may service to characterise their actions *at a particular point in time* but say relatively little about their general view of the world or 'level of consciousness'. Indeed, it might be suggested that the use of the polar terminology ('revolutionary/reformist') is a function of bourgeois intellectual schematisation, which imagines that workers are only 'revolutionary' if they mount the barricades and 'reformist' or 'integrated' if they do not, and which therefore fails to identify the realities which drive workers to action or condemn them to passivity. I would suggest that the same workers can be both revolutionary and reformist at different points in time and yet their motivation remain the same. To a large extent it is the surrounding terrain which determines the appropriate form of action (or quiescence), as we will see.

So far it has been suggested that some forms of apparently radical action tell us less about working-class attitudes than historians have often imagined. This is even truer of other supposed indicators of militancy or its absence. Voting figures, for example, have often been taken to demonstrate the ideological identity of workers; yet what they actually tell us is far from clear. In Germany before the First World War more workers voted for a socialist party than in any other country. It would be rash, however, to conclude from this that German workers were more 'socialist' than their counterparts elsewhere. This might have been the case, but it was not necessarily the case. It could just as easily be explained by the fact that the SPD was the only party in Wilhelmine Germany which clearly represented the immediate economic interests of the industrial proletariat (and significantly had done so during the period of the Anti-Socialist Law of 1878-90, when most trade unions had been dissolved). It is true that the electoral propaganda of the SPD placed great stress on the 'class nature' of the Prusso-German state; but it hardly required an acquaintance with the writings of Marx to bring this home to the average German worker: the existence of discriminatory franchises in several of the *Länder*, the policy of agricultural protection pursued by successive Reich governments after 1879 and even the system of taxation which favoured East Elbian distilleries discussed in a previous chapter in this book made clear that government was by and for a privileged few and that the unfortunate consumer had to pay through the nose for this sorry state of affairs.[22] A further possible explanation for the high socialist vote in Imperial Germany may relate to the difficulties faced by unskilled workers in heavy industry when they tried to organise, difficulties to which I will return: the absence of strong economic organisation amongst such groups perhaps meant that the SPD was the only vehicle through which they could express their material discontents.

Conversely, electoral support for non-radical parties is no sure indication of the existence of a non-revolutionary and 'moderate' working class, as has sometimes been assumed for Germany in the wake of the First World War.[23] It is true that the moderate Majority SPD won far more votes than the more radical Independent Social Democratic Party, USPD (the newly founded KPD boycotted the election), in January 1919. However, many of those SPD voters gave their allegiance to more radical groupings very soon thereafter, as is evidenced by the erosion of the SPD vote and the rapid expansion of support for not only the USPD but also the Communists and even ultra-leftist organisations. This demonstrates the volatility of working-class allegiances and how dangerous it is to have a static view of their ideological identity. Furthermore, the events of 1918/19 in Germany witnessed SPD voters joining campaigns for socialisation in the Ruhr against the wishes of their ostensible representatives.[24] To restate the point, working-class action and consciousness have proved to be remarkably volatile.

Party membership might seem to be a far more reliable guide to the ideological identity of the working class than voting behaviour: party members were expected to invest time, energy and money in party activities and might well be expected, therefore, to have a clearer understanding of political issues and a greater commitment to their respective organisations. This may be true; but even here there are serious difficulties. We have already seen that some Russian Mensheviks carried what were to all intents Bolshevik placards in July 1917. Similarly we know that many Russian workers found it difficult to distinguish between the positions of the Menshevik and Bolshevik leaderships in the course of the 1905 Revolution.[25] In Germany in the course of the November Revolution of 1918 and in the subsequent upheavals in the Ruhr and in Saxony party political labels are equally misleading. In November 1918 there is considerable evidence that workers were confused about the differences between the various socialist factions. In the Ruhr in early 1919 some SPD members pursued policies widely at variance with those of their official leaders, as happened again in Saxony in 1923. Perhaps even more strikingly, there were miners in the Ruhr in 1919 who belonged to both the KPD and to various anarcho-syndicalist organisations! It was not just the SPD which failed to establish a dominance over the (often vivid) imagination of its proletarian rank and file.[26]

It is perhaps not surprising that working-class attitudes should prove so difficult to classify and so volatile in time of great social upheaval, as in the cases mentioned above. However, the extent to which membership of a political party indicates an identity between the party's official theory and the attitudes of the rank and file is far from clear even in more serene days. This has been demonstrated by a vast literature on the attitudes of the SPD membership in Wilhelmine Germany. Hans-Josef Steinberg has shown that the official (and rather castrated) Marxism of Karl Kautsky meant little to even the leadership of the SPD, with a few significant exceptions.[27] Studies of the borrowing records of workers' libraries seem to reveal little interest in Marxism.[28] It has been claimed that the SPD's membership shared some of the nationalistic, monarchist and even anti-Semitic values of Wilhelmine society.[29] The choral societies, festivals and sports activities of Social Democracy did little to generate radical class consciousness and perhaps served to integrate workers into the prevailing economic and social order.[30] Günther Roth, the major progenitor of this argument of 'negative integration', and Peter Stearns have assembled quotations from SPD members disclaiming any revolutionary ambitions.[31] Exactly what all of this tells us is debatable, as Richard Evans has already shown in the Introduction: it is surely significant that workers belonged to specifically *working-class* cultural organisations rather than those of the middle class. It is also the case that the book-borrowing habits of workers were not identical to those of their social superiors.[32] But it cannot be doubted that membership of German Social Democracy did not necessarily mean a commitment to the values of revolutionary Marxism. Some workers paid their party dues to enjoy the enormous range of social amenities it provided, some to enjoy the economic benefits of insurance schemes and some because they were lonely.

II

Conversely, membership of a political party whose national leadership moved increasingly to the right in the years immediately before the First World War does not necessarily indicate that the rank and file of the SPD underwent a similar process of 'embourgeoisement', as I have argued elsewhere.[33] Furthermore, and this is where many of the preceding chapters in this volume become relevant, what the cultural activities of the SPD and in particular its leisure activities tell us about working-class aspirations in general is open to question on a number of grounds. In particular, the formal culture of the SPD's ancillary institutions is only part of a much broader picture. There were whole areas of working-class life in Wilhelmine Germany which did not integrate easily into the usual picture of 'respectability': pilfering in the Hamburg docks, widespread extramarital sexual practice and the absence of any stigma attaching to illegitimacy, violence in the wake of suffrage demonstrations and the daily life of youth gangs, heavy drinking, even, *perhaps*, industrial sabotage.

The existence of this 'non-respectable' side of proletarian behaviour in industrial Germany in the late nineteenth and early twentieth century, however, raises a whole series of problems of interpretation. In the first place it might be conjectured that we are talking about two distinct working-class cultures. Perhaps there was a 'respectable' working class and a 'rough' working class. Certainly the official organs of the SPD often argued in this way, attributing violence and unseemliness to the unorganised and uneducated 'Lumpen'.[34] I would be less prepared to dismiss such a contention out of hand than some of the other contributors to this volume, though I would not go so far as Karl Heinz Roth and Eckhard Brockhaus in drawing a great divide between the lives and attitudes of the skilled and unskilled.[35] Crime rates were lower in SPD-dominated areas, a fact on which leading Social Democrats and not only those of the right congratulated themselves. Richard Evans' article on 'Red Wednesday' in Hamburg reveals tensions between a justified claim that even the organised metalworkers and building workers could not be controlled by the local SPD leadership and the extent to which their direct action can really be assimilated to that of the crime-ridden *Gängeviertel*.[36] Furthermore, where the SPD had sunk deep roots in communities before the First World War, there the

Communist Party had difficulty in making any headway subsequently, thus suggesting that exposure to the SPD and its organs did have some impact on working-class perceptions.[37] In this sense, and only in this sense, would I agree with Keith Nield and Geoff Eley that the achievements of German Social Democracy before 1914 should not be underestimated.[38] As the membership of the SPD remained restricted to skilled workers before 1914 and as they played a major role in its creation, it might further be conjectured that the 'respectability' of the SPD's self-image was not the *consequence* of the deliberate policy of the party but rather an outcrop of the pre-existing values of skilled workers and artisans; and that therefore the tension between the SPD and the values of some workers which Michael Grüttner and Stephen Bajohr identify as increasing after 1918 perhaps existed at an earlier date. Clearly more work needs to be done in this area.

Having said this, however, it is true that the preceding articles cast justifiable doubt on the concept of two cultures, of a 'respectable' SPD membership and a riotous remainder (who, incidentally, were always in the great majority). Grüttner makes it clear that pilfering on the Hamburg docks had more to do with opportunity and the economic conjuncture than anything else; though it was also true that those principally engaged in pilfering in the early 1890s were weakly unionised. As James Roberts shows, SPD members could also be heavy drinkers. Equally David Crew explains how industrial sabotage could be the act of organised and educated trade union members operating in certain unfavourable circumstances, whilst Stephen Bajohr suggests that differential patterns of illegitimacy within the working class only became really marked in the Weimar Republic. None of this is remarkable for the reasons provided by Richard Evans in his Introduction to this volume: 'the boundary lines between proletariat and sub-proletariat . . . employed and unemployed, permanently engaged and casually hired, were fluid, shifting and hard to discern' in the German economy which expanded so rapidly before the First World War and was in a state of almost permanent crisis thereafter. Hence broad investigation gives the lie to many archetypes of the Wilhelmine working class derived from limited indices. Not only the examination of the formal politics of the SPD but even a study of its cultural institutions leaves many questions unanswered.

The discussion of sabotage, drinking, illegitimacy, youth gangs and pilfering in this book raises additional problems of terminology and causality. The SPD rank and file may have combined heavy drinking with a clear dislike of alcoholism. Berlin youth gangs may have preyed on other sections of the community but clearly subscribed to some internal code of behaviour. Many proletarian illegitimate births were legitimised by marriage after a relatively short time. Hamburg dockers did not believe it improper to steal from their employers, yet did not steal from one another. In short, these various forms of behaviour may not have corresponded to certain ideals of morality, but that does not mean that those who engaged in them were devoid of any ideas of what was right and proper. Rather, they subscribed to a set of collective values which often came into conflict with those of bourgeois morality and on occasions and increasingly after 1918 with those of the SPD. Furthermore, the increase in pilfering in Hamburg corresponded to changes in work structures and severe deprivation for some groups of workers, whilst thieving amongst the youth gangs of Weimar also correlated to some extent with economic recession. In such circumstances theft might best be regarded as neither immoral nor as the symbol of an alternative morality, but rather as a necessity.

If it is difficult to categorise these various aspects of proletarian social life, it is even more difficult to establish what is perhaps most important and interesting, namely the relationship between that social life and politics. In certain ways the various facets of working-class existence discussed here do help to explain or at least elucidate the growing gulf between the SPD and certain sections of the German working class after the First World War. There was some overlap, as Eve Rosenhaft shows, between membership of KPD paramilitary organisations and the Berlin youth gangs, though it was far from total and the party experienced all kinds of difficulties in imposing its will on its unruly membership. The gulf which opened up between the illegitimacy rates of skilled workers and their less skilled contemporaries in the Weimar Republic also overlapped with political variables: the areas of high proletarian illegitimacy were also areas of KPD support. The attempts of the SPD and Free trade unions to stop pilfering in the Hamburg docks after the First World War clearly created tensions between those organisations and what had been their earlier constituency. This, of course, constitutes the value of the preceding chapters: they demonstrate that divisions within the German working class cannot simply be reduced to those of formal politics.

Here, however, we are confronted with the problem of ascribing some causal role to such developments. It is clear that the divisions within the ranks of German labour were not only divisions of political affiliation but reached down into the less tangible realms of social 'attitudes' and 'values'. This does not mean, however, that such differences in values were the *cause* of the fratricidal strife which doomed the German working class to defeat. And none of the contributors makes any such claim. For to do this effectively one would also have to analyse not only developments in the home and the neighbourhood, which figure most prominently in these papers, but also at work. The divisions within the Frankfurt working class, for example, may well have correlated to changes in work practices, as the change in the social composition of Communist support charted by James Wickham in recent articles has suggested.[39] Equally, as Michael Grüttner shows, the level of pilfering in Hamburg had a great deal to do with the reorganisation of dock work and the strength of trade union organisation. Nor is it clear how various 'cultural' values correlate with 'radical' or 'reformist' activities. There may be some correlations, as suggested above; but David Crew demonstrates that even an act of industrial sabotage or violence does not necessarily indicate the existence of revolutionary sentiments. A trade union member faced with intransigence on the part of his employers and lacking support from colleagues organised in a Catholic union might well see such an act as a means of securing reformist rather than revolutionary ends, i.e. as a tactic to achieve a wage increase, for example. Clearly, therefore, the context in which such an act takes place is crucial to any understanding of it.

III

The study of working-class culture, therefore, once again presents a picture in which workers were not the mere recipients of ideas from above and in which official party institutions did not lead unreflecting proletarian sheep. If party membership is no infallible guide to the attitudes of workers, membership of trade unions tells us even less. In the first place, trade union membership in many industrial sectors has witnessed huge fluctuations over very short periods of time: in some German unions before the First World War there was an annual turnover of membership in excess of 100 per cent.[40] In France the rapid mobilisation of thousands of new trade unionists and their involvement in strike waves between 1917 and 1920 was followed by an equally rapid demobilisation: after the failure of the 1920 general strike the membership of the CGT fell from 2,000,000 to 600,000 within a few months.[41] The same thing happened in both Italy and Germany in the three years after the First World War.[42] Even in less troubled Britain the TUC, which had achieved a membership of 8 million by 1920, lost two and a half million of these in the next two years and even more members after the failure of the general strike in 1926.[43] This might suggest that trade union membership was a brief experience for some workers and a recurrent one for some others. It clearly makes it very difficult to assess working-class aspirations from the statements and behaviour of trade union leaders. Indeed, there are numerous cases in which conflict between those leaders and their working-class rank and file can be identified, as in the mines and engineering plants of Wilhelmine Germany[44] and in the factory occupations in Milan in 1920.[45] More problematic than the evidence of trade union membership, however, is the interpretation of the failure to organise, a failure which characterised the overwhelming majority of the European working class, especially women and the unskilled, before 1914. There is a whole series of explanations of this failure which does not have to rely on the assumption that such apparent inaction necessarily implies 'tacit acceptance' of or 'integration' into the prevailing social and political order. The weak bargaining position of the unskilled and the consequent possibility of easy dismissal, the hold exerted by employers like Krupp, Stumm and Thyssen over their employees through the provision of company housing, pension schemes, blacklists of agitators – especially easy to operate effectively in German heavy industry given the degree of capital concentration – were quite sufficient to deter all but the most courageous from embarking upon risky confrontation, especially where such confrontation entailed the risk of encounters with the police and government troops, leading often to imprisonment and on occasion death. Other factors militated against proletarian organisation as well: a high turnover of the labour force in any given factory, the low expectations of many who came from depressed rural backgrounds, functional divisions and skill differentials within the labour force, ethnic and religious divisions. Given such obstacles, failure to organise by no means necessarily denoted a satisfaction with the *status quo* or an absence of class consciousness. That this is so is demonstrated by the fact that many of those who became active in militant industrial action and radical politics at the end of the First World War in Italy and Germany and who played an active role in the France of the Popular Front were precisely those who had not been mobilised by political or economic organisations previously.[46] There is also evidence that the workers who participated in the most adventurous ultra-leftist politics in the Ruhr in 1920 had even belonged to the so-called 'Yellow' (i.e. bosses') unions before 1914.[47]

Finally — and here few would disagree — membership of an economic organisation in no way necessarily guarantees any desire for *political* as distinct from economic change. Many organisations of skilled British artisans in the first half of the nineteenth century had 'no politics' rules, whilst unionised miners did not wish to be associated with the Chartists and their political agitation.[48] In Germany in the course of the 1848 Revolution and again in the 1860s the relatively powerful unions of printers and cigar workers refused to associate themselves with movements for political reform, at least initially.[49] In the same country there existed in the years before the First World War a bakers' union which was explicitly monarchist in sympathy; whilst the largest union of German white-collar workers, the Deutschnationaler Hand-lungsgehilfenverband (German National Union of Commercial Employees) subscribed to an ideology that was anti-socialist, imperialist and racist.[50]

What, then, of the evidence to be gained from the study of strikes, which has emerged as a major preoccupation of recent labour history? It has been claimed with some justification that strikes are the most direct reflection of working-class aspirations and far more revealing of what workers really want than the statements of their supposed political representatives.[51] In the nineteenth and early twentieth century strikes required considerable commitment from their participants: the striker would be bound to encounter financial hardship, might well lose his job, might be arrested and might even be shot or cut to death by the sabre or bayonet of troops regularly used to protect blacklegs and break picket lines. Hence, so the argument goes, by close investigation of the demands of strikers we should gain some insight into what really mattered to workers; and by examining who did and did not go on strike we should be able to identify those workers who were and were not militant.

First, even those who support this line of argument would accept that there is no necessary correlation between industrial militancy and political radicalism. We have already seen that Engels was bemused by the way in which Britain had experienced countless labour disputes and seen the rise of strong union organisation and yet at the same time remained relatively immune to working-class political radicalism. In Germany workers with considerable economic grievances often petitioned the Kaiser for help against their employers and genuinely seemed to expect help from that remote quarter. Such was true of metalworkers in Solingen, Silesian weavers and miners in the Ruhr.[52] Printers were — and often still are — militant on the issues of wages and

job security and yet few of them supported the movements of the revolutionary left in the inter-war period. Industrial militancy was — and
often still is — generated by the erosion of pay differentials; yet such
militancy clearly runs in the face not only of ideas of proletarian revolution but even of working-class solidarity. Going on strike, therefore,
tells us little about the *political* persuasion of workers except, of course,
in the rare cases in which strikes have taken place to achieve specific
political ends, such as suffrage reform — though even that might have
been desired for instrumental reasons.

Conversely, the low strike rates of some groups of workers do not
provide incontrovertible evidence of satisfaction with prevailing circumstances or the absence of any class consciousness for precisely the
reasons already given to explain the failure of some workers to organise:
absence of bargaining power, effective employer controls, etc. Amongst
some groups of workers it is possible to postulate the existence of a
traditional resignation in the face of adversity, born of impotence and
low expectations. But in no way does this necessarily correspond to the
absence of any sense of class identity. After all, one version of an acute
awareness of social deprivation and one which makes a clear distinction
between 'them' and 'us' simply states that there will 'always be rich
and poor' — Stearns even gives an example of an SPD member saying
precisely this![53] More to the point, there is evidence, as mentioned
earlier, that workers excluded from the ranks of both economic and
political protest before the First World War were some, though by no
means all, of those who constituted the rank and file of the councils'
movement in Germany in 1918, who mobilised in the French strike
wave of 1919/20 and again in 1936, and who were active in the Italian
factory occupations of 1919/20 also. Here, in fact, is a clear indication
that their previous inaction should not necessarily be construed as an
indication of the absence of discontents but was rather the consequence
of various economic and political controls which were only removed
with the collapse of the *ancien régime* in the wake of the First World
War.[54] Furthermore, detailed studies of individual firms over a long
period of time may reveal a mass of discontents which, for one reason
or another, are never articulated in industrial action or organisation but
are none the less real. This is certainly shown by Rudolf Vetterli's study
of the iron and steel firm of Georg Fischer at Schaffhausen in Switzer-
land between 1890 and 1930.[55] For what Vetterli demonstrates,
contrary to the popular archetype, is that labour relations in Switzer-
land were far from the smooth, untroubled waters of bourgeois
imagination. There were many occasions on which a large part of the

work-force expressed discontent about wage rates, the behaviour of foremen, attempts to increase productivity; yet the firm experienced no real strike, except the general one of 1918, until 1924. Once again this suggests that proletarian quiescence on the industrial front may have been the consequence of workers recognising that industrial action would probably prove abortive, especially as the Fischer concern dominated job opportunities in the area and possessed a work-force that was highly differentiated in its skills and its interests.

There is a further problem with strikes as an indicator of working-class attitudes. It may well be significant that when workers strike their major demands relate to one kind of issue rather than another: some claim to have detected a move away from issues of job control to wages, for example.[56] However, it is not clear that one can make as much of the fact that strike demands concentrate on immediate 'bread and butter' questions as some historians imagine: in the case of German miners in the Second Reich, for example, it has been argued that the restricted nature of strike demands indicates an absence of political radicalism.[57] I fail to see how such conclusions can be drawn from strike demands alone; for strikes are not normally concerned with directly political issues. In a sense they are by definition 'economistic', except in highly exceptional historical situations. They need to be analysed in conjunction with party-political allegiance and other aspects of working-class behaviour before any such conclusions can be drawn. It is also possible to postulate that workers will restrict their demands to those that can be at least in part realised through strike action, even where they have much grander aspirations. Many of the SPD members who were prepared to demonstrate for suffrage reform in Hamburg in 1906 doubtless participated in industrial action on the part of the unions where no mention was made of this particular issue, for example.

Just as membership of a radical or moderate political organisation tells us less than we might imagine, therefore, so also is it incorrect to assume that the failure of workers to appear on the barricades or participate in industrial action necessarily denotes 'integration' into the prevailing social order or an acceptance of it. Where death is the almost certain consequence of a particular course of action, or poverty and unemployment, people rarely risk their lives for causes that are lost. It could even be argued that the failure of the inter-war European working class to engage in adventurist revolutionary action reflected an accurate assessment of objective possibilities, as witnessed, for example, by the tragic events in Austria in 1934.[58] Indeed, what is amazing is that so many were prepared to sacrifice their lives in the struggle against a mighty and vicious counter-revolution.

There are other indicators that one might examine to establish the presence or absence of a radical working-class consciousness: what workers themselves said about their experiences and aspirations (but working-class autobiographers are, of course, rare and by dint of that atypical); the content of the popular songs of a period and other aspects of folk culture (though workers in the SPD regularly sang revolutionary songs and religious hymns in one and the same evening, once again testifying to the difficulties of pigeon-holing proletarian attitudes); what workers chose to read (though this obviously depended in part on what was available, and it is also debatable how much the reading public absorbs from its would-be mentors and some people do read material with which they are not necessarily in ideological sympathy). The problem of fitting working-class attitudes into rigorously consistent theoretical models is further demonstrated by the complex phenomenon of working-class nationalism. It has sometimes been argued, for example, that the popular enthusiasm manifested in the streets of Berlin, London, Vienna, Paris, even Moscow, in August 1914 demonstrated an absence of radical commitment on the part of the proletarian masses and an overriding commitment to the national state. Now it may well be that in a fully articulated political theory nationalism and political radicalism are mutually exclusive; but it is far from clear that such is the case in daily reality. There were South Wales miners with traditions of domestic militancy who none the less volunteered to fight for the British Empire in 1914, just as some former socialist radicals in Germany supported the war effort of the Reich.[59] These workers were 'nationalist'; yet their nationalism may have been very different to that of the ruling élite. To support the Fatherland in its hour of need did not imply satisfaction with the prevailing political and social arrangements. This was certainly the case for some German Social Democrats who supported their government's war effort: they did so not only because they believed that Germany was about to be invaded by barbarous Russia but also because they thought that their patriotism would oblige the Wilhelmine state to make concessions to the economic and political aspirations of the German working man.[60]

In the assessment of working-class attitudes towards their economic and social environment there is a further area of potential investigation which has perhaps been rather underexplored hitherto: productivity rates. Obviously there are enormous difficulties in both establishing and then interpreting the data. Many of the rises and falls in productivity rates are beyond the deliberate intervention of workers: sheer physical exhaustion, the introduction of new technology, etc. However, falling productivity in unchanged working conditions would seem to register discontent on the part of the work-force. Indeed, such seems to have been the case in some European firms shortly before the outbreak of the First World War in response to an attempt on the part of employers to speed up work processes.[61] In the context of effective governmental repression, as in the Third Reich, when no real possibility of overt industrial or political resistance exists, it is even possible to argue, as does Tim Mason,[62] that falling productivity rates may be interpreted as a form of opposition, especially where the labour law has been criminalised.

IV

Where all of this leads, except to pessimistic ignorance in the face of the sphynx-like ranks of the industrial working class, is debatable. Where it most certainly does not lead, however, is to the conclusion that workers are never 'radical', never concerned with political change and social revolution. It may well be that material problems, often problems of survival, let alone anything else, problems in their working conditions, have always dominated working-class existence; although the ways in which workers have responded to these problems have varied enormously from place to place and time to time, and have been mediated by received experience and expectations. All it means is that it makes little sense to want to pigeon-hole workers into archetypal 'revolutionaries' or 'reformists' once and for all. To say that the worker's existence has been dominated by immediate material concerns is not to deny him his dignity; nor is it to dispute his capacity for political reflection. The whole point, in fact, is that immediate concerns can lead to noble enterprises. The movement for workers' control on 'Red Clydeside' at the end of the First World War, for example, was partly inspired in the first instance by the loss of authority, status and control on the part of engineering workers on the shop floor and in a sense was an attempt by this highly skilled and formerly privileged group to retain its traditional benefits. Yet at the end of the day the demand for 'workers' control' was truly revolutionary, involving the abolition of capitalist ownership and work relations.[63] Similarly, the deprivations of war led the proletariat of Moscow and Petrograd to overthrow two political systems in 1917. In the mines of the Ruhr in early 1919 and

again in 1920 the desire of the pitworkers to win a shorter working day
and achieve some degree of job security led to confrontation with an
SPD government and its trade union allies, clashes with troops, disillusion-
ment with Social Democratic politics and even drove some miners into
the arms of a short-lived anarcho-syndicalist movement.[64]

This suggests that there are objective circumstances which of necessity
transform economic demands into political and sometimes very radical
political struggles. Where governments wage wars and those wars can
be identified as the prime cause of material deprivation, as in Russia
and Germany after 1914, there the rectification of material grievances
entails the ending of hostilities and therefore either a change in government policy or the overthrow of governments. Where attempts to strike
or form trade unions were thwarted by the intervention of government
troops or repressive labour legislation, there the attempt to articulate
economic grievances led to demands for changes in the law and government, and on occasion to revolutionary politics. Such was to a certain
extent the case in early-nineteenth-century Britain, where the Combination Acts, the use of spies and *agents provocateurs*, the deportation of
unionists, the employment of troops to quash peaceful demonstrations
led protestors to demand a change in the governmental system. As
E.P. Thompson has remarked, 'In the end, it is the political context as
much as the steam engine, which had the most influence upon the
shaping of the consciousness of the working class.'[65] In France too the
repression of working-class industrial action in the 1830s and 1840s led
to insurrections in Paris in 1832 and 1834 and in Lyons in 1831 and
1834, as well as to the formation of revolutionary secret societies with
both a middle-class and a working-class membership, as in Auguste
Blanqui's *Société des Saisons*.[66] Equally, the suppression of many
trade unions and other forms of working-class associational life in
Germany under the Anti-Socialist Law (1878-90) led some workers to
look to the SPD and the political arena for a solution to their problems.[67]
Most obviously of all, the rapid politicisation of workers with economic
grievances was brought about by the violent intervention of troops.
The radicalisation of many Ruhr miners between 1918 and 1920
stemmed from the brutal actions of the Freikorps;[68] whilst the violence
and militancy of Spanish workers in the late nineteenth and early
twentieth century was in many ways a reaction to vicious state repression, especially in the guise of the Guardia Civilia and subsequently of
Moroccan troops.[69] Most infamously of all, the Russian Revolution
of 1905 began as loyalist unionists petitioned the Tsar but were then
attacked by troops.[70] In fact the 1905 Revolution demonstrates a

proposition developed by Rosa Luxemburg at the time:[71] there are situations in which it is simply impossible to separate economic from political struggle, especially in authoritarian and repressive regimes in which even the economic organisation of workers is not tolerated. Conversely, the relative absence of state intervention in the processes of collective bargaining in late-nineteenth-century Britain meant that workers' horizons did not necessarily extend beyond the purely economic struggle; and this may explain why British workers were relatively slow to form their own political, as distinct from economic, organisations.

Other factors can also lead from economic grievance to political struggle, of course, especially where the weakness of labour or the intransigence of employers precludes success as the result of exclusively industrial conflict. We have already seen that the militancy of French anarcho-syndicalists and the timing of French strike waves could be so explained. The changing fortunes of British Chartism in the 1830s and 1840s also suggest that it was workers who had participated in abortive industrial struggles previously who turned to politics for a remedy for their economic problems; and that they did so in circumstances of economic depression, when high unemployment had drastically reduced their bargaining power and consequent industrial muscle. In a sense insurrection and violent action reflected the desperation of the handloom weaver.[72] It may even be possible to explain the high socialist vote in Germany in terms of industrial impotence. To talk of the industrial impotence of the German working class may sound crazy: by 1914 something like a quarter of the total labour force had been organised, a figure only bettered by the British trade union movement and that of Austria. Germany also possessed one of the largest industrial unions in the world, the giant Metalworkers' Union, with around half a million members. However, German employers and especially those in heavy industry revealed an almost total hostility to independent working-class organisation before 1914. This becomes abundantly clear if one looks at the number of workers covered by collective agreements in British and German industry. In Britain in 1910 900,000 miners, 500,000 railway workers, 460,000 textile operatives and 230,000 metalworkers benefited from such agreements. The equivalent figures for Germany only three years later are staggeringly different: 16,000 textile workers, 1,376 metalworkers and a mere 82 miners.[73] The high degree of capital concentration in German heavy industry also enabled employers to operate effective black-lists of agitators and their control over the labour force was further increased by the provision of company housing and welfare schemes. In such circumstances the prospects of successful industrial action were remote until the utterly changed political context of 1918, when, significantly, the workers in this sector began to enter the ranks of protest on a huge scale.

It has been claimed that such arguments, which derive working-class political action from initially economistic motives, are 'reductionist', in so far as they ignore the relative autonomy of politics and ideology.[74] The problem with this objection, at least as raised by Geoff Eley and Keith Nield, is that it rests on an *assertion* of the autonomy of the political realm rather than a demonstration of that autonomy. In fact I have not claimed that all aspects of working-class political action can be explained directly by reference to solely economic grievances. First, I have argued that the actions of the state play a crucial role in shaping labour protest; and secondly, I have tried to show that in certain cases working-class political action can be explained without any necessary reference to the role of imported ideology and formal organisation. In short, this is an exercise in the application of Ockham's razor. However, there is a further empirical justification for the position stated in this chapter: the European working class turned to independent politics only in certain cases and in cases in which the state intervened in the daily lives of workers in both the factory and the home. In their understandable desire to stress the autonomous roots of working-class action and political practice, Eley and Nield criticise those who have emphasised the crucial role of the German state in creating Social Democracy and its culture and imagine that that culture was successful in creating a relatively unified oppositional labour movement. However, it can be pointed out that unity did not survive the dissolution of the Wilhelmine state; that in Britain, where the state's interventionist role declined in the second half of the nineteenth century, labour did not develop an independent politics on any significant scale and remained divided by sectional interests; and that the extent of state interference in proletarian existence in the Second Reich was truly enormous. It was not just that the formal organisations of labour were proscribed at certain times or that Social Democrats were excluded from state employment or that the SPD press was censored. Interference went much further than that, as many of the chapters in this volume demonstrate. In Brunswick the authorities refused to allow unmarried mothers to employ the title 'Frau'; their permission was needed for marriage and they attempted to prevent concubinage between the unmarrried. In Berlin between the wars, as Eve Rosenhaft shows, much of the hostility of youth was directed against the creation of new state institutions which performed surveillance as well as social service functions. The drinking habits of Ruhr miners were not exempt from governmental interference either: shift workers who were only free after pubs closed formed their own *Schnapskasinos*, but these were subjected to close police scrutiny and a series of running battles between the miners and the police over such drinking clubs helped to politicise their members, who sometimes invited SPD party locals to hold meetings on their premises.[75] Clearly, therefore, state interference was a major influence in the rapid and large-scale politicisation of German labour. Equally, it has been demonstrated that the radicalisation of Ruhr miners in 1919 and 1920 correlates closely with the interventions of counter-revolutionary Freikorps;[76] and that of Asturian miners in 1934 can likewise be described as a 'defensive' reaction.[77]

To be sceptical about what certain indices tell us about working-class attitudes and about the role of formal organisation and theory is not to deny that ideology in the more general sense of a received or changing set of ideas and values, as distinct from imported political theory, was relevant to the action of certain groups of workers. Indeed, it is precisely here that the preceding articles are significant. Artisanal values of independence, self-respect and the dignity of labour obviously played a major role in the generation of protest in early-nineteenth-century England.[78] Violence in industrial relations, in social conflict and even in the paramilitary activities of Communists and Nazis in Weimar Germany during the depression could also mirror a more generally violent society, as has been argued in the case of Hamborn during the revolutionary upheavals in Germany at the end of the First World War and of youth gangs in Berlin in the late 1920s and early 1930s.[79] It can hardly be accidental that socialism appealed to some sections of the Spanish working class and anarchism to others, depending partly on factory structure and the differing expectations which came from different rural backgrounds.[80] However, this last point also crystallises my central argument: for when the social composition of the Spanish socialist movement changed in the 1930s as a result of the influx of rural labourers from Andalusia and Estremadura, so too did the party's style of action. In fact it swung to the left, found it increasingly difficult to control its membership and came, in a sense, to resemble the anarchist movement more closely than had previously been the case.[81] To admit the importance of ideology in this general and informal sense, however, is clearly not the same as to believe the Leninist theory of 'consciousness from without', which ascribes the determining role to professional revolutionaries. What I have attempted to show is that a 'revolutionary' working class was the product of the pressures of the factory and the state, of inherited values and changing circumstances in both public and private life; and that therefore it is most misleading to focus attention upon the supposed 'leaders' of the working class. Above all, it is simply impossible to stereotype the complexity and volatility of working-class thought and action.

Notes

1. Karl Marx and Friedrich Engels, *The Holy Family* (1845) in *Marx-Engels Gesamtausgabe* (Moscow, 1927), 1/3, p. 207.

2. Karl Marx, *The Poverty of Philosophy* in *MEGA* 1/6, pp. 226f.

3. Karl Marx and Friedrich Engels, *The Communist Manifest* in *MEGA* 1/6, pp. 533f.

4. I realise that to talk of the transition from economic to political struggle is, in a sense, to beg the question from the start, in so far as it makes assumptions about the primacy of economics. However, there is empirical validation for this position. In the first place, some labour movements have developed independent economic but not political organisations; and second, trade union organisation did historically pre-date independent working-class politics.

5. See his remarks in *Karl Marx and Friedrich Engels on Britain* (Moscow, 1962), pp. 28-33 and 567f.

6. For Gramsci see his *Prison Notebooks* (London, 1971). For a recent application of his theory to English labour history see R.Q. Gray, *The Labour Aristocracy in Victorian Edinburgh* (Oxford, 1976); and for a general plea in favour of Gramsci's model of 'hegemony' and of its value for social history see Geoff Eley and Keith Nield, 'Why does Social History Ignore Politics?', *Social History*, vol. 5, no. 2 (1980), pp. 249-71. I have doubts about the general viability of a theory that was designed to explain developments in the Italian *mezzogiorno*. I have even more serious doubts about statements which claim that the cultural organisations of the working class 'constitute the concrete terrain from which the working class can *force* a re-negotiation of hegemonic class relations'. This very broad definition of the concept of 'hegemony' as a process of negotiation actually dissolves the concept of *hegemony* and seems to incorporate almost any aspect of inter-class relationships.

7. For Kautsky see R.J. Geary 'Karl Kautsky and the Development of Marxism', unpublished PhD, University of Cambridge, 1971, pp. 137ff. For Lenin see his *Collected Works* (Moscow, 1961), vol. 5, pp. 383f.

8. John Foster, *Class Conflict in the Industrial Revolution* (London, 1974).

9. See, for example, J. Barrington Moore, *Injustice. the Social Bases of Obedience and Revolt* (White Plains, NY, 1978).

10. Leon Trotsky, *The History of the Russian Revolution* (London, 1967), vol. 1, Ch. 1.

11. Robert F. Wheeler, ' "Ex oriente lux?". The Soviet Example and the German Revolution, 1917-1923' in Charles L. Bertrand (ed.), *Revolutionary Situations in Europe, 1917-1922* (Montreal, 1977), p. 46.

12. J.L.H. Keep, *The Russian Revolution: a Study in Mass Mobilisation* (Westfield, 1976).

13. Marc Ferro, *La Révolution de 1917* (Paris, 1967), pp. 456-66.

14. J.L.H. Keep, *The Rise of Social Democracy in Russia* (Oxford, 1966),

p. 46; Allan K. Wildman, *The Making of a Workers' Revolution. Russian Social Democracy 1891-1903* (Chicago, 1967), pp. 94f, and Franco Venturi, *Roots of Revolution. A History of the Populist and Socialist Movements in Nineteenth Century Russia* (London, 1960), pp. 517, 539 and 552.

15.   Jean Reynaud, *Les Syndicats en France* (Paris, 1963); Peter N. Stearns, *Revolutionary Syndicalism and French Labour* (New Brunswick, 1971).

16.   Quoted in Edouard Dolléans, *Histoire du Mouvement Ouvrier* (Paris, 1946), vol. 2, p. 130. It should be noted that Griffhuelhes is not just saying that he does not read Sorel but that he reads *no* theory.

17.   This is the central argument of Stearns, *Revolutionary Syndicalism.*

18.   Robert J. Holton, 'The Crowd in History: Some Problems of Theory and Method', *Social History*, vol. 3, no. 2 (1978), p. 231.

19.   Edward Shorter and Charles Tilly, *Strikes in France 1830-1968* (New York, 1979).

20.   The debate as to whether strikes can be regarded as 'political' or not is central to the argument between Stearns on the one hand and Shorter and Tilly on the other.

21.   For radicalism in the German Revolution see Dick Geary, 'Radicalism and the German Worker: Metalworkers and Revolution, 1914-1923' in Richard J. Evans (ed.), *Society and Politics in Wilhelmine Germany* (London, 1978).

22.   It might also be argued that radicalism amongst British labour in the 1830s and 1840s and especially its anti-governmental orientation had not a little to do with economic policy and the Corn Laws. See Asa Briggs, *Chartist Studies* (London, 1977), pp. 38ff; David Jones, *Chartism and the Chartists* (London, 1975), pp. 120f; and Malcolm Thomis, *The Town Labourer and the Industrial Revolution* (London, 1974), p. 26.

23.   This evidence plays a central role in the 'moderate' interpretation of the 1918 Revolution. See, for example, A.J. Ryder, *The German Revolution of 1918* (Cambridge, 1967).

24.   Geary, 'Radicalism'. See also Manfred Bock, *Syndikalismus und Linkskommunismus von 1918-1923* (Meisenheim an Glan, 1969); Robert F. Wheeler, *USPD und Internationale* (Frankfurt am Main, 1975); Ossip K. Flechtheim, *Die KPD in der Weimarer Republik* (Frankfurt am Main, 1971); Georg Eliasberg, *Der Ruhrkrieg von 1920* (Bonn, 1974); Jürgen Tampke, *The Ruhr and Revolution* (London, 1979); Erhard Lucas, *Märzrevolution im Ruhrgebiet* (Frankfurt am Main, 1970) and *Marzrevolution 1920* (1973); David Morgan, *The Socialist Left and the German Revolution* (London, 1975).

25.   Solomon M. Schwarz, *The Russian Revolution of 1905* (Chicago, 1967), p. 111.

26.   Dick Geary, 'The Ruhr: From Social Peace to Social Revolution', *European Studies Review*, vol. 10 (1980), pp. 503f and 'Radicalism', pp. 270-3.

27.   Hans-Josef Steinberg, *Sozialismus und Sozialdemokratie* (Hanover, 1969).

28.   Dieter Langewiesche and Klaus Schönhoven, 'Arbeiterbibliotheken und Arbeiterlektüre im Wilhelmischen Deutschland', *Archiv für Sozialgeschichte*, vol. XVI (1976), pp. 135-204.

29.   Hans-Ulrich Wehler, *Sozialdemokratie und Nationalstaat* (Göttingen, 1972); Peter Domann, *Sozialdemokratie und Kaisertum unter Wilhelm II* (Wiesbaden, 1974); Werner Blessing, 'The Cult of Monarchy. Political Loyalty and the Workers' Movement in Imperial Germany', *Journal of Contemporary History*, vol. 13, no. 2 (1978), pp. 357-6; Rosemarie Leuschen-Seppel, *Sozialdemokratie und Antisemitismus im Kaiserreich* (Bonn, 1978).

30.   Dieter Dowe, 'The Workers' Choral Movement before the First World War', *Journal of Contemporary History*, vol. 13, no. 2 (1978), pp. 269-76; Horst Ueberhorst, *Frisch, Frei, Stark und Treu. Die Arbeitersportsbewegung in Deutsch-*

land 1893-1933 (Düsseldorf, 1973; Klaus Tenfelde, 'Mining Festivals in the Nineteenth Century', *Journal of Contemporary History*, vol. 13, no. 2 (1978), pp. 377-412, and in the same issue of that journal (pp. 175f) Gerhard A. Ritter, 'Workers' Culture in Imperial Germany: Problems and Points of Departure for Research'.

31. Günther Roth, *The Social Democrats in Imperial Germany* (Totowa, NY, 1963, pp. 195ff; Harvey Mitchell and Peter N. Stearns, *Workers and Protest* (Ithaca, NY, 1971), pp. 209ff.

32. Langewiesche and Schönhoven show, for example, that workers were far more likely to borrow 'political' novels.

33. For accounts of the 'embourgeoisement' of the SPD see Harry J. Marks, 'Sources of Reformism in the Social Democratic Party of Germany', *Journal of Modern History*, vol. XI, no. 3 (1939); J.P. Nettl, 'The German Social Democratic Party as a Political Model', *Past and Present*, no. 30 (1965), pp. 65-95; Roth, *Social Democrats*. For a critique see Dick Geary, 'The German Labour Movement, 1848-1919', *European Studies Review*, vol. 6 (1976), pp. 297-330.

34. See the quotation in James Roberts' chapter above, p. 88.

35. See David Crew's chapter above, pp. 108-41.

36. Richard J. Evans, ' "Red Wednesday" in Hamburg: Police, Social Democrats and Lumpenproletariat in the Suffrage Disturbances of 17 January 1906', *Social History*, vol. 4, no. 1 (Jan. 1979), pp. 1-31. See also Rosa Luxemburg's remarks in Mary Alice Walters (ed.), *Rosa Luxemburg Speaks* (New York, 1970), pp. 149ff.

37. Flechtheim, *KPD*, pp. 63f; Richard N. Hunt, *German Social Democracy 1918-1933* (Chicago, 1970), pp. 93-130.

38. Eley and Nield, 'Why does Social History Ignore Politics?', p. 264.

39. James Wickham, 'Working-class Movement and Working-class Life' (papers delivered to the fourth meeting of the SSRC Research Seminar Group in Modern German Social History, University of East Anglia, July 1980).

40. Mitchell and Stearns, *Workers and Protest*, p. 139.

41. Mayone Ruth Clark, *A History of the French Labour Movement* (Berkeley, 1930), pp. 85ff.

42. Gerhard Braunthal, *Socialist Labour and Politics in Weimar Germany* (New York, 1978), p. 88; Flechtheim, *KPD*, p. 70; Werner T. Angress, *Stillborn Revolution. The Communist Bid for Power in Germany, 1921-1923* (Princeton, 1963), pp. 72ff; Denis Authier and Jean Barrot, *La Gauche Communiste en Allemagne 1918-1921* (Paris, 1976), pp. 121 and 164; Adrian Lyttleton, 'Revolution and Counter-revolution in Italy' in Bertrand, *Revolutionary Situations*, pp. 69ff.

43. Henry Pelling, *History of British Trade Unionism* (London, 1966), pp. 180 and 188.

44. Klaus Tenfelde, 'Linksradikale Strömungen in der Ruhrbergarbeiterschaft 1905 bis 1919' in Hans Mommsen and Ulrich Borsdorf (eds.), *Glück auf, Kameraden! Die Bergarbeiter und ihre Organisationen in Deutschland* (Cologne, 1979), pp. 199-224.

45. Paolo Spriano, *L'occupazione della fabbrice* (Turin, 1964).

46. Geary, 'Radicalism', pp. 276-83; Martin Blinkhorn, 'Industrialisation and Social Protest in Italy', unpublished MS; Albert S. Lindemann, *The 'Red Years'* (Berkeley, 1974), pp. 253-70; Hans-Ulrich Ludewig, *Arbeiterbewegung und Aufstand* (Husum, 1978), p. 84; Dolléans, *Mouvement Ouvrier*, vol. 3 (Paris, 1953), pp. 152ff; Shorter and Tilly, *Strikes*, pp. 132-6; Antoine Prost, *La GGT à l'Epoque du Front Populaire* (Paris, 1964), pp. 66 and 104.

47. Eliasberg, *Ruhrkrieg*, p. 48.

48. Jones, *Chartism*, p. 138.

49. Ulrich Engelhardt, *'Nur vereinigt sind wir stark'. Die Anfänge der deutschen Gewerkschaftsbewegung 1862/63 bis 1869/70* (Stuttgart, 1976); Dieter Dowe. *Aktion und Organisation* (Hanover, 1970), pp. 244-8; Jörg Schadt, *Die Sozialdemokratische Partei in Baden* (Hanover, 1971), pp. 32f.

50. Mitchell and Stearns, *Workers and Protest*, p. 145; I. Hamel, *Völkischer Verband und nationale Gewerkschaften* (Frankfurt am Main, 1967).

51. Mitchell and Stearns, *Workers and Protest*, pp. 165-81. Such a claim is also central to Stearns' analysis of French anarcho-syndicalism, to Shorter and Tilly's analysis of French strikes and to similar work on German industrial behaviour. See, for example, David Crew, *Town in the Ruhr: a Social History of Bochum, 1860-1914* (New York, 1979), Ch. 6; Albin Gladen, 'Die Streiks der Bergarbeiter' in Jürgen Reulecke (ed.), *Arbeiter an Rhein und Ruhr* (Wuppertal, 1974), pp. 113-67; and Stephen Hickey, 'The Shaping of the German Labour Movement' in Evans, *Society and Politics*, pp. 226-37.

52. David Footman, *Ferdinand Lassalle* (New York, 1969); Richard W. Reichard, *Crippled from Birth. German Social Democracy 1844-1870* (Iowa, 1969), pp. 165 and 190.

53. Mitchell and Stearns, *Workers and Protest*, p. 21.

54. For an expansion of this argument see Geary, 'The Ruhr'.

55. Rudolf Vetterli, *Industriearbeit, Arbeiterbewusstsein und gewerkshaftliche Organisation* (Göttingen, 1978).

56. Patrick Joyce, 'The Culture of the Craft and the Culture of the Factory', unpublished paper delivered to the Lancaster/German Historical Institute Conference on Artisans and Workers in Britain and Germany in the Early Stages of Industrialisation, November 1980.

57. See note 51 above.

58. See the section on 'Revolutionary Success and Failure' in Ch. 4 of my book *European Labour Protest 1848-1939* (Croom Helm, 1981).

59. This was the case with Konrad Haenisch and Paul Lensch in the SPD. For Britain see J.T. Ward and W.H. Fraser, *Workers and Employers* (London, 1980), pp. 193f.

60. Gerald Feldman, *Army, Industry and Labour in Germany, 1914-1918* (Princeton, 1966), p. 30.

61. Peter N. Stearns, *Lives of Labour. Work in a Maturing Industrial Society* (London, 1975), pp. 126-69, 193f and 219f.

62. Tim Mason, *Arbeiterklasse und Volkgemeinschaft* (Opladen, 1975).

63 James Hinton, *The First Shop Stewards' Movement* (London, 1973).

64. Eliasberg, *Ruhrkrieg*; Lucas, *Märzrevolution*; Tampke, *Ruhr*; Bock, *Anarcho-syndikalismus.*

65. E.P. Thompson, *The Making of the English Working Class* (London, 1978), p. 216.

66. Dolléans, *Mouvement Ouvrier*, vol. 1, pp. 172-9; John Plamenatz, *The Revolutionary Movement in France 1815-1871* (London, 1952).

67. Vernon L. Lidtke, *The Outlawed Party* (Princeton, 1966); Günther Bergmann, *Das Sozialistengesetz im rechtsrheinischen Industriegebiet* (Hanover, 1970).

68. Such an argument is central to Eliasberg, *Ruhrkrieg*, and to Ludewig, *Arbeiterbewegung und Aufstand.*

69. Gerald Brenan, *The Spanish Labyrinth* (Cambridge, 1962), pp. 156f; Adrian Schubert, 'Revolution in Self-Defence: the Radicalisation of the Asturian Coal Miners, 1921-1934', unpublished MS.

70. Schwarz, *1905.*

71. Robert Looker (ed.), *Rosa Luxemburg. Selected Political Writings* (London, 1972), pp. 117-34.

72.   Thompson, *The Making*, pp. 52ff; Jones, *Chartism*, pp. 153-8; J.T. Ward (ed.), *Popular Movements c. 1830-1850* (London, 1970), pp. 108 and 121; Gareth Stedman Jones, 'England's First Proletariat', *New Left Review*, no. 90 (1975), pp. 52ff.

73.   Stearns, *Lives of Labour*, pp. 165 and 180f.

74.   Eley and Nield, 'Why does Social History Ignore Politics?', pp. 261ff.

75.   Niethammer and Brüggemeier, 'Schlafgänger, Schnapskasinos und industrielle Kolonie' in Jürgen Reulecke and Wolfhard Weber (eds.), *Fabrik, Familie, Feierabend* (Wuppertal, 1978).

76.   Eliasberg, *Ruhrkrieg*, and Ludewig, *Arbeiterbewegung und Aufstand*.

77.   Schubert, 'Revolution in Self-Defence'.

78.   This is the central thesis of Thompson, *The Making*.

79   Erhard Lucas, *Arbeiterradikalismus: Zwei Formen von Radikalismus in der deutschen Arbeiterbewegung* (Frankfurt am Main, 1976); Eve Rosenhaft, 'The German Communists and Paramilitary Violence 1929-1933', unpublished PhD thesis, Cambridge, 1979.

80.   Martin Blinkhorn, 'Industrialisation and Social Protest in Spain', unpublished MS.

81.   Gabriel Jackson, *The Spanish Republic and the Civil War 1931-1939* (Princeton, 1965), pp. 79f.

NOTES ON CONTRIBUTORS

Stefan Bajohr was born in Bad Harzberg, West Germany, in 1950 and studied history, sociology and political science at the universities of Bielefeld, Zurich and Marburg, taking his MA in 1977 and his doctorate in 1978. He is the author of *Die Hälfte der Fabrik* (Marburg, 1979), a history of women's work in Germany from 1914 to 1945, and articles on oral history and the history of women in the Third Reich. After holding a scholarship from the Friedrich Ebert Foundation from 1975 to 1978, he taught at the University of Marburg during 1979-80 and is now an Academic Adviser in the Office of the Federal Chancellor in Bonn. Together with Gerd Hardach he is currently preparing a book on the everyday life of working-class families in Brunswick.

David F. Crew was born in London in 1946 and studied at McMaster University, Ontario, graduating in 1967. He took his MA and PhD at Cornell University in 1970 and 1975, and was Assistant Professor of History at Columbia University, New York, from 1974 to 1980. He has held Fellowships from the German Academic Exchange Service and the American Council of Learned Societies. He is the author of *Town in the Ruhr: a Social History of Bochum 1860-1914* (New York, 1979) and of articles on social and regional mobility and patterns of protest in the German working class before 1914. Since 1980 he has been Fellow and College Lecturer, Fitzwilliam College, Cambridge. He is currently preparing a book on 'Socialism and Society in Germany and France, 1890-1920'.

Richard J. Evans was born in Woodford, Essex, in 1947 and studied history at Jesus and St Antony's Colleges, Oxford, graduating in 1969 and obtaining his doctorate in 1972. From 1972 to 1976 he was Lecturer in History at the University of Stirling, Scotland. He has held Research Scholarships from the FVS Foundation of Hamburg and the German Academic Exchange Service. He is the author of *The Feminist Movement in Germany 1894-1933* (London, 1976) and editor of *Society and Politics in Wilhelmine Germany* (London, 1978). He has published studies on the history of women, the working class and the labour movement in Germany. Since 1976 he has been Lecturer in European History at the University of East Anglia. In 1980 he was

Visiting Associate Professor of History at Columbia University, New York, and in 1981 he held a Fellowship of the Alexander von Humboldt Foundation at the Free University of Berlin. He is currently researching into aspects of poverty, crime and disease in Germany before 1914.

Dick Geary was born in 1945 in Leicester and studied history at King's College, Cambridge from 1964 to 1970, gaining his doctorate in 1971. From 1970 to 1973 he was a Research Fellow of Emmanuel College, Cambridge. Since 1973 he has been Lecturer in French and German Studies at the University of Lancaster, where he is currently head of the Department of German Studies. He has written a number of articles on the German labour movement, on Karl Kautsky and on socialism, and is the author of review articles on Marxist theory, the rise of Fascism and the social history of the Ruhr area. His book *European Labour Protest 1848-1939* was published by Croom Helm in 1981. He is currently completing a book on the German labour movement.

Michael Grüttner was born in 1953 in Baden-Baden, studied history, sociology and philosophy at the University of Hamburg, and has been working there since 1977 on a dissertation on the social history of dock workers in Hamburg from 1886 to 1914. He is the author of a number of publications on the social history of the working class and on city planning in nineteenth- and twentieth-century Germany, including studies of the Hamburg dock strike of 1896, published in a recent volume on the history of strikes in Germany edited by Klaus Tenfelde and Heinrich Volkmann, and of the slum-clearance programmes of 1892-1935 in Hamburg. He is at present completing his dissertation.

James S. Roberts was born in 1950 in Gainesville, Florida, and studied at Northwestern University, graduating in 1972. From 1972 to 1979 he studied and taught at the University of Iowa, taking his PhD in 1979 and returning in 1980 as Visiting Assistant Professor. He has held Fellowships from the German Academic Exchange Service and the Family and Community History Center at the Newberry Library, Chicago. He is the author of a number of articles on drink and the working classes in late-nineteenth- and early-twentieth-century Germany. Since 1980 he has been Lecturer in History at Stanford University, California. He is currently preparing a book on 'Drink, Temperance and the Working Class in Germany' and is researching on female employment patterns and on the cultural significance of 'Payday' in the nineteenth-century German working class.

Eve Rosenhaft was born in New York City in 1951 and studied at McGill University, Montreal, graduating with a BA in 1974. From 1974 to 1978 she studied at King's College, Cambridge, taking her PhD in 1979. During 1975-6 she was a Fellow of the Institute for European History, Mainz, and from 1978 to 1981 was a Research Fellow of King's College, Cambridge. Since 1981 she has been Lecturer in German studies at the University of Liverpool. She is the author of *Between 'Individual Terror' and 'Mass Terror'*, a study of the German Communists and the armed struggle against Fascism from 1929 to 1933, to be published in 1982, and of a number of articles on the problem of political violence. She is currently preparing a general social and political history of the Communist Party of Germany.

INDEX